THE LANGUAGE OF THE
FOREIGN BOOK TRADE

Abbreviations • Terms • Phrases

Second Edition

JERROLD ORNE
University Librarian, University of North Carolina

Chicago, 1962
AMERICAN LIBRARY ASSOCIATION

Preface

The primary purpose of this second edition of *The Language of the Foreign Book Trade,* as of the first edition of 1949, is to provide a needed working tool in the major foreign languages for librarians. It should also be useful to workers in the book trade, whose work may be hampered by lack of language training, and to publishers and booksellers who work with foreign publications. With the rapid acceleration of communications and the increasing distribution of European publications there is an ever more urgent need for linguistic competence. Since most people do not readily acquire many languages, a multilingual glossary of book-trade terms is a necessity. Eleven languages are represented in the present text: Czech, Dano-Norwegian, Dutch, French, German, Italian, Polish, Portuguese, Russian, Spanish, and Swedish.

The first principle of selection for inclusion of terms, abbreviations, and phrases in this text is that of current usage, primarily as found in foreign booksellers' catalogs. The aim has been to define the language as used in these catalogs. This purpose accounts, in part, for the number of terms defined in each language. Countries which have an active book trade are represented by a larger number of terms. Russia, Czechoslovakia, and Poland enforce rigorous regimentation on booksellers, and consequently the number of catalogs in these countries is limited. In order to fill out the usual terminology for these languages (all of which are new to this edition), it has been necessary to use some retrospective materials. Current sources, however, are used for all the other languages, and it can be stated with certainty that the definitions in the sections of this dictionary that reflect an active book trade represent current usage.

The second edition of *The Language of the Foreign Book Trade* contains approximately 16,000 definitions, as compared with approximately 6000 for the first edition. A basic list of nearly one thousand terms that are principally employed in the book trade is included for every language. A term which is common in one language, however, may not be listed in another. The differences between the various vocabularies lie essentially in peripheral areas of terms less or little used. Nor can it be said that every word included in the lists is peculiar to the book trade. Although most words of a general nature are not included, some common terms which are constantly encountered in the book trade will be found. Where there are variant meanings of a word, only the definition employed by the book trade is cited. The paper and printing trades have been exhaustively treated in other publications. A few words are included whose forms are identical in English and the foreign language. These are not superfluous if they do no more than reassure the wary user who has previously been deceived by a cognate form with a totally different meaning. In general, the simplest and shortest definition is used.

The material is organized in a form most convenient for the user. Each language is in a separate list, and the languages follow one another in alphabetical order without reference to any grouping. Danish and Norwegian have been combined in one alphabet for obvious reasons.

Within each language the needs of the user again have determined the arrangement. Words are alphabetized letter by letter, and abbreviations, terms, and phrases are all combined in one alphabet. Where there are variant spellings of a term with the same meaning, the variants are arranged as separate entries, not as parts of one entry. For example, in the Dano-Norwegian section "blaek" and "blekk" both mean "ink." Instead of both terms being placed on one line, separated by a comma, they are listed as two separate entries in alphabetical order. A similar arrangement is employed for the plural form when the plural does not follow in alphabetical order. For example, in the German section the plural of "Blatt" is "Blätter," and the latter is listed alphabetically, not on the same line with "Blatt."

Diacritical marks are ignored in alphabetizing all foreign terms. For example, the German umlaut "ä" is considered as "a" not "ae." In Spanish dictionaries words beginning with "ch" usually are found at the end of the C-word entries. Here they are arranged alphabetically. The Russian text is preceded by an alphabet, as an added guide for those who need it. In every language the rule followed has been to alphabetize by letter for the benefit of the user not familiar with the language and its various forms. This procedure obviously is in contradiction to linguistic principles, but this dictionary has no pretentions toward such principles. It is organized for a specific purpose — to be a working tool for librarians, bookmen, and publishers — and the simplified approach will come closer to accomplishing this purpose than any other.

Some of the problems encountered in the earlier edition are equally present at this time. In some languages — notably Danish, Norwegian, and Portuguese — the languages are in transition. Orthography is in a state of continuous flux, sometimes reinforced by official edicts and sometimes not. In the case of Norwegian, there are conflicts between people and classes of the country itself concerning spelling and words, despite official edicts. In Portuguese, there are problems of changes in the language within Brazil as well as differences between the Portuguese of the mother country and that of Brazil. Spanish requires consideration of differences in current usage as between Spain, Mexico, and other Latin-American Spanish-speaking countries. There is almost no need to mention the currently incredible rate of language change within the central and east European countries which affects the text. In every case an effort has been made to obtain group preference of individual differences.

With few exceptions each language has been examined by two readers or revisers and, in some cases, four or more. A serious effort has been made to assure the validity of the language in the eyes of a person to whom it is native. Where possible, collaborators have been selected not only for their knowledge of the language, but for their familiarity with the book trade.

The labors of those concerned have been of a most devoted character; the results are certainly far beyond my most ardent hopes. To all of those who joined me in the task of writing and rewriting, my boundless appreciation cannot adequately be expressed — were I capable of it — even in the words of the eleven languages of the text. Were it not for my collaborators' highly developed professional sense and the generosity of their respective institutions, this dictionary could not have been completed.

The Czech text is one of the few due essentially to a single contributor. Dr. Paul L. Horecky, assistant chief of the Slavic and Central European Division of the Library of Congress, is its author. The Dano-Norwegian list had two principal contributors as well as a native reviewer. Mr. Jens J. Christoffersen, assistant manager of Kraus Periodicals, Mamaroneck, New York, and Dr. Harry Bergholz, chief bibliographer at the University of North Carolina Library, both made extensive revisions to the original text. To strengthen the Norwegian parts of this text we obtained the collaboration of Mrs. Gert Hall, a visiting scholar temporarily at the Duke University Library. The first revision of the Dutch text by Dr. Harry Bergholz was painstakingly reviewed, expanded, and improved by Mr. Hugo B. Corstius in the firm of Martinus Nijhoff, The Hague, Netherlands. The French text is my own, with very considerable revisions and additions derived from new materials. The German text is properly attributable to Dr. Harry Bergholz, with able assistance by Mr. Frederick Altman, managing head of Kraus Periodicals.

The Italian text has been amplified and improved by a considerable amount of new materials passing through my own hands. The possibility of including Slavic texts was suggested by the early work of Miss Leila Moran at the U.S. Dept. of Agriculture Library in this field. She generously shared her counsel and materials with us. From her brief list an extension was made by Mr. Stephan G. Prociuk, a researcher at the University of North Carolina. Further expansions were made by Dr. Janina Wojcicka, Polish and Slavic research librarian in the Slavic and

Preface

Central European Division of the Library of Congress, and by Mrs. Helena Gierasimowicz, now a graduate student in the University of North Carolina Library School. Brazilian Portuguese was represented among our collaborators by Mrs. Esmeralda Javens, a native Brazilian, briefly a member of the University Library staff. Dr. David Griffin of the School of Languages, Foreign Service Institute, U.S. Dept. of State, gave the text final and painstaking review.

The Russian text is almost exclusively the work of Mrs. Angele Avizonis, a member of the catalog department staff at the University of North Carolina, with able assistance from her husband, Dr. Konstantinas Avizonis, professor of history at Elon College in North Carolina. Dr. Paul Horecky, mentioned above, offered useful suggestions for this text also. The Spanish text is essentially my own work, with added review by Dr. Francisco Aguilera, assistant chief of the Hispanic Foundation at the Library of Congress, and Dr. David Griffin, mentioned above. For the Swedish text we again had the collaboration of the versatile Dr. Harry Bergholz and Mr. Jens J. Christoffersen. Another member of the University Library staff of short but timely period, Mrs. Margareta Kirschner, helped to assure the currency of this list. To all of these, and inevitably to their husbands, wives, and friends frequently consulted, I here express my heartfelt gratitude. The labor is long and the rewards few; their willingness to work at this task merits a high tribute to their sense of professional responsibility.

Grateful recognition must be made here also of the boundless patience and perseverance of Mrs. Musella Wagner, faithful producer of the reams of copy which flowed through the numerous revisions of each text. Some of these texts had as many as six revisions, yet she ground out each new copy without complaint. Without her help our efforts would never have reached the publisher.

In every case the character and content of each text, insofar as they are good, are a tribute to my numerous collaborators. Where there may be errors or omissions, these must be my own responsibility, for the final form and content of the text are largely a matter of personal judgment which I have reserved for myself. It is my hope that my colleagues will find this work useful and find me ever grateful for either the praise or the criticism that it may warrant.

Jerrold Orne

Contents

CZECH

a jiní: and others
a tak dále: etc.
abecední: alphabetical
abecední rejstřík: alphabetical
  index
abecední uspořádání: alphabetical
  order
abecední věcný rejstřík: alphabetical subject index
abonent(i): subscriber(s)
abonnement: subscription
abonovaný: subscribed
adaptace: adaptation
adresa: address
adresář(e): directory(ies)
adresát: addressee
aj. see a jiní
akademie: academy
aktovka(y): portfolio(s)
akvarel(y): water color(s)
alba: albums, books of plates
album: album, book of plates
aldinka: Aldine
almanach(y): almanac(s)
alternativní název: alternate title
americký: American
anály: annals
analytický: analytical
anglický: English
anonymní: anonymous

anonymní dílo(a): anonymous
  work(s)
anotace: annotation(s)
anotovaný katalog: annotated
  catalog
antedatovaný: antedated
antikva: antiqua, roman type
antikvář: antiquarian bookseller
antikvariát: secondhand bookstore
antikvární kniha: secondhand book
antologie: anthology
apokryf(y): apocrypha, apocryphal
  book(s)
arabeska(y): arabesque(s)
arabská(é) číslice: Arabic
  numeral(s)
arch(y): sheet(s), folio(s)
archiv: archives, records
archiválie: archives, records
archivní materiál: archives,
  documents
atd. see a tak dále
atlas(y): atlas(es)
aukce: auction
aukční katalog: auction catalog
autentický: authentic
autobiografie: autobiography(ies)
autograf(y): autograph(s)
autor: author, writer
autoreferát: author's summary

1

autoři: authors, writers
autorisované vydání: authorized
  edition
autorisovaný překlad: authorized
  translation
autorské právo: copyright
autorství: authorship

b.m. *see* bez místa
b.m.a.r. *see* bez místa a roku
b.r. *see* bez roku
báchorka(y): fairy tale(s)
bádání: research
bajka(y): fable(s)
barev. *see* barevný
barevná(é) ilustrace: illustra-
  tion(s) in color
barevná litografie: chromolithography
barevná(é) rytina(y): color
  engraving(s)
barevné(á) vyobrazení: illus-
  tration(s) in color
barevný: in color
barevný dřevoryt: woodcut in
  color
barevný tisk: color printing
báseň: poem
básně: poems
básnictví: poetry
beletrie: belles-lettres, fiction
bez copyrightu: without copyright
bez místa: no place of publication
bez místa a roku: no place and
  no date
bez názvu: no title
bez roku: no year, no date
bez titulního listu: title page
  missing
bezdřevný papír: wood-free
  paper
běžné číslo: current issue
bezplatně: without charge, free
bezplatný výtisk: free copy
bianco: blank
bibliofil: bibliophile
bibliofilské vydání: bibliophile
  edition

bibliografická informace: bibliographic information
bibliografická(é) práce: bibliographic work(s)
bibliografická(é) vzácnost(i): rare
  book(s)
bibliografický(é) seznam(y): bib-
  liography(ies)
bibliografický(é) soupis(y): bibliographic list(s)
bibliografie: bibliography(ies)
biblový papír: Bible paper
bílý: white
biografie: biography(ies)
bordura(y): border(s)
breviář(e): breviary(ies)
briliant: brilliant
brož. *see* brožovaný
brožovaná(é) kniha(y): booklet(s),
  paperbound book(s)
brožovaný: sewed, stitched
brožura(y): pamphlet(s), unbound
  book(s)
bukinista: dealer in secondhand
  books
bulharský: Bulgarian

č. *see* číslo
čára(y): line(s)
čárová(é) mědirytina(y): line
  engraving(s)
časopis(y): journal(s), periodi-
  cal(s)
časopisectví: periodical press,
  periodical publishing
část(i): part(s), section(s)
celokožená vazba: full-leather
  binding
celoplátěná vazba: cloth binding
celoroční předplatné: annual
  subscription rate
celostránková(é) ilustrace: full-
  page illustration(s)
celostránkové(á) vyobrazení: full-
  page illustration(s)
cena: price
cena netto: net price
ceník(y): price list(s)

censura: censorship
censurované vydání: expurgated
  edition
černý: black
červený: red
český: Czech
cestovní deník(y): travel
  diary(ies)
chyba(y): mistake(s), error(s)
chybí: missing, wanting, lacking
chybí konec: end missing
chybí začátek: beginning missing
čínský: Chinese
čís. see číslo
číslo(a): number(s), issue(s)
číslo svazku ve sbírce: serial
  number, series number
číslovaná(é) stránka(y): numbered page(s)
číslování: numeration
číslovaný(é) list(y): numbered
  leaf(ves)
číslovaný(é) výtisk(y): numbered
  copy(ies)
citace: quotation
čítanka(y): reader(s)
citát(y): quotation(s)
cizozemský: foreign
článek: article, section
články: articles, sections
črta(y): sketch(es)
čtrnáct(ý): fourteen(th)
čtrnáct dní: fortnight
čtrnáctideník: fortnightly,
  biweekly
čtrnáctidenně: fortnightly,
  biweekly
čtvrtletně: quarterly
čtvrtletník: quarterly
čtvrtý: fourth
čtyři: four
čtyřicátý: fortieth
čtyřicet: forty
cyrilice: Cyrillic alphabet

data: dates
datování: dating
datum: date

definitivní vydání: definitive
  edition
délka: length
deník(y): diary(ies)
denně: daily
desátý: tenth
deset: ten
deska(y): cover(s)
dětská(é) kniha(y): children's
  book(s), juvenile book(s)
devadesát(ý): ninety(ieth)
devatenáct(ý): nineteen(th)
devátý: ninth
devět: nine
diagr. see diagram
diagram(y): diagram(s)
diář(e): diary(ies), journal(s)
díl(y): part(s), volume(s)
dílo(a): work(s)
dílo na pokračování: work to be
  continued, publication in
  installments
dílo poctěné cenou: prize-
  winning work
dílo v jednom svazku: one-volume
  work, omnibus volume
dílo více původců: work by
  several authors
disertace: dissertation(s),
  thesis(es)
distributor knih: book distributor
divadelní hra: play, drama
dobová vazba: contemporary
  binding
dobový: contemporary
dobrodružná literatura: adventure
  books
dobrý: good
dodatek: appendix, supplement
dodatky: appendixes, supplements
doklad(y): document(s), act(s)
dokumentace: documentation
dokumentární: documentary
dolní ořízka: bottom edge, lower
  edge
domácí: domestic
doplněk: supplement
doplněné vydání: enlarged edition

3

doplňkový(é) sešit(y): supplementary part(s)
doplňkový(é) svazek(svazky): supplementary volume(s)
doplňky: supplements
doslov: epilogue
doslovný překlad: literal translation
dovoz: import
dovozní právo: import regulations
dražba: auction
dřevořez(y): woodcut(s)
dřevoryt(y): wood engraving(s)
druhý: second, other
dubleta(y): duplicate(s), duplicate copy(ies)
duplikát(y): duplicate(s), duplicate copy(ies)
dva: two
dvacátý: twentieth
dvacet: twenty
dvanáct(ý): twelve(twelfth)
dvanácterka: duodecimo
dvouměsíčník: bimonthly
dvouročník: biennial
dvousloupcový: in double columns

edice: edition(s)
ediční plán: publishing plan
encyklopedie: encyclopedia(s)
epigraf(y): epigraph(s)
erb(y): coat(s) of arms, escutcheon(s)
exemplář(e): copy(ies), issue(s)

faksimilovaný(é) přetisk(y): facsimile reproduction(s)
faktura(y): invoice(s)
falcování: folding
falsifikát(y): falsification(s), forgery(ies)
fascikl(y): fascicule(s)
fiktivní autor: fictitious author
foliant(y): large volume(s), folio(s)
folie: gold leaf
formát: format

fotografický otisk: photographic copy
fotografický přetisk: photographic facsimile, photoprint
fotografie: photograph(s)
fotogravura(y): photoengraving(s)
fotokopie: photocopy(ies)
fotolitografie: photolithography
fotostat(y): photostat(s)
francouzský: French
fysická mapa: physical map

glosa(y): gloss(es)
glosář(e): glossary(ies)
gotické písmo: Gothic script, Old English
grafický(é) list(y): engraving(s), print(s)
grafika(y): graphic art; engraving(s), print(s)

hadrový papír: rag paper
hedvábný papír: silk paper
heliogravura: heliogravure, phototypography
heslo(a): catchword(s), heading(s)
hladká(é) ořízka(y): cut edge(s), smooth edge(s)
hlava(y): chapter(s)
hlavní název: main title
hlavní názvy: main titles
hlavní redaktor: editor in chief
hlazený papír: glazed paper, glossy paper
hlubotisk(y): intaglio print(s)
hnědý: brown
hodnota: value, price
horní okraj stránky: head margin, top margin
horní ořízka: top edge
hřbet knihy: back, spine

identifikace: identification
iluminace: illumination
ilustrace: illustration(s)
ilustrace v textu: illustrations in the text
ilustrátor: illustrator

ilustrovaná obálka: illustrated
cover
ilustrované vydání: illustrated
edition
ilustrovaný: illustrated
informace: information
iniciála(y): initial(s), initial
letter(s)
inkunábule: incunabulum(a)
italský: Italian

jaro: Spring
jasný: light, clear
jazyk(y): language(s)
jeden: one
jedenáct(ý): eleven(th)
jediné vydání: only edition
jednobarevné vyobrazení:
monochrome illustration
jednosvazkové dílo: one-volume
work
jednosvazkový výbor z děl:
selected works in one volume
jednotlivé(á) číslo(a): separate
issue(s)
ještě nevyšlo: not yet published
jmenný rejstřík: index of persons
jméno: name, appellation
jméno původce: name of author
jubilejní sborník: *Festschrift,*
jubilee publication
jubilejní vydání: jubilee edition

k disposici: available, at the
disposal
kalendář(e): calendar(s)
kaligrafie: calligraphy
kancionál(y): hymnal(s)
kapesní atlas: pocket atlas
kapesní formát: pocket-size
kapesní slovník: pocket
dictionary
kapesní vydání: pocket edition
kapitola(y): chapter(s)
karton: pasteboard
kartuš(e): cartouche(s)
katalog: catalog
každý: each

kniha(y): book(s)
knihkupec: bookseller, bookdealer
knihkupectví: bookstore
knihomol: bookworm
knihopisné poznámky: annotations
knihovna: library
knihovnice: woman librarian(s)
knihovník(níci): librarian(s)
knihtiskárna: printing house,
printing office
knihvazač: bookbinder
knihvazačství: bookbinding
knížečka(y): booklet(s)
knížka(y): small book(s),
booklet(s)
knižní aukce: book auction
knižní obchod: book trade
knižní výzdoba: book decoration
knižní značka(y): bookplate(s),
ex libris
kolace: collation
kolektiv autorů: collective
authorship, joint authors
kolektivní dílo: collective work,
joint work
kolem: about, approximately
kolibří kniha(y): miniature book(s)
kolofon: colophon
kombinovaná vazba: half binding,
half-bound
komentář(e): commentary(ies)
komentované vydání: annotated
edition
kompilace: compilation(s)
komplet: complete set
konec: conclusion, end
konfiskované vydání: seized
edition
konspekt: outline, syllabus
kopie: copy, transcript
korigovaný: corrected
kování: clasps, metal ornaments
kožená vazba: leather binding
koženka: leatherette, imitation
leather
kozinka: goatskin
krásná literatura: belles-lettres
krátký: short, brief

kronika(y): chronicle(s)
kuriosa: curiosa
kursiva: cursive, italics
kůže: leather

latinisované jméno: Latinized
  name
latinka: roman type
legenda(y): legend(s), caption(s)
lepenka: cardboard, pasteboard
lepenková vazba: hard cover
lept(y): etching(s)
leptaný: etched
léta: years
leták(y): broadside(s), handbill(s)
léto: Summer
letopis(y): annals, chronicle(s)
levné vydání: cheap edition
lichá(é) stránka(y): odd page(s)
lidové vydání: popular edition
linka(y): line(s)
lis: press
list(y): leaf(ves), sheet(s),
  folio(s)
listina(y): document(s)
listina sepsaná vlastní rukou:
  holograph
lístkové vydání: loose-leaf
  edition
lit. *see* literatura
literární dílo(a): literary work(s)
literární pozůstalost: work
  unpublished at the death of
  a writer
literatura: literature
literatura pro mládež: juvenile
  literature
litografie: lithography

maďarský: Hungarian
magazin(y): magazine(s)
malý: little
mapa(y): map(s), chart(s)
mapa světa: world map
marginálie: marginal notes,
  marginalia
marmorovaný papír: marbled
  paper

marokén: morocco leather
masové vydání: popular edition
mědiryt(y): copperplate illus-
  tration(s)
mědirytectví: chalcography, line
  engraving
mědirytina(y): copperplate en-
  graving(s)
měsíčně: monthly
mesíční zpráva: monthly report
mesíčník: monthly publication,
  monthly
mezera(y): gap(s)
mikrofilm: microfilm
mikrofilmová kniha: book on
  microfilm
mikrofilmování: microfilming
miniaturní kniha(y): miniature
  book(s)
ministerstvo: ministry
místní vydání: local edition
místo tisku: place of printing
místo vydání: place of publication
modrý: blue
monografie: monograph(s)
mp. *see* mapa

na pokračování: to be continued
na př. *see* na příklad
na příklad: for example
na rubu: verso
na skladě: in stock
na ukázku: on approval
nabídka(y): offer(s), tender(s)
nadpis(y): superscription(s)
nahoře: above
náhradní výtisk(y): replacement
  copy(ies)
náklad(y): edition(s)
nakladatel: publisher
nakladatelská obálka: publisher's
  cover, original cover
nakladatelská sbírka: publisher's
  series
nakladatelská vazba: publisher's
  binding
nakladatelská značka: publisher's
  mark, signet

nakladatelské družstvo: publishing co-operative
nakladatelské knihkupectví: publishing and bookselling firm
nakladatelské údaje: imprint
nakladatelství: publishing house, publishing firm
nákupní cena: purchase price
naléhavý: urgent
nálepka(y): label(s)
nápis(y): inscription(s)
národní bibliografie: national bibliography(ies)
nárožnice: corner(s)
následující: following
nástin: outline, layout
naučný slovník: encyclopedic dictionary
název: title
název kapitoly: chapter title, chapter heading
název na vazbě: binder's title
název sbírky: series title
název série: series title
název svazku: volume title
nazvaný: entitled
názvy: titles
neautorisované vydání: unauthorized edition
neautorisovaný překlad: unauthorized translation
nečíslovaná(é) stránka(y): unnumbered page(s)
nečíslovaný: unnumbered
nečíslovaný(é) list(y): unnumbered leaf(ves)
nedatovaný: undated
nedokončené vydání: unfinished edition
nejnovější číslo: latest issue (of a periodical)
neklížený papír: unsized paper
německý: German
není k disposici: not available
neoříznutá kniha: uncut book
neoříznutý okraj stránky: uncut edge, untrimmed edge
nepoškozená kniha: a book in good condition
nepotřebný výtisk: surplus copy
nepřetržité číslování: consecutive numbering
nepřetržité stránkování: consecutive pagination
nerozřezaná kniha: book with leaves uncut
nestránkováno: unpaginated
netto: net price
neúplný: incomplete, odd
nevázaná kniha: unbound book
nevydaná díla: unpublished works
nezměněné vydání: unchanged edition
notace: notation(s)
nové vydání: new edition, reissue
novela(y): novelette(s), short novel(s)

obal(y): book jacket(s), wrapper(s)
obalená kniha: book with jacket
obálka: cover, envelope
obálka knihy: cover of a book
obálkový název: cover title
obraz(y): picture(s), illustration(s)
obrázek: illustration
obrázková kniha: picture book
obrázky: illustrations
obrazová příloha: illustrated supplement
obsah: table of contents, summary
obyčejný: ordinary
ocelorytina(y): steel engraving(s)
ocenění: appraisal, evaluation
od začátku do konce: cover-to-cover, from top to bottom
oddíl(y): section(s), division(s)
odhad: estimate, appraisal
odkaz(y): reference(s)
odpovědný redaktor: editor in charge
odstavce: paragraphs, items
odstavec: paragraph, item
ohnutý roh listu: dog-eared
okraj(e): margin(s)
oktáv: octavo
omezený náklad: limited edition

7

opis(y): copy(ies)
opotřebovaná kniha: used book, worn book
oprava: correction; repair, restoration
opravené vydání: revised edition
orig. *see* originál
originál: original
ořízka(y): edge(s)
oříznutá kniha: trimmed book
oříznutý okraj stránky: trimmed edge
oslí ucho: dog-eared
osm: eight
osmdesát: eighty
osmdesátý: eightieth
osmerka: octavo
osmnáct(ý): eighteen(th)
osmý: eighth
osobní jméno: first name, given name
otisk(y): copy(ies), print(s)
ověření: verification
ozdoba(y): decoration(s), ornament(s)
označení: designation, mark
oznámení: announcement, notice
oznamovatel(e): bulletin(s), gazette(s)

padělek: forgery, falsification
padesát(ý): fifty(ieth)
paměti: memoirs, recollections
pamflet(y): lampoon(s)
papír: paper
paragraf(y): paragraph(s), paragraph mark(s)
pastelová kresba: pastel drawing
patisk(y): counterfeit edition(s), forgery(ies)
patitul: bastard title, half title
patnáct(ý): fifteen(th)
pátý: fifth
pečet': seal
pergamen: parchment
pergamenová vazba: vellum binding
pergamenový papír: parchment

paper, vellum paper
periodicita: frequency
periodika: periodicals
periodikum: periodical
perokresba(y): pen and ink drawing(s)
perová vazba: loose-leaf binding
pět: five
písemnictví: literature
písmeno: letter, type
písmo: writing, handwriting
plagiát: plagiarism
plátěná vazba: cloth binding
plátno: cloth
plíseň: mildew
plochý hřbet: flat back
počet stránek: number of pages
počet svazků: number of volumes
pod názvem: under the title
podnázev: subtitle
podobizna(y): portrait(s)
pododíl(y): subdivision(s)
podpis(y): signature(s)
podrobný: detailed
podtrhávati: to underline
podzim: Fall
poesie: poetry
pohádka(y): fairy tale(s)
pojednání: treatise(s), essay(s)
pokračovací dílo: publication appearing in parts, continuation
pokračování: continuation, sequel
polemika: polemical writing, polemics
polokožená vazba: half-leather binding
pololetně: semiannually
polopergamenová vazba: half-vellum binding
poloplátěná vazba: half-cloth binding, half-linen
poloúřední tiskovina: semiofficial publication
polský: Polish
populární: popular
pořadí: sequence, arrangement
portrét(y): portrait(s)
poškození: damage, injury

poškozený výtisk: damaged copy,
  defective copy
poslední: last, latest
poslední autorisované vydání:
  definitive edition
poslední vydání: last edition,
  latest edition
posmrtné vydání: posthumous
  edition
pošta: mail
poštovné: mailing charges,
  postage
potištěná stránka: printed page
pouzdro: case, box
povídka(y): tale(s), short
  story(ies)
povinný výtisk: legal deposit
  copy
pozn. *see* poznámka
poznámka(y): note(s), footnote(s)
poznámka(y) na okraji: marginal
  note(s)
poznámka(y) pod čarou: foot-
  note(s)
poznámka(y) vydavatelova:
  publisher's note(s)
práce: work(s), transaction(s)
Praha: Prague
pramen(y): source(s)
právě vyšlo: just published
právo nakladatelské: copyright
před názvem: before the title
předběžná cena: probable price,
  approximate price
předběžné vydání: preliminary
  edition
předběžný: preliminary
předmluva: foreword, preface
přednázev: bastard title, half
  title
předplacení: advance payment,
  subscription
předplatitel(é): subscriber(s)
předplatné: subscription payment
předpokládaný autor: probable
  author
přehled(y): survey(s), outline(s)

přehlédnuté vydání: revised
  edition
překlad(y): translation(s)
překladatel(é): translator(s)
přeložiti: to translate
přemístění: rearrangement
přepis: transcription, transliteration
přepracované dílo: reworked book
přepracované vydání: rewritten
  edition
přepracování: rewriting,
  adaptation
přepychová vazba: de luxe binding
přepychové vydání: de luxe edition
přestalo vycházet: ceased publication, publication completed
přestavění: rearrangement
přetisk(y): reprint(s)
přetisk zakázán: copyright
převázaný: rebound, recased
příjmení: surname
příl. *see* příloha
příloha(y): supplement(s),
  appendix(es)
přípisek: postscript
příručka(y): handbook(s),
  reference book(s)
příruční slovník(y): pocket
  dictionary(ies)
příspěvek: contribution
příspěvky: contributions
přívazek: bound together with
pro služební potřebu: for official
  use
prodejní cena: retail price,
  catalog price
prospekt: prospectus
proza: prose
prozatimní vazba: temporary
  binding
prozatimní vydání: provisional
  edition
průměr: average
průsvitka: paper mark, watermark
průvodce: guidebook, directory
první: first

9

první vydání: first edition,
first printing
prvotisk(y): incunabulum(a)
půlročník: semiannual publication
puncovaná(é) rytina(y): stippled
engraving(s)
původ: origin, provenience
původce(i): author(s)
původní: original, authentic
původní název: original title
původní vydání: original edition

rabat: discount
řada: series, set
ražení: tooling, embossing
razítko: stamp, signet
recense: review
recensní výtisk: review copy
redakce: editing, editorial office
redakční: editorial
redaktor: editor
redigoval: edited by
referát: abstract, report
rejstřík(y): index(es), list(s)
rekreační literatura: light
reading
reprodukce: reproduction(s),
copy(ies)
restaurace: restoration(s)
resumé: résumé, synopsis
revidované vydání: revised
edition
revise: revision
revue: review, critique
řezaná kožená vazba: goffered-
leather binding
roč. see ročně
ročenka(y): yearbook(s), annual(s)
ročně: yearly, annually
ročník(y): annual volume(s)
rodové jméno: family name,
last name
rok(y): year(s)
rok tisku: year of imprint,
date of printing
rok vydání: year of publication,
date of publication

román(y): novel(s)
romanopisec(pisci): novelist(s)
roz. see rozebráno
rozebraná kniha: out-of-print
book
rozebráno: out-of-print
rozměr knihy: size of book, format
rozměr listu: size of leaf
rozmnoženo: mimeographed copy,
processed copy
rozmnožený strojopis: mimeographed copy, processed copy
rozřezaná kniha: cut pages
rozsah: extent, scope
rozšířené vydání: enlarged edition
rubrika(y): rubric(s)
rudý: red
rukopis(y): manuscript(s)
rukověť'(i): handbook(s),
outline(s)
rumunský: Romanian
ruský: Russian
různé: miscellaneous, diverse
rytci: engravers
rytec: engraver
rytectví: engraving
rytina(y): print(s), engraving(s)

s názvem: entitled
safián: crushed morocco
satinový papír: glazed paper
sběratel(é): collector(s)
sbírka(y): collection(s), series
sbírka knih: book collection
sbírka ve sbírce: subseries
sbírka(y) zákonů: collection(s)
sborník: collective work, commemorative volume
schází: missing, wanting
schválené vydání: approved
edition
schváleno k tisku: approved for
publication
sebrané spisy: collected works
šedesát(ý): sixty(ieth)
šedivý: gray
sedm: seven
sedmdesát(ý): seventy(ieth)

sedmnáct(ý): seventeen(th)
sedmý: seventh
šedý: gray
sekce: section(s)
série: series
sešit(y): issue(s), part(s),
   section(s)
šest: six
sestavovatel: compiler
šestnáct(ý): sixteen(th)
šestý: sixth
seznam(y): list(s), index(es)
seznam ilustrací: list of illustrations
seznam vyobrazení: list of illustrations, table of illustrations
signální výtisk: advance copy
signet: printer's device, signet
šířka knihy: width of a book
šíti: sewing, stitching
sklad knih: bookstore, book stock
školní vydání: school edition
slabikář: primer, first reader
slepotisk: blind tooling;
   letterpress
sleva: discount
slovesnost: literature
slovník(y): dictionary(ies),
   lexicon(s)
souběžný: parallel
souborný název: collective title
souborný rejstřík: general index,
   composite index
současný: contemporary, current
soudobý: contemporary, current
souhrn: summary, résumé
soukromý tisk: privately printed
soupis(y): list(s), roster(s)
španělský: Spanish
speciální: special
spisovatel(é): writer(s)
spisovatelka(y): woman writer
   (women writers)
spodní okraj stránky: bottom of
   a page, lower margin
spoluautor: coauthor, joint
   author
spolupráce: co-operation,

collaboration
spolupracovník(níci): collabo-
   rator(s)
sr. see srovnej
srovnej: to compare
starý(é) tisk(y): old print(s),
   old book(s)
štírcí knihový: bookworms
štírek knihový: bookworm
štítek: label, lettering piece
štítky: labels, lettering pieces
sto: one hundred
str. see strana
strana(y): page(s)
stránka(y): page(s)
stránkování: pagination
středisko: center
stříbrný: silver
strojopis: typescript
stručný: concise
studie: essays, studies
stý: one hundredth
subskribent(i): subscriber(s)
subskripce: subscription(s)
subskripční cena: subscription
   price
sv. see svazek
svazek: volume, tome, fascicle
svazky: volumes, tomes, fascicles
systematický rejstřík: classified
   index

tajný(é) tisk(y): clandestine
   publication(s)
technický: technical
teletina: calfskin
tisíc: thousand
tisk: print, printing
tisk z hloubky: intaglio print
tisk z výšky: relief print
tiskárna: printing establishment
tiskařská značka: printer's mark,
   printer's device
tiskařské údaje: imprint
tištěno jako rukopis: privately
   printed
titul(y): title(s)
titulní list: title page

titulní stránka: title page
transkripce: transcription
transliterace: transliteration
třetí: third
tři: three
třicátý: thirtieth
třicet: thirty
třináct(ý): thirteen(th)
třísloupcový: in three columns
tržní cena: current price
tučné písmo: boldface type
tuzemský: domestic
týdeník: weekly
typografie: typography, printing

učebnice: textbook(s), manual(s)
ukazatel(é): register(s), index(es)
ukázkové(á) číslo(a): sample
  issue(s)
umělecká literatura: fiction
umělecké vydání: art edition
unikát(y): unique copy(ies)
unikátní: unique
úplné vydání: complete edition
úplný: complete
úprava knihy: book decoration
úřední tiskovina(y): official
  publication(s)
úřední vydání: official edition
úryvek: fragment
úspěšná kniha: best seller
uspořádání: arrangement, order
ústřední: central
úvod: introduction, foreword

v: in
v. *see* viz
v.t. *see* viz též
v tisku: in press, in print
vadný výtisk: defective copy,
  damaged copy
varianta(y): variant(s)
váz. *see* vázaný
vázaná kniha: bound book
vázaný: bound
vazba s dřevěnými deskami:
  wooden boards
včetně: including

vědecká(é) společnost(i): learned
  society(ies)
vědecké(á) pojednání: treatise(s),
  study(ies)
vedlejší název: alternative title
vedoucí redaktor: editor in chief
velikost: size, format
velikost knihy: size of book,
  format
velín: vellum
velké(á) písmeno(a): capital
  letter(s)
věnování: dedication
vepřovice: pigskin
věstník(y): bulletin(s), journal(s)
více nevyšlo: no longer published,
  all published
vícebarevná(é) ilustrace: colored
  illustration(s)
vícebarevné(á) vyobrazení: polychrome illustration(s)
vícebarevný: multicolored,
  polychrome
vícejazyčné dílo: multilingual work
vícesvazkový: in several volumes,
  multivolume
viněta(y): vignette(s)
viz: see
viz na rubu: see verso
viz též: see also
vlastní životopis: autobiography
vlastním nákladem: published by
  the author
vlastnoruční podpis(y): auto-
  graph(s)
vložka(y): insert(s), inset(s)
vodoznak(y): watermark(s)
volný list: loose-leaf
volný překlad: free translation
volný výtisk: free copy
vpisek: interpolation
vročení: date of imprint, year of
  issue
všeobecná díla: general works
vtlačený nápis: tooling, embossing
výběr: selection
výbor: selections, anthology
vybrané spisy: selected works

vyčerpávající bibliografie: comprehensive bibliography
vycházeti: to appear, to be
published
vyd. *see* vydání
vydal: edited by
vydání: edition(s)
vydání pro mládež: edition for
children
vydávaný: published by
vydavatel(é): publisher(s)
vydavatelské právo: right of
publication, copyright
vydavatelský arch: publisher's
sheet, publisher's signature
vydavatelství: publishing house,
publishing firm
vyjde v nejbližší době: to appear
soon
vynechání: omission(s)
vyobrazení: illustration(s)
vyplaceně: postpaid
výroční zpráva(y): annual
report(s)
výška knihy: height of the book
vyškrábaný text: erasure in text
vyškrtnouti: to erase, to delete
vysvětl. *see* vysvětlivka
vysvětlivka(y): footnote(s),
explanatory note(s)
výt. *see* výtah
výtah: abstract, abridgment
výtisk(y): copy(ies), issue(s)
výzdoba knihy: book decorations
vzácné knihy: rare books
vzácný(é) tisk(y): rare book(s)
vzpomínky: memoirs

zabavené vydání: confiscated
edition
zachovalá kniha: in good condition, as new
záhlaví: heading(s), caption(s)
zahraniční: foreign
zakázané knihy: prohibited
books, censored books
zakázané vydání: banned
edition

zaniklý časopis: discontinued
periodical
zápisky: memoirs
zařazovati: to insert, interpolate
žargon: jargon
zastaralý: antiquated, out of date
zastavený(é) časopis(y): discontinued periodical(s)
závěr: conclusion
záznam(y): entry(ies), item(s)
zcela přepracované vydání: completely revised edition
zdarma: no charge, free
zelený: green
zeměpisný: geographical
zima: Winter
životopis(y): biography(ies)
životopisec: biographer
životopisný slovník: biographical
dictionary
zkrácené vydání: abridged edition
zkratka(y): abbreviation(s),
contraction(s)
zlacení: gliding
zlatiti: to gild
zlato: gold
zlatý: golden
zlomek: fragment
zlomkovitý: fragmentary
zlomky: fragments
žlutý: yellow
značka(y): mark(s)
znak(y): mark(s), sign(s)
znovu otisknouti: to reprint
zpěvník(y): songbook(s)
zprac. *see* zpracovaný
zpracování: arrangement,
adaptation
zpracovaný: elaborated
zpráva: report, account
zprávy: proceedings
zrevidovaný: revised
žurnalista: journalist
žurnalistika: journalism
zvláštní otisk(y): special re-
print(s), offprint(s)
zvláštní vydání: special edition
zvláštnosti: curiosa, specialties

DANO-NORWEGIAN

a. *see* andre
aaben: open
aar: year
aarg. *see* aargang
aargang: year, volume
aarh. *see* aarhundrede
aarhundrede(r): century(ies)
aarlig: annual
aarsberetning(er): annual
  report(s)
abonnement: subscription
adskillige: several
aegte bind: raised bands
aeldre: older, earlier
aeldste: oldest
aendrede: changed, revised
aendret: changed, revised
aeseløre: dog-ears
aeske: box
afbildn. *see* afbildning
afbildning(er): illustration(s),
  picture(s)
afbleget: faded
afbrudt: interrupted, irregular
afd. *see* afdeling
afdeling(er): part(s), section(s),
  volume(s)
afhandling(er): essay(s), paper(s),
  treatise(s)
aflang: elongated

afpudset: trimmed
afrevet: torn off, torn out
afrundet: dulled, rounded
afskåret: cut off, excised
afskrabning(er): scratch(es),
  chafing
afslidt: dulled, rounded
afsluttet: concluded, completed
afsnit: section(s), paragraph(s)
aftryk: printing(s), edition(s)
aktmaessig: documentary
aktmessig: documentary
aktstykke(r): document(s)
akvarel(ler): water color(s)
akvatinta: aquatint
alle slags: all sorts of
alm. *see* almindelig
almanak: almanac
almenfattelig: popular
almindelig: common, ordinary
alminnelig: common, ordinary
alt det udkomne: all published
alt i alt: altogether
alt som udkom: all published
alt som utkom: all published
alt udk. *see* alt udkomne
alt udkomne: all published
amatør: amateur, collector
amatørbind: amateur binding
anastatisk: anastatic

and. *see* andre
anden: second, other
andre: others
anerkendt(e): recognized
anerkjent: recognized
anetavle: genealogical table
anføre: mention, indicate
anført: listed, indicated
angitt(e): indicated
angivne: indicated
anmaerkning(er): note(s)
anmeldelse(r): review(s)
anmerkning(er): note(s)
anmode: inquire, request
anmodning(er): request(s)
anmrkn. *see* anmerkning
annoncer: advertisements
annonser: advertisements
anonym: anonymous
antaget forfatternavn: pseudonym
antal: number
antall: number
antikva skrift: roman type
antikvar: antiquarian bookdealer
antikvariat: antiquarian dealer's
  shop
antikvarisk: used, secondhand
antologi: anthology
anvisning: instruction
aquatinte: aquatint
aquatintstik: aquatint(s),
  etching(s)
år: year(s)
arabesk: arabesque
arb. *see* arbeid
arbeid(er): work(s)
årbog (bøger): yearbook(s)
årg. *see* årgang
årgang: year, annual volume
årh. *see* århundrede
århundrede(r): century(ies)
ark: quire(s), signature(s),
  sheet(s)
arkiv: archives
arksignatur: signature
årstal: year
årstallet: year
artikler: articles

association-eksemplar: association copy
atlasbind: atlas volume(s)
åtte(nde): eight(h)
atten(de): eighteen(th)
auka: augmented
auktion: auction sale
autograf: autograph, signature
autotypi(er): halftone engraving(s)
avbildende: showing, representing
avbildn. *see* avbildning
avbildning(er): illustration(s),
  picture(s)
avd. *see* avdeling
avdeling: part, section
avhandling(er): essay(s),
  treatise(s)
avis(er): newspaper(s)
avisanmeldelse(r): newspaper
  review(s)
avissaertrykk: reprint from
  newspaper
avisudklip: newspaper clipping(s)
avisutklipp: newspaper clipping(s)
avlang: oblong
avslutning: conclusion, end
avslutte: conclude, complete
avsnitt: section(s)
avtrykk: printing(s), edition(s)
avvikende: differing
avviker: differs, deviates

b. *see* bind
baandvaerk: scrolls, tracery
baerer: contains
bag: back, rear
bagerst: at the very end
bagomsl. *see* bagomslag
bagomslag: back wrapper
bagside: verso
bak: back
bakerst: at the very end
bakgrunn: background
bakomsl. *see* bakomslag
bakomslag: back wrapper
bakperm: back cover
bakside: verso
bånd(s): tie(s)

banderole

banderole: lettered scroll
bastardskrift: bastard type
bearb. *see* bearbeidet,
 bearbejdet
bearbeidelse: adaptation
bearbeidet: revised, adapted
bearbejdelse: adaptation
bearbejdet: revised, adapted
bedårende: delightful
bedste: best
begge: both, either
begraenset: limited
begrenset: limited
begyndelse: beginning
begyndelseblad: preliminary
 leaf(ves)
begynnelse: beginning
beklippet: clipped, trimmed
bemaerkn. *see* bemaerkninger
bemaerkninger: notes, remarks
bemerkninger: notes, remarks
beregnet: calculated, intended
beretning: report
berømt: famous
berører: affects, touches
besk. *see* beskadiget, baskåret
beskaaret: trimmed, cropped
beskad. *see* beskadiget
beskadiget: damaged, broken
beskåret: trimmed, cropped
beskrevet: described
beskrivelse: description
beskrivende: descriptive
beslag: decoration
beslaglagt: confiscated,
 suppressed
besørget: executed
bestaar: consists
bestående av: consisting of
består: consists
beste: best
bestemt: destined
bestilling: order, ordering
betydelig: considerable,
 important
betydningsfuld(e): remarkable,
 significant
betydningsfuld(este): (most)

 remarkable
bevaret omslag: wrappers preserved, bound in
bib.b. *see* biblioteksbind
bibliofiludgave: de luxe edition
bibliofilutgave: de luxe edition
bibliogr. *see* bibliografi
bibliografi: bibliography
bibliografisk: bibliographic
bibliotek: library
bibliotekarie: librarian
biblioteksbind: library binding
bibliotekstempel: library stamp
bidr. *see* bidrag
bidrag: contribution(s)
bidragyder(e): contributor(s)
bilag: annex, supplement
bill. *see* billede
billedbilag: pictorial appendix,
 supplement
billedbog: picture book
billedbok: picture book
billede(r): illustration(s), pic-
 ture(s)
billedraekke: series of pictures
billedside(r): picture page(s)
billedtavler: pictorial plates
billedtekst: caption, legend
billig: cheap, inexpensive
bind: volume(s), binding
bindebånd: ties
bindfarge: color of binding
bindfarve: color of binding
bindflade(r): side(s) of binding
bindflate(r): side(s) of binding
bindnummer: volume number
bindside(r): side(s) of binding
bindsignatur: volume number
biografi(er): biography(ies)
biografisk: biographical
bl. *see* blad, blank
blå: blue
blaa: blue
blad: leaf, sheet; journal
blade: leaves, sheets; journals
blader: leaves, sheets; journals
bladornament(er): scrollwork
bladrand(e): page margin(s)

16

blaek: ink
blaeknotater: notes in ink
blaekplet: inkspot
blandede: mixed, miscellaneous
blandet: mixed, miscellaneous
blandinger: miscellany
blandt: among
blank: blank
blekk: ink
blekkflekk(er): inkspot(s)
blindpresning: blind tooling
blindpressing: blind tooling
blindtryk: blind tooling
blindtrykk: blind tooling
blindtrykt: blind-stamped,
  blind-tooled
bll. see blade
blokbog: block book
blokka: blocks
blokker: blocks
blomstermotiv: floral design
blomsterornament: floral design
blyant: pencil
blyantsindstreget: pencil scored
blyantsindstregn. see
  blyantsindstregning
blyantsindstregning(er): pencil
  scoring(s)
blyantsmaerke(r): pencil mark(s)
blyantsmrk. see blyantsmaerker
blyantsskrevet: penciled
blyantstrek(er): pencil mark(s)
blyantsunderstregninger: pencil
  underscoring
bog: book
bøger: books
bogbind: binding, bookbinding
bogbinder: binder
bogdekoration: book decoration
bogejermaerke(r): ex libris
bogelsker: booklover
bogform: format
bogfortegnelse: bibliography
bogh. see boghandel
boghandel: book trade; bookstore
boghandler(e): bookdealer(s)
bogillustrationskunst: art of book
  illustration

bogkunstner: illustrator
bogladepris: list price
boglomme: pocket
bogmaleri: illumination
bogsamling: collection of books,
  private library; lot
bogstav(er): letter(s)
bogtr. see bogtryk, bogtrykt
bogtryk: print, printing; letterpress
bogtrykarbejde: example of
  printing
bogtrykker: printer
bogtrykkeri: printing firm
bogtrykkermaerke(r): printer's
  mark(s), device(s)
bogtrykt: printed
bogudsalg: book sale
bogudstyr: book design
bogven(ner): bibliophile(s)
bøjelig: flexible, limp
bok: book
bok-: for further compounds beginning with "bok" see also
  entries beginning with "bog"
bøker: books
bokmål: special form of literary
  Dano-Norwegian
boksamling: collection of books;
  lot
bokutsalg: book sale
bord(er): border(s), decoration(s)
bordeauxfarvet: wine-colored
bordure: border, decorative
  framework
bordyre(r): border(s)
bortkommet: lost, gone
bortraderet: erased
bortradert: erased
bortset fra: apart from, except
bortskåret: cut off, excised
borttaget: obliterated
bøttepapir: handlaid paper
bra: nice, fair
brandskade: burn
bred: wide
bredde: width
brev: letter, correspondence

17

breve: letters, correspondence
brever: letters, correspondence
brevfacsimile: facsimile letter
brevsamling: collection of letters
brevveksling: correspondence
brist: defect
brocheret: paper-bound, in
  wrappers
brochure: pamphlet, booklet
broderet: embroidered
broget: varicolored
broncespaender: bronze clasps
bronzeret: reddish-brown
brosjert: paper-bound, in
  wrappers
brosjyre(r): pamphlet(s)
brud: break
brugsspor: trace(s) of use
brukket: broken
brun: brown
brunet: browned
brunflekket: foxed, browned
brunplettet: foxed, browned
brunskjold. see brunskjoldet
brunskjoldet: foxed
bundet: bound

cartouche: cartouche
censur: censorship
chagr. see chagrin
chagrin: shagreen
ciseleret: chased, finely tooled;
  chiseled
ciselering: tooling, goffering

d. see del
dagbog(bøger): diary(ies)
dansk: Danish
dårlig: worthless, poor
dater: dates
dateret: dated
datert: dated
dato: date
debutbog: first book
debutbok: first book
ded. see dedikation
dediceret: dedicated, inscribed
dedik. see dedikasjon

dedikasjon: dedication, inscription
dedikation: dedication, inscription
defekt: defective, imperfect
deilig(e): lovely, charming
dejlig(e): lovely, charming
dekkel(kler): board(s)
dekorasjon(er): decoration(s)
dekoration(er): decoration(s)
dekorativ: decorative, ornamental
dekoreret: decorated
del: part
dele: parts
deler: parts
dels: in part, partly
delt: divided
deltitel: part title
delv. see delvis
delvis: partly
deraf: of which
derav: of which
derefter: thereafter
deretter: thereafter
deriblandt: including
dessuten: in addition
desuden: in addition
desvaerre: unfortunately
det udk. see det udkomne
det udkomne: all published
detailleret: detailed
detailtegning(er): detail drawing(s),
  diagram(s)
detaljert: detailed
devise: device, motto
diag. see diagram
diagram(mer): diagram(s)
digt(e): poem(s)
digterverker: poetic works
digtsamling: collection of poems
dikt(e): poem(s)
diktning: creative writing(s),
  poetry
disp. see disputats
disputats: dissertation
disputatsudgave: thesis edition
diss. see disputats
div. see diverse
diverse: several, various
dobbeltbind: double bands

dobbeltblad: double sheet
dobbeltsid. *see* dobbeltsidig
dobbeltsidig: two-sided, two-page
dobbeltspaltet: two-column
doktoravhandling: doctoral thesis
dokument(er): document(s)
dokumentarisk: documentary
dr.avh. *see* doktoravhandling
drevet: embossed
duodez: duodecimo
dupliceret: mimeographed
duplikeret: mimeographed
dybrødt: dark red
dybtryk: offset printing
dybtryksgengivelse(r): reproduction(s) by offset
dybtrykshaefte(r): issue(s) with offset illustrations
dyptrykk: offset printing
dyr: expensive

een: one
efterår: Fall, Autumn
efteråret: Fall, Autumn
eftergjordt: artificial
efterl. *see* efterladt
efterladt(e): posthumous
efterord: postscript
efterskr. *see* efterskrift
efterskrift: postscript, postface
eftersøgt: sought after, rare
efterspill: epilogue
efterspurgt: in great demand, sought after
eftertragtet: sought after
eftertryk: pirated edition, reprint
egenhaendig: autograph, in one's own handwriting
egenhendig: autograph, in one's own handwriting
eget forlag: published by the author
egne: own, personal
egnet: suitable, appropriate
egtraesplade(r): oak board(s)
ei: one
eks. *see* eksemplar

eksempelsamling(er): collection(s) of examples
eksempl. *see* eksemplar
eksemplar(er): copy(ies)
eksempler: examples
ekspedere: to forward, to send
ekspl. *see* eksemplar
ekstranummer: special issue, edition
el. *see* eller
eleg. *see* elegant
elegant: elegant, elegantly
elfenbenpergament: ivory vellum
elfte: eleventh
ell. *see* eller
eller: or, otherwise
ellers: or, otherwise
elleve: eleven
ellevte: eleventh
emaljebind: enamel binding
emner: subjects
en: a, one
en del: some
endel: somewhat, some
endelig: final
endelige udgave: definitive edition
endvidere: further
enestående: unique
eneste: only
engelsk bind: limp binding
enhvert: every, each one
enk. *see* enkelt
enkelt: single; plain, rustic
enkelte: a few
enkelthefte(r): separate issue(s)
enkeltvis: singly, separately
ens. *see* ensartet
ensartet: uniform
ensfarget: of one color
ensformig: uniform
erindringer: memoirs
erratablad: errata sheet
erstattet med: replaced by
et: a, one
et par: a few, a couple
ethvert: every, each one
ett: a, one
etter: after

19

etterlatte skrifter: posthumous
  works
etterspurt: sought for
ettertraktet: sought after
eventuelle: possible, possibly
eventyr: tale(s)
exlibris: bookplate
expl. *see* eksemplar

f.eks. *see* for eksempel
få: few
faa: few
faareskind: sheepskin
facsimileaftryk: facsimile
  reprint
facsimilia: facsimiles
faellesbd. *see* faellesbind
faellesbind: bound together,
  series binding
faellesomsl. *see* faellesomslag
faellesomslag: wrappers for
  series
faellespublikation: companion
  publication
faellesregister: general index
faks. *see* faksimile
faksimile: facsimile
faksimile-avtrykk: facsimile
  reprint
faksimilebilag: supplement
faksimileret: reproduced in
  facsimile
falmet: faded
fals(e): joint(s); guard(s)
farge(r): color(s)
farve(r): color(s)
farvebilag: color plate(s)
farvefot. *see* farvefotografi
farvefoto(s): color photograph(s)
farvefotografi(er): color photo-
  graph(s)
farveillustr. *see* farveillustra-
  tion
farveillustration(er): color
  illustration(s)
farvelagt: colored, in colors
farvelitografi(er): color litho-
  graph(s)

farvetavle(r): colored plate(s)
farvetr. *see* farvetryk
farvetryk: color print, color
  printing
farvetrykk: color print, color
  printing
farvetrykt: printed in color
farvetvl. *see* farvetavle
fastgjort: affixed
fastklaebet: reglued
fedtplet(ter): grease stain(s)
fellesbind: bound together, series
  binding
felt(er): panel(s)
fem: five
femte: fifth
femten(de): fifteen(th)
femti(ende): fifty(ieth)
ferdig: ready
festskrift: commemorative
  volume
fig. *see* figur
figur(er): figure(s), illustration(s)
filet(er): fillet(s)
fineste: finest, best
fingeret: fictitious
finstilt: in small print
fint: neatly
fire: four
firkant: square, quadrangle
firti(ende): forty(ieth)
fjerde: fourth
fjernet: removed, erased
fjorten(de): fourteen(th)
fl. *see* flere
flade ophøjede bind: flat raised
  bands
flammet: marbled
flekk(er): spot(s)
flekket: spotted
flere: more, several
flerfarvet: multicolored
fleste: most
fletvaerk: interlacings
flexibel: flexible
flg. *see* følgende
fløjl: velvet
fløjlsagtig: velvet-like

fløjlsbind: velvet binding
fløjlsforet: velvet-lined
flot: elegant
flott: elegant
fløyelsbind: velvet binding
fløyelsforet: velvet-lined
flygeblad: flyleaf; broadside
flyveblad: pamphlet, broadside
flyveskrift(er): pamphlet(s),
  broadside(s)
foderal: slipcase
fol. *see* folio
folder: folder, portfolio
foldet: folded
følge: series, sequence
følgende: following
folieret: foliated
foliering: foliation
folio: folio
folkebog: popular book, chapbook
folkelig: popular
folkeudgave: popular edition
før: before, prior to
for det meste: mostly
for eksempel: for instance
for hånden: present
for- og bagomslag: front and
  back wrappers
for- og bagperm: front and back
  cover
for oven: on top
for.s. *see* forfatterens
forandret: altered, changed
foranstående: preceding
forår: Spring
foråret: Spring
forarbejdet: prepared
forbedring(er): correction(s),
  improvement(s)
fordansket: put into Danish
fordanskning: Danish version
fordekkel(kler): front cover(s)
fordekl. *see* fordekkel
fordybet: embossed
foregående: preceding
forelaesning(er): academic
  lecture(s)
foreløbig: preliminary, interim

førende: leading, first class
foreste: front, foremost
forestillende: representing
foret: lined
foretaget: executed; practiced
forf. *see* forfatter, forfatterens
  forlag
forf.s. *see* forfatterens
forfalskning: forgery
forfatter: author
forfatterens: of the author
forfatterens forlag: published by
  the author
forfatterrettighed: copyright
forfatterskab: authorship
forfattet: written, authored
forgyldning: gilt decoration(s)
forgyldt: gilt, decorated with gold
forhandlinger: proceedings
forhøjning(er): raised decoration(s)
fork. *see* forkortet
forklaring: explanation
forkort. *see* forkortelse
forkortelse(r): abbreviation(s)
forkortet: abridged
forkortet titel: short title
førkrigsudgave: prewar edition
forl. *see* forlag
forlaegger: publisher
forlaengst: a long time ago
forlag: publishing firm
forlagsrett: copyright
forlagt: published
format: format
formered: enlarged
formering: edge of book cover
formindsket: reduced in size
fornem(t): exquisite(ly)
fornyet: restored, renewed
forøgede: enlarged
forøget: enlarged
forøk. *see* forøket
forøket: enlarged
foromsl. *see* foromslag
foromslag: front wrapper
forord: preface
foroven: on top
forperm: front cover

forreste: front, foremost
forreven: torn
forrevet: torn
forrige: previous, last
forsaavidt: insofar as
forsalg: advance sale
forsats: flyleaf
forsatsbl. *see* forsatsblad
forsatsblad: flyleaf
forside: front cover, recto
forsk. *see* forskellig
forskell. *see* forskellig
forskellig(e): various, different
forskjellig(e): various, different
forsnit: fore edge
forsøg: essay, essays
første: first
forstaerket: reinforced
førstetryk: first impression
førstetrykket: first impression
førsteudgave: first edition
forsynede: furnished, provided;
   supplied
forsynet: furnished, provided;
   supplied
fort. *see* fortitel
fortaelling(er): short story(ies),
   tale(s)
fortale: preface
fortegn. *see* fortegnelse
fortegnelse(r): catalog(s), list(s)
fortiden: the past
fortil: in front
fortitel: half title
fortløbende: continuous
fortraeffelig: excellent
fortrinlig: excellent
fortrolig: confidential
fortryk: preprint, advance copy
fortsaettelse bindende: buyer
   agrees to continue subscription
fortsat: continued, to be continued
foruden: besides
foruten: besides
fot. *see* fotografi
foto: photograph
fotogr. *see* fotografi, fotografisk
fotografi(er): photograph(s)

fotografisk: photographic
fotogravure(r): photoengraving(s)
fotokopi: photostat
fotolitografi: photolithograph(y)
frakturskrift: black-letter type
fremmed: foreign
fremragende: outstanding
fremstillet: produced, printed;
   related, told
fremstilling: production, account
fribl. *see* friblad
friblad: flyleaf
frise(r): frieze(s), border(s)
frisk: fresh
friskhed: freshness
friskt: fresh
front. *see* frontispice
frontisp. *see* frontispice
frontispice: frontispiece
fugtpl. *see* fugtplettet
fugtplet(ter): damp stain(s)
fugtplettet: damp-stained, foxed
fugtrand(e): damp stain(s)
fugtskjold(er): damp stain(s)
fugtskjoldet: damp-stained
fuldført: completed
fuldst. *see* fuldstaendig
fuldstaendig(t): complete(ly)
fuldt: entirely
fullkommen: perfect
fullstendig(t): complete(ly)
futteral: slipcase
fyldig: copious, ample
fylt: filled

gaaet tabt: lost
gået ind: discontinued
gamalnorsk: Old Norwegian
ganske: quite
gav ut: edited
gave: gift
gedechagrin: shagreen
gedeskind: goatskin, morocco
geiteskinn: goatskin, morocco
genfortalt: retold
gengivelse: reproduction
gengivet: reproduced
genindbundet: recased

gennemarbejdet: reworked, adapted
gennemgående: throughout
gennemgang: review
gennemillustr. *see* gennemillustreret
gennemillustreret: illustrated throughout
gennemset: edited, slightly revised
gennemsk. *see* gennemskudt
gennemskudt: interleaved
genoptryk: reprint
genudgivelse: new edition; reissue
gjengivelse: reproduction
gjennemgående: throughout
gjennomskutt: interleaved
glanspapir: fancy paper
glat: smooth
glatt: smooth
glimrende: excellent, brilliant
glittet: coated, polished
glosar: glossary, word list
glose(r): gloss(es)
gnavet: gnawed
godt: good, fine
gotisk: gothic
graf(er): graph(s)
grafisk: graphic
granitol: a patent book cloth
granskning: research
grav. *see* graveret
graveret: engraved
gravert: engraved
grøn: green
grønn: green
groteskskrift: block letter
grov: rough, rustic
grundlaeggende: basic, fundamental
grundtraek: basic outline
gruppe: group
gul: yellow
guld: gold
gulddek. *see* gulddekoration
gulddekoration: gold decoration
guldlinier: gold fillets

guldpraegning: gold stamping
guldpresset: gold-stamped
guldsn. *see* guldsnit
guldsnit: gilt edges
guldtrykt: printed with gold
gull: gold
gullsnitt: gilt edges
gulnet: yellowed
gulplettet: yellow-spotted, foxed
gulvpap: heavy gray paperboard
gummistempel: rubber stamp

h. *see* halv, hefte
haandb. *see* haandbog
haandbog(bøger): handbook(s)
haandgjort: handmade
haandindbundet: handmade binding
haandkoloreret: hand-colored
haandskrevet: handwritten
haandskrift: manuscript, handwriting
haandtegning: sketch, drawing
haefte(r): part(s), fascicle(s), issue(s); pamphlet(s)
haefteomslag: wrappers
haeftesubskription: parts issued to subscribers
haeftet: sewed
haiskinn: sharkskin
hajskind: sharkskin
hajskindbind: sharkskin binding
halv: half
halvårlig: semiannual
halvb. *see* halvbind
halvbind: half volume; half binding
halvbuckrambind: half-buckram binding
halvdel: half
halvfrans: half calf
halvhundre: fifty
halvlaeder: half leather
halvlaerred: half cloth
halvmaanedskrift: semimonthly publication
halvmånedlig: semimonthly
halvpergament: half vellum
halvpluviusin: half leatherette, fabrikoid

23

halvsaffian: half morocco
halvsh. *see* halvshirting
halvshirting: half cloth
halvtonaetsning: halftone engraving
halvtreds: fifty
halvtredsindstyve: fifty
halvtres: fifty
halvtresinstyve: fifty
håndb. *see* håndbog
håndbog: handbook
håndbok: handbook
håndbundet: hand-bound
håndg. *see* håndgjort
håndgj. *see* håndgjort
håndgjort: handmade
håndindbundet: hand-bound
håndkoloreret: hand-colored
håndmalede: hand-painted
håndskrevet: handwritten, autographed
håndskrift(er): manuscript(s)
haves også separat: available also separately
hefte(r): part(s), fascicle(s), issue(s); pamphlet(s)
hefteomslag: wrappers
hefteskrift: publication issued in parts
heftet: stitched, sewed
heftn. *see* heftning
heftning: stitching
helbind: full binding
helbuckrambd. *see* helbuckrambind
helbuckrambind: full-buckram binding
helfabrikoidlaeder: full imitation leather
hellaeder: full leather
hellaederspejlbind: full-leather paneled binding
hellaerred: full cloth
hellaerredsmappe: full-cloth portfolio
helldr. *see* hellaeder
hellerretsbind: full-cloth binding
helmaroquin: full morocco

helpergament: full vellum
helpluv. *see* helpluviusin
helpluviusin: full leatherette, fabrikoid
helruskindbind: full suede
helsaffianbd. *see* helsaffianbind
helsaffianbind: full morocco
helsh. *see* helshirting
helshirting: full cloth
helside(s): full page
helsidesbilde: full-page illustration
helsidesplanche(r): full-page plate(s)
helskb. *see* helskindbind
helskind. *see* helskindbind
helskindbind: full-leather binding
helt: all, entirely
helvti: half
henved: approximately, nearly
her: here, with this item
her og der: in some places
heraf: of which, of this, of these
herav: of which, of this, of these
heri: in which, in this, in these
herunder: under this heading
hft. *see* hefte, heftet
hftr. *see* hefter
hidtil: so far
hist. *see* historisk
historisk: historical
hittil: so far
hjørne(r): corner(s)
hjørnebeslag: cornerpieces
hjørneroset(ter): corner rosette(s)
hjørnestempler: corner decorations
hjorteskind: buckskin, doeskin
hlaeder. *see* halvlaeder
hldr. *see* halvlaeder
høj: high
hollandsk: Dutch
høst: Fall, Autumn
høsten: Fall, Autumn
høstnr. *see* høstnummer
høstnummer: Fall issue
hov. *see* hoved
hoved: head, principal

hovedpart: the majority, most of which; main part
hovedparten: the majority, most of which; main part
hovedredaktør: editor in chief
hovedregister: general index
hovedsagelig: principally
hovedtitel: main title
hovedvaerk: principal work, main work
hovedverk: principal work, main work
høyre: right-hand
hpluv. see halvpluviusin
hprgt. see halvpergament
hsh. see halvshirting
hshirt. see halvshirting
hul(ler): hole(s)
hullet: holed
hundreaarige: centennial
hundred(e): hundred(s)
hundrede: hundredth
hver: each
hver enkel: each one separately
hvert enkelt: each one separately
hvid: white
hvidt: white
hvitt: white
hvoraf: of which
hvorav: of which
hvormed: with which, together with
hvorpå: upon which

i alt: altogether
i anl. see i anledning
i anledn. see i anledning
i anledning: on the occasion
i samtidens stil: in contemporary style
i teksten: in the text
iagttagelser: observations
ialt: altogether
ib. see indbundet
identisk: identical
ifølge: according to
ikke almindelig: uncommon
ikke i boghandelen: not for

general sale, privately printed
ikke i handelen: not for general sale, privately printed
ill. see illustrasjon, illustreret
illum. see illuminerede
illuminerede: illuminated, colored
illumineret: illuminated, colored
illustr. see illustrasjon
illustrasjon(er): illustration(s)
illustration(er): illustration(s)
illustrationsmateriale: illustrations, illustrative material
illustrator: illustrator
illustreret: illustrated
illustrert: illustrated
imit. see imiteret
imiteret: imitated
imitert: imitated
imod: against
imot: against
imponerende: impressive
indbinding: binding
indbindningspris: binding price
indbøjet: folded in
indbundet: bound
indeholder: contains
indenfor: within, inside
inderside: inner side
indgående: extensive, extensively
indgik i: merged with
indheftet: bound in
indhold: contents
indholdsfortegnelse: index
indholdsfortgn. see indholdsfortegnelse
indholdsregister: table of contents
indklaebet: tipped in
indlagt: laid in; enclosed
indledning: introduction
indledningsord: prefatory note
indmalet: painted in
indrammet: framed
indramning: framing
indre: inner, inside
indsat: inserted
indskrift: inscription
indskudt: inserted
indstr. see indstreget

25

indstreget: underlined, scored
indstregninger: underscoring
indtil: until, up to
indtrykt: printed in, embossed
indvendig: inside
initial(er): initial letter(s)
inkunabel(bler): incunabulum(a)
inl. *see* inledning
inledning: introduction
inledningsark: first signature
innb. *see* innbundet
innbinding: being bound, binding
innbundet: bound
inneh. *see* inneholder
inneholder: contains
innhold: contents
innholdsfortegnelse: index
innklebet: pasted in
innlagt: laid in; enclosed
innledn. *see* innledning
innledning: introduction
innsiden: inside
innskudt: inserted
inst. *see* institutt
institutt: institute
istandsat: remade, renewed
itu: broken

jaevn: ordinary
jansenistbind: Jansenist binding
japanpapir: Japanese paper
jevnfør: compare, see
jfr. *see* jevnfør
jordslaaet: mildewed, foxed
jubilaeumsbog: jubilee book
jubilaeumsskrift: jubilee publication
jubileumsbok: jubilee book
julebog(bøger): Christmas gift
   book(s)

kaliko: calico, cloth
kalv: calf
kalveskind: calfskin
kalveskinn: calfskin
kammarmorsnit: marbled
   edge(s), combed edge(s)
kantet: edged, bordered

kantforgylning: gilding on edges of
   covers
kapitael: capital letter
kapitaelbånd: headband
kapitel: chapter
kapitelinitial(er): chapter initial
   letter(s)
kapitler: chapters
kardusomslag: blank wrapper
karikatur(er): caricature(s)
karikatyr(er): caricature(s)
kart. *see* kartonert
kart(er): map(s), chart(s)
kartbilag: map supplement
kartnbd. *see* kartonbind,
   kartonbundet
kartografi: cartography
karton. *see* kartonert
karton: boards, pasteboard;
   slipcase
kartonbd. *see* kartonbind
kartonbind: board binding
kartonbundet: bound in boards
kartonert: bound in boards
kartong: boards, pasteboard;
   slipcase
kartonnage: boards; slipcase
kartonneret: bound in boards
kartouche: cartouche
kartskiss(er): sketch map(s)
kartuche: cartouche
kartusche: cartouche
kassette: slipcase
katalog(er): catalog(s)
kemityperet: engraved in zinc
kender(e): expert(s), connois-
   seur(s)
kgl. *see* kongelig
kildehenvisn. *see* kildehenvisning
kildehenvisning(er): reference(s)
   to sources
kildehistorisk: based on original
   sources
klaebet op: pasted up
klebet inn: pasted in
klipp: clipping
klippet: clipped
klumme(r): column(s)

knap: button, knob
knapp(er): button(s), knob(s)
kniplingsmønster: lacelike
  pattern
knop(per): boss(es)
knudestempel(pler): nodular
  stamp(s)
knytebånd: fastening ribbon
kobb. see kobbere
kobber(e): copper engraving(s)
kobberplade(r): copperplate(s)
kobberst. see kobberstik
kobberstik: copper engraving(s)
kobberstukket: copper engraved
kobberstukne: copper engraved
kobbertavler: engraved plates
kodeks: codex
kol. see koloreret
kold: cold, dry point
koldnaalsradering(er): dry-point
  etching(s)
kollationering: collatior
kolofon: colophon
kolor. see koloreret
koloreret: colored
kolorering: coloring
kolorert: colored
kommentar(er): commentary(ies)
kommenteret: commented
kommentert: commented
komp. see komplet, komponeret
kompilation: compilation
kompilator: compiler
komplet: complete
komplett: complete
komponeret: composed, designed
komponeret bind: original publisher's decorated binding
komposisjon(er): composition(s)
komposition(er): composition(s)
konfiskeret: confiscated
konfiskert: confiscated
kongelig(e): royal
kongl. see kongelig
konkordans: concordance
kontant: cash
konto: account
kopperstikk: copper engravings

kort: map(s), chart(s); brief
kortbilag: supplement of maps
kortblade: map sheets
kortfatt. see kortfattet
kortfattet: concise, brief
kortmappe: portfolio of maps
kortplancher: map plates
kostbareste: most expensive
kostede: brought, sold for
kostet: brought, sold for
kostumekobber: engraved plates
  of costumes
kpl. see komplet
kplt. see komplet
kraftig: forceful, heavy
krideret: fine-coated (paper)
kritik(er): review(s)
kritiker(e): reviewer(s)
krøllet: crushed, crinkled
krønike(r): chronicle(s)
kronologisk: chronological
krusedulle: flourish, paraph
kse. see kassette
kundskab: knowledge, study
kunst: art
kunstbilag: art supplement
kunstbog(bøger): art book(s)
kunstgengiv. see kunstgengivelse
kunstgengivelse(r): art reproduc-
  tion(s)
kunstlaeder: imitation leather,
  leatherette
kunstner(e): artist(s)
kunstnerisk: artistic
kunsttr. see kunsttryk
kunsttryk: art printing
kunsttrykpapir: art paper, fine-
  coated paper
kunstudgave: de luxe edition
kuriøs: curious, quaint
kursiv: italics
kvadratisk: square
kvart: quarto
kvartalskrift: quarterly publication
kvartark: quarto sheet
kvarto: quarto
kvartside: quarto page

27

kyndig: experienced, expert

laeder: leather
laederkapitael: leather headband
laedermosaik: inlaid leatherwork
laederryg: leather back
laenkebind: chained binding
laer: leather
laerde selskaber: learned so-
　cieties
laerde selskaper: learned so-
　cieties
laerebog: textbook
laerebok: textbook
laerredsbd. see laerredsbind
laerredsbetrukket: cloth-covered
laerredsbind: cloth binding
laerredsbundet: clothbound
laerredsfals(e): cloth joint(s),
　guard(s)
laerredskant(er): cloth edging(s)
laerredsryg: cloth back
laerredsside(r): cloth cover(s)
laerrygg: cloth back
laesebog: reader, textbook
landkart: map(s)
landkort: map(s)
landtoning(er): view(s)
lang: long
langnarvet: long-grained
langs: along
lap: patch
lapp: patch
lappet: patched
latinske bogstaver: roman script
lav: low
ldrryg. see laederryg
ledet: directed
ledsaget: accompanied
leksikon: encyclopedia, diction-
　ary
lerret: cloth
lesebok: textbook
let: slight, slightly
lett: slight, slightly
lette: light, slight
leveres: be furnished, delivered
levering: delivery; fascicle, part

lex-8vo. see lexikon-octavo
lexikon-octavo: large octavo
liden: small
lidt: a few, a little
lige: straight
lige side: verso
lige utkommet: just published
ligeledes: likewise
liggeled: also, likewise
lilje(r): fleur(s)-de-lys
lille: short, small
lille smule: a little
linie(r): line(s)
linieforgyldn. see linieforgyldning
linieforgyldning: gold fillets
linieret: lined, ruled
linietaelling: marginal line
　numbers
linje(r): line(s)
linjemønster: pattern of lines
linoleum-snit: linoleum-cut plate
linosnit: linoleum-cut plate
lit. see litografi
liten: small
litograferet: lithographed
litografert: lithographed
litografi: lithographed plate,
　lithography
litografisk: lithographic
litt: slightly
litteraturheft(e): bibliographic
　issue(s)
livserindringer: memoirs
livsskildring: biography
lødig: fine
lødigste: finest
lomme: pocket
lommebog: pocketbook, almanac
løs: loose, unstuck
løs-ryg: hollow back
løse ark i mappe: loose signatures
　in portfolio
løst monteret: loosely mounted
luksusudg. see luksusudgave
luksusudgave: de luxe edition
lydefri: perfect, flawless
lydefrit: perfect, flawless
lys: light-colored, pale

lyst: light-colored, pale
lysebrun: light brown
lystryk: photolithograph(s),
  photolithography
lystryksgengiv. *see* lystryks-
  gengivelse
lystryksgengivelse(r): reproduc-
  tion(s) in photolithography

m.fl. *see* med flere
m.m. *see* med mere
maanedsskrift: monthly
maerke(r): mark(s)
maerkelig: strange, unusual
makuleret: damaged
makulert: damaged
maleri(er): painting(s)
malet: painted
månedlig: monthly
månedsskrift: monthly
manga: many, numerous
mange: many, numerous
manglende: missing
mangler: lacking, missing
manuskript: manuscript
manuskriptsamling: collection
  of manuscripts
mappe(r): portfolio(s)
margen(er): margin(s)
margin-notater: marginal notes
marginalnotater: marginal notes
markspist: worm-eaten
marmor. *see* marmoreret
marmoreret: marbled
marmorering: marbling
marokin: morocco
maroquin: morocco
maroquintitelfelt: morocco
  title piece
maskinmanuskript: typescript
maskinopsk. *see* maskinopskåret
maskinopskåret: trimmed by
  machine
maskinskr. *see* maskinskrevet
maskinskrevet: typed
maskinskript: typescript
mat: tarnished, without luster
med flere: with several others

med hvide blade: interleaved
med kyndig hand: by an expert
  craftsman
med meget: etc., etc.
med mere: among others, *inter alia*
medaillon: medallion
medaljong: medallion
medarb. *see* medarbeider
medarbeider: collaborator
medbundet: bound with, bound in
medforfatter: coauthor, joint author
medindbd. *see* medindbundet
medindbundet: bound with
medl. *see* medlem
medlem(mer): member(s)
medt. *see* medtaget
medtaget: damaged, worn
medtatt: damaged, worn
medvirkning: collaboration, co-
  operation
meget sjaelden: very rare
meget sjelden: very rare
mellem mangt: among others
memoirer: memoirs
merke: mark
messingsbeslag: brass decorative
  ornamentation
messingspaende(r): brass clasp(s)
mg. *see* manga, mange
mgl. *see* mangler
middelalder: Middle Ages
middelalderen: Middle Ages
middelalderlig: medieval
middelmaatig: mediocre
midte: center
midtre: central
mimeograferet: mimeographed
mindealbum: commemorative
  album
mindeskrift: commemorative
  volume
mindeudg. *see* mindeudgave
mindeudgave: commemorative
  edition
mindre: smaller, minor, less
miniaturebog: miniature book
minneskrift: commemorative
  volume

29

minneutgave: commemorative
edition
modsat: opposite
monografi: monograph
monteret: mounted
montert: mounted
mørkeblå: dark blue
mørkebrun: dark brown
mørkegrøn: dark green
mosaik: mosaic, inlaid
motiv(er): motif(s)
motsatt: opposite
motto: motto, epigraph
ms. *see* manuskript
mskript. *see* manuscript
mugplet: mildew spot
mus. *see* notetrykk
myke: flexible
mykt: flexible

n.p. *see* nedsat pris, ny pris
n.p.o. *see* navn på omslag
n.p.s. *see* navn på smudsbladet
n.p.smt. *see* navn på smudstitelblad
n.p.t. *see* navn på titelblad
naest: next to, after
naesten: almost
naestnyeste: penultimate, next
to the last or latest
naestsidste: penultimate, next
to the last or latest
naevnt: mentioned
narv(er): grain, scoring
navn: name
navn på friblad: name on flyleaf
navn på omslag: name on cover
navn på smudsbladet: name on
flyleaf
navn på smudstitelblad: name on
half-title page
navn på titelblad: name on title
page
navne- og sagregister: index of
names and subjects
navne- og sakregister: index of
names and subjects
navneliste: list of names
navnetrekk: signature
30

nederste: bottom, lower
nedkratset: disfigured by scribbling
nedre: bottom, lower
nedsat pris: reduced price
neste: next
nettopris: net price
nevnt: mentioned
ngl. *see* nogle
ni: nine
niende: ninth
niger: morocco
nigerskind: morocco
nitten(de): nineteen(th)
nitti(ende): ninety(ieth)
no. *see* nummer
nodebilag: music supplement
nodetillaeg: music supplement
noe: some, somewhat, a little
noen: some
noget: some, somewhat, a little
nogle: some
nøgleroman: *roman à clef*
nøjagtig: exact
norsk: Norwegian
notater: notes
note(r): annotation(s)
notemateriale: annotations
notesbog: notebook
notetrykk: printed music
notitser: notes
noveller: short stories, tales
nr. *see* nummer
nulevende: contemporary
numm. *see* nummereret
nummer: number
nummereret: numbered
nummerering: numbering, pagination
nummerert: numbered
nummr. *see* nummereret
nutidig: modern, present-day
ny: new
ny pris: list price
nyare: newer
nydelig: nice
nyere: newer
nyerhvervelse(r): recent acqui-
sition(s)

nyeste: newest, most recent
nyindkøb: recent acquisitions
nynorsk: New Norwegian
nyt: new
nytaarsbog: New Year publication
nytryk: reprint(s), reprinting
nytt: new

o. *see* omslag, over
o.a. *see* og andre
o.m. *see* også med
o.m.a. *see* og mange andre
o.o. *see* originalt omslag
o.s.v. *see* og så videre
oaseged: deep-grained morocco
ødelagt: destroyed
off. *see* offentlig
offentlig: public
officiel(t): official(ly)
offisiell: official(ly)
offset: offset
offsettryk: offset printing
ofte: often
og andet: and others
og andre: and others
og mange andre: and many others
og så videre: et cetera
også: also
også med: (bound) together with
øjensynlig: obvious
okart. *see* originalkartonnage
oksehud: oxhide
omarb. *see* omarbeidet,
  omarbejdet
omarbeidet: revised
omarbejdet: revised
omfattende: comprehensive
omfatter: comprises
omgitt (av): surrounded (by),
  framed (with)
omgivet (af): surrounded (by),
  framed (with)
omhandler: deals with
omhdl. *see* omhandler
omhyggelig(t): careful(ly)
omkranset: framed, surrounded
omkring: around
omredigeret: revised, re-edited

omredigering: revision
omrids: outline
omriss: outline
oms. *see* omsett
omsett: translated
omsl. *see* omslag
omslag: wrapper
omstillet: transposed
omtrent: approximately
omtrykt: reprinted
ønsket: desired
ophøjede bind: raised bands
opkl. *see* opklaebet
opklaebet: mounted
opl. *see* oplag
oplag: printing, edition
oplagstal: number of copies
  printed
oplysende: explanatory
oplysn. *see* oplysning
oplysning(er): explanatory note(s)
oplyst: explained, interpreted;
  enlightened
oppbd. *see* originalpapbind
opphøjde: raised
oppklebet: mounted
oppl. *see* opplag
opplag: printing, edition
oppslagsbok: reference book
opptrykk: reprint
opr. *see* oprindelig
oprindelig: original
opprinnelig: original
opsiktsvaekkende: startling,
  sensational
opskaaren: opened (with paper
  knife)
opslagsvaerk: reference work
optegnelser: notes
optr. *see* optryk
optryk: reprint
optrykt: reprinted
or. *see* original
ordbog: dictionary
ordbok: dictionary
orden: order (sequence)
ordliste: vocabulary, word list
ordnede: arranged

ordnet: arranged
ordre: order (purchase)
ordsamling: vocabulary, word list
organ: publication
orienterende: exploratory
orig.skb. *see* originalskindbind
orig-ms. *see* original-manuskript
origb. *see* originalbind
original: original
original-manuskript: author's manuscript
originalbind: original binding
originalgrafik: original engravings, etchings
originalkartonnage: original paperboard binding
originalpapbind: original boards
originalradering(er): original etching(s)
originalshirting: original cloth
originalskindbind: original leather binding
originalt omslag: original wrapper
originaludgave: original edition
originalutgave: original edition
orm(e): worm(s)
ormaedt: worm-eaten
ormehul(ler): wormhole(s)
ormstukken: worm-eaten
ornert: decorated
oshirt. *see* originalshirting
osv. *see* og så videre
otte(nde): eight(h)
otti(ende): eighty(ieth)
ov. *see* over
oven. *see* for oven
ovenfor: above
ovennaevnte: above-mentioned
ovenstående: above
over: over, about, of
overalt: universally
overdaadigt: abundantly; exquisitely
overdådig: abundantly; exquisitely
overordentlig: extraordinary

overs. *see* oversat, oversigt
oversaettelse: translation
oversaetter(e): translator(s)
oversat: translated
oversatt: translated
oversetter(e): translator(s)
oversigt: summary, survey
oversigtstavle: synoptic table
oversikt: summary, survey
overskrift: superscription, heading
oversnit: top edge
øverste: upper
overstreget: crossed out, canceled
overtrukket: covered, coated
øvre: upper
øvrige: remaining, others

p. *see* pagina
på lager: in stock, available
på stort papir: on large paper
paa forlangende: on request
paa hovedet: upside down
paany: again, anew
påbegyndt: started
paent: neat, nice
pag. *see* pagineret, paginering
pagina(ae): page(s)
pagineret: paginated, numbered
paginering: pagination
påklaebet: pasted on, mounted
påklistret: pasted on, mounted
pamflet: pamphlet
påny: again, anew
pap: cardboard
papaeske: pasteboard box
papbd. *see* papbind
papbind: boards
papir(er): paper(s)
papirbind: boards
papkart. *see* papkartonnage
papkartonnage: box, slipcase
papomslag: paperboard covers
papp: cardboard
pappb. *see* pappbind
pappbind: boards
pappermer: cased binding
paraferet: initialed
paralleltekst: parallel text

påsat: affixed, superimposed
påsatt: affixed, superimposed
påtrykt: printed on, imprinted
pen: neat, fine
pene: neat, fine
pennetegning(er): pen and ink
   drawing(s)
pent: neat, fine
perfekt: perfect
pergament: parchment, vellum
pergamentforstaerkning(er):
   vellum reinforcing(s)
pergamenthåndskrift(er): vellum
   manuscript(s)
pergamentryg: parchment back(s)
pergt. see pergament
perkal: calico
perkalin: buckram
perm: side
personal- og real-register: index
   of persons and subjects
personliste: list of persons
personregister: index of names
pirattryk: pirated publication(s)
pjece: pamphlet, booklet
pl. see plettet, planche
plan(er): map(s), plan(s)
planche(r): plate(s)
plano: unfolded
plansje(r): plate(s)
pletfri: spotless
plettet: spotted
plettfri: spotless
pluv. see pluviusin
pluviusin: leatherette, fabrikoid
poleret: polished, calendered
polert: polished, calendered
polykrom: multicolored
pompøs: grandiose, impressive
porfyr: porphyry
port. see portraet
porto: postage
portofrit: prepaid
portr. see portraet
portr.-stik. see portraetstik
portraet(ter): portrait(s)
portraetstik: engraved portrait
portraettegninger: portrait
   drawings
portrett(er): portrait(s)
pr. see pro
praeget: stamped, tooled
praegtig: magnificent, splendid
pragteksemplar: beautiful copy
pragtfuld: splendid
pragtvaerk: de luxe work
praktverk: de luxe work
prektig: splendid
presset: tooled, stamped
pris(er): price(s)
prisbelønnet: prize-winning
priv. see privat
privat: private, privately
privatbind: three-quarter binding
privattryk: privately printed
privilegium: permit to publish
pro: per, each
prospekt(er): view(s)
prøve(r): specimen(s), sample(s)
proveniens: provenance
prøveoversaettelse: tentative
   translation
provinstryk: provincial publication
prydet: adorned
prydinitial(er): ornamental
   initial(s)
pseud. see pseudonym
pseudonym: pseudonym
publ. see publikasjon
publikasjon(er): publication(s)
publikation(er): publication(s)
punkteret: stippled

quartal: quarter

r. see rekke
raakant: deckled edges
rabat: discount
radering(er): etching(s)
raekke(r): series
ramme: frame, border
rand: edge, margin
randbemaerkning(er): marginal
   note(s)
randbemerk. see randbemerkning

33

randbemerkning(er): marginal note(s)
randforsiring: ornamental border
randnotater: marginal notes
rankevaerk: scrolls, interlaced pattern
raritet: rarity
ratebetaling: installment payment
recension: review
red. *see* redaksjon, redaktør, redigeret
redaksjon: editorship
redaktion: editorship
redaktør: editor
redegørelse: report
redigeret: edited
redigert: edited
referat: report
registerbind: index volume
rekke(r): series
remme: ties
ren: clean
renset: expurgated
renskrift: fair copy
rep. *see* repareret
reparation: repair
repareret: repaired
reparert: repaired
reproduceret: reproduced
reprodusert: reproduced
rest: the balance, the rest
restaureret: restored, repaired
restaurering: restoring, repair
restoplag: remainders
resumé: summary
ret: rather
rettelse(r): correction(s)
rettleiing: introduction
rev. *see* revideret
revet: torn
revne: crack, split
revnet: split
revideret: revised
revidert: revised
rift: tear
rig: rich
rigt: richly
rik: rich

rikt: richly
rk. *see* raekke
rocaille: shell-like pattern
rød: red
rødkridtet: marked with red pencil
rødlig: reddish: fawn-colored
roman: novel
rovtryk: pirated publication(s)
rubriceret: rubricated
rubrik: rubric, heading
rubrisert: rubricated
rudeformet: lozenze-shaped
rudemønstret: checkered design
rulle(r): scroll(s)
ruskindbd. *see* ruskindbind
ruskindbind: suede binding
ruslaeder: Russian leather
rustplet(ter): foxing
rustplettet: foxed
ryg: back, spine
rygdekoration: ornamentation on spine
rygfals: back joint
rygfelt(er): panel(s) on back or spine
rygforg. *see* rygforgyldning
rygforgyldn. *see* rygforgyldning
rygforgyldning: gold tooling on back
rygg: back, spine
rygskilt: label, lettering piece
rygtitel: spine title

s. *see* side
s.p.t. *see* stempel paa titelblad
saaledes: thus, in this condition
saelges: sold, available
saerdeles: especially
saerlig: special
saernummer: special issue
saerpraeget: unusual
saertilbud: special offer
saertr. *see* saertryk
saertryk: separate, reprint
saerudg. *see* saerudgave
saerudgave: special edition, de luxe edition

34

saerutgave: special edition,
  de luxe edition
saffian: morocco
saffiansryg: morocco back
saffiansrygg: morocco back
sagregister: subject index
sakregister: subject index
således: thus, in this state
salg: sale
samarb. *see* samarbeid
samarbeid: collaboration
saml. *see* samlet, samling
samlebind: collective work
samlede: collected, compiled
samlede verker: collected works
samler(e): collector(s)
samlet: collected, compiled
samlevaerk: composite work
samling(er): collection(s)
samlingsverk: collective work
samme: same
sammelbind: collective volume
sammen med: together with
sammenbragt: gathered
sammenbundet: bound together
sammendrag: abstract
sammenfold. *see* sammenfoldet
sammenfoldet: folded
sammenlagt: laid together
sammenlignende: comparative
sammenstykket: mended
samt: and, together with
samt. *see* samtidig
samtid. *see* samtidig
samtidig: contemporary
samtlig: entire, complete
sarsenett: book cloth
sart(e): delicate
schatteret: hatched
scholier: scholia, critical notes
se: see
segl: seal
seks: six
seksten(de): sixteen(th)
seksti(ende): sixty(ieth)
selskab(er): society(ies)
selskap(er): society(ies)
selvbiografi: autobiography

selvportraet: self-portrait
selvskrevet: autograph, in one's
  own handwriting
selvstaendig: independent
senere: later
sep. *see* separat
separat: separate, separately
sepia: sepia
serie: series
serpr. *see* serprent
serprent: separate, offprint
sett: set
shb. *see* shirtingsbind
shirt. *see* shirting
shirting: cloth
shirtingrygg: cloth spine, half
  cloth
shirtingsbd. *see* shirtingsbind
shirtingsbind: cloth binding
shirtingsomslag: cloth wrapper
shirtomsl. *see* shirtingsomslag
shr. *see* shirtingrygg
side: page, side
sideforgyldning: gold tooling on
  sides
sideløbende: facing, opposite
sider: pages, sides
sidetal: number of pages, pagination
sidetitel: cover title
sidste: last, final
sidstnaevnt: last mentioned
sign. *see* signeret
signatur: signature; letter or
  number denoting signature
signeret: signed
signert: signed
silkebind: silk binding
silkeforsats: silk end papers
silkemoiré: watered silk, tabby
simpel: simple, unpretentious
siselert: goffered
siste: last, final
sjaeld. *see* sjaelden
sjaelden: seldom found, rare
sjaeldenhed: rarity
sjaeldneste: rarest
sjagreng: shagreen

sjelden: rare
sjeldenhet: rarity
sjette: sixth
sjirting: cloth
skadet: damaged
skaeg: bearded edge(s)
skaev: askew, crooked
skb. *see* skindbind
skildring(er): description(s)
skimmelplet: mildew
skind: leather
skindafstødning(er): rubbing
   damage(s) to leather
skindbind: leather binding
skindindlaeg: leather intarsia
skindkanter: leather edges
skindryg: leather back
skindtit. *see* skindtitel
skindtitel: leather title piece
skinn: leather
skinnbind: leather binding
skinnrygg: leather spine, half
   leather
skisse(r): sketch(es)
skitse(r): sketch(es)
skizze(r): sketch(es)
skjev: askew, crooked
skjold(er): stain(s)
skønhedsfejl: blemish(es)
skønnlitteratur: fiction, belles-
   lettres
skr. *see* skinnrygg
skrabet: scratched, scraped
skramme: scratch
skrammet: scratched, scraped
skrapet: scratched, scraped
skravering: azure tooling
skrevet: written
skrift(er): work(s), writing(s)
skriftmaal: literary language
skrivepapir: writing paper,
   ledger paper
skriver(e): writer(s), scribe(s)
skrivter: works, writings
skrotstik: dotted print(s)
skuespil: play, drama
skygget: hatched
slaegtstavle(r): genealogical

table(s)
slidt: worn, frayed
slitt: worn, frayed
slutning: end, conclusion
slutt: end
sluttede: closed up, ended
slutvignet: tailpiece
slyngning(er): tracery, scroll(s)
sm. *see* smukt
smaapletter: small spots
smaaskrifter: miscellanea
smaedeskrift(er): lampoon(s)
småflekker: small spots
småfortaelling(er): short story(ies)
smagfuld: tasteful
smakfull: tasteful
smal: narrow, thin
småskr. *see* småskrifter
småskrifter: miscellanea
smt. *see* smudstitel
smudset: dirty, soiled
smudsig: dirty, soiled
smudsomslag: dust jacket
smudstitel: half title, bastard title
smudstitelblad: half-title page
smuk: nice
smukkest(e): nicest
smukt: handsomely
smusset: dirty, soiled
smussig: dirty, soiled
smussomslag: dust jacket
smusstitel: half title, bastard title
smykket: adorned
snavset: dirty, soiled
snit: edges
snitmaleri: fore-edge painting
snitt: edges
søgt: sought
søkort: chart(s)
sol. *see* solid
solgt: sold
solid: strong, well-made
sølv: silver
sølvspaender: silver clasps
som altid: as always
som ny: as new
som regel: as a rule, in general
som vanlig: as usual

sommer: Summer
sommeren: Summer
sørgespil: tragedy
sort: black
sortkunst: mezzotint process
spaende(r): clasp(s)
spaenderest(er): remnant(s) of
  clasps
spaettet: speckled
spalte(r): column(s)
special: special
specielt: especially
spejl: panelwork; lining
spejlbind: leather binding with
  panel designs, "mirror" binding
spenner: clasps
spesiell: special
spesielt: especially
spiralheftet: spiral binding
splittet: split, cracked
spor: trace(s)
spraengt: sprinkled
spraenkt: sprinkled
sprukket: cracked
ss. *see* sider
st. *see* stempel
st.hft. *see* stift heftet
st.p.t. *see* stempel paa titelblad
staalstik: steel engraving(s)
stadig: stable, steady
staerkt: strongly, considerably
staffage: adornments
stålstikk: steel engraving(s)
stamtavle(r): genealogical table(s)
stand: state, condition
standardudgave: standard edition
standset: ceased
steintrykk: lithograph,
  lithography
stempel(pler): stamp(s), mark(s)
  left by a stamp, stamping tool
stempel paa titelblad: stamp on
  title page
stemplet: stamped
stens. *see* stensilert
stensilert: mimeographed
stentrykt(e): lithographed
sterk: strongly, greatly

sterkt: strongly, greatly
stift heftet: boards
stik: engraving(s)
stikk: engraving(s)
stikordskatalog: subject catalog
stikordsregister: subject index
stilfuld: stylish, tasteful
stivheftet: boards
stødt: mutilated, crushed
stoffbind: cloth binding
stor: large
storartet: excellent
storhefte(r): large part(s),
  fascicle(s)
større: larger, greater
størrelse: size
største: largest, greatest
størstedelen: the largest part
stort: large
støvet: dusty
stregbordure: gilt lines, fillets
stregfilet(er): line fillet(s)
stregforgyldning: gold tooling in
  line designs, fillets
streker: lines, marks, markings
striemappe: canvas portfolio
strimmel: wrapper
stukket: engraved
stukne: engraved
styg: ugly, bad
stygg: ugly, bad
stykke(r): part(s), piece(s)
subskript. *see* subskription
subskription: subscription
subskription er bindende for hele
  vaerket: subscribers contract
  for entire work
superexlibris: ownership stamp
suppl. *see* supplement
supplement: supplement
supplementshefte: supplementary
  issue
supplerende: supplementary
supplert: supplemented
supprimert: suppressed
svaert: heavy, thick
svag: slight
svak: slight

svensk: Swedish
svineskind: pigskin
sytten(de): seventeen(th)
sytti(ende): seventy(ieth)
syv(ende): seven(th)

tab: loss
tab. *see* tabel
tabel(ler): table(s)
tallrik(e): numerous
talr. *see* talrig
talrig(e): numerous
tavle(r): plate(s)
tb. *see* tabel
tegn. *see* tegning
tegnede: drawn
tegner(e): artist(s), illustrator(s)
tegnet: drawn
tegngr. *see* tegninger
tegning(er): drawing(s)
teikning(ar): drawing(s)
tekst: text
tekstbd. *see* tekstbind
tekstbilag: text supplement
tekstbind: text volume
tekstbl. *see* tekstblad
tekstblad: text page
tekstfigurer: illustrations in the text
tekstforklaring(er): textual explanation(s)
teksthefte: text part; issue
tekstkritisk(e): critical
tekstrettelse(r): correction(s) in the text
teksttab: loss of text
teksttap: loss of text
temmelig: rather, fairly
textbidrag: textual contribution(s)
textrevision: revision of text
ti(ende): ten(th)
tiaar: decade
tiår: decade
tidebog: Book of Hours
tidl. *see* tidlig
tidlig: early
tidligst: earliest, first
tidsskr. *see* tidsskrift

tidsskrift(er): journal(s), magazine(s), periodical(s)
tidsskriftraekke: run (of a journal)
tiende: tenth
til bogladepris: at list price
til minde om: in commemoration of
til priser: at prices
tilblivelse: origin
tilbud: offer
tilbyde: offer
tildels: partly
tilegnelse: dedicatory note
tilegnet: dedicated to
tilføjelse(r): addition(s)
tilføyde: added
tilføyelse(r): addition(s)
tilhørende: belonging to
tilhørt: belonged to
tillaeg: supplement, appendix
tillaegsbind: supplementary volume
tilleg: supplement, appendix
tilligemed: together with
tilrettelagt: arranged
tilsammen: together, in all
tilskrift(er): handwritten note(s)
tilskrivn. *see* tilskrivning
tilskrivning: handwritten notes
tilsmudset: soiled
tilstand: state
tilstede: extant, present
tilstraekkelig: sufficient
tit. *see* titel
titel: title
titel-etiket: title label
titelbilde: frontispiece
titelbillede: frontispiece
titelbl. *see* titelblad
titelblad: title page
titelfelt: title piece, label
titelkobber: engraved frontispiece; engraving on title page
titelskilt: label on spine
titelvignett: vignette on the title page
to: two

38

tolv(te): twelve (twelfth)
tomefelt: volume label
tonede: shaded, tinted
tonet: shaded, tinted
tontryk: tint(s)
topp: top
tospaltet: two-column
tr. *see* trykkeri, trykt
traepermer: wood boards
traeplade(r): wood board(s)
traeskårne: woodcut
traesn. *see* traesnit
traesnit: woodcut(s)
traesnitvignetter: woodcut
  vignettes
traktat: treatise
tre(dje): three (third)
tredive: thirty
tredivte: thirtieth
tredjedel: third
treliniet: three-line
trepermer: wooden boards
tresidet: three-sided
tresnittillustrasjoner: woodcut
  illustrations
tretten(de): thirteen(th)
tryk: printing, prints
trykfejl: misprint(s)
trykk: printing, prints
trykkeri: printing office
trykning: printing
trykpapireksemplar: edition on
  special paper, usually large
  paper edition
trykpapirekspl. *see* trykpapireksemplar
trykt: printed
tsd. *see* tusind
tus. *see* tusen
tuschmanér: chiaroscuro
tusen: thousand(s)
tusende(r): thousand(s)
tusind: thousand(s)
tusinde(r): thousand(s)
tv. *see* tvaer
tvaer: oblong
tvaerfolio: oblong folio
tvende: two

tverr: oblong
tvl. *see* tavle
tyding: translation
tyk: thick, heavy
tykk: thick, heavy
tykkelse: thickness
tynd: thin
tyndpapir: Bible paper
tynn: thin
tynt: thin
type(r): type
tysk: German
tyve(nde): twenty(ieth)

u. *see* uddrag
u.a. *see* uden aar, uden aarstal
u.å. *see* uden år
u.st. *see* uden sted
u.st.o.å. *see* uden trykkested og år
ualmindeligt: unusual, uncommon
ualminnelig: unusual, uncommon
uberørt: untouched, intact
ubesk. *see* ubeskaaret
ubeskaaret: untrimmed, with
  deckled or rough edge
ubeskåret: untrimmed, with
  deckled or rough edge
ubetydelig: insignificant, slight
ubrugt: unused, as new
udarb. *see* udarbejdet
udarbejdet: compiled
udateret: undated
udbedret: repaired
udbedring: repair, correction
udbudt: offered
udbyde: offer
uddr. *see* uddrag
uddrag: extract(s), selection(s)
uddragne: selected, excerpted
uden aar: without date
uden år: without date
uden aarstal: without date
uden sted: without place
uden trykkeaar: without date
uden trykker: without printer
uden trykkested: without place of
  publication
uden trykkested og år: without

39

place or date
udfoldeligt: folding
udfoldningskobbere: folded engravings
udførlig: detailed
udførligt: detailed
udført: executed
udg. *see* udgave, udgivet
udgave(r): edition(s)
udgave for ungdommen: juvenile edition
udgivelse: publication, issuance
udgiver: editor, publisher
udgivet: edited
udk. *see* udkom
udkast: draft
udkom: published
udkommer ikke mere: no longer published
udkommer om kort tid: to appear shortly
udm. *see* udmaerket
udmaerket: excellent, distinguished
uds. *see* udsolgt
uds.i.b. *see* udsolgt i boghandelen
udsalg: sale
udsdt. *see* udsendt
udsendelse: issuing, distribution
udsendt: distributed, issued
udskaering: excision
udskåret: cut out, carved
udslettet: erased
udsmykket: adorned, ornamented
udsmykning: decoration
udsn. *see* udsnit
udsnit: excerpt, excised portion
udsogt: choice
udsolgt: out of print
udsolgt i boghandelen: out-of-print
udtog: excerpt, abstract
udtømmende: exhaustive
udtvaering: rubbing
udv. *see* udvalg, udvalgt
udvalg: choice, selection
udvalgt: chosen, selected
udvendig: external

udvidet: increased, enlarged
uens: unlike, differing
uens. *see* uensartet
uensartet: disparate, not uniform
ufarget: uncolored, natural
ufarvet: uncolored, natural
uforandret: unchanged
ufriskt: soiled
ufuldendt: unfinished
ufullstendig: incomplete
ugeblad: weekly
ugeskrift: weekly
uhyre: exceedingly
uib. *see* uindbundet
uillustr. *see* uillustreret
uillustreret: without illustrations
uillustrert: without illustrations
uindbundet: unbound
uinnbundet: unbound
ukeblad: weekly publication
ukendt: unknown, unlisted
ukentlig: weekly
ukjent: unknown, unlisted
ukomplet: incomplete
ulastelig: impeccable, irreproachable
ulike: unlike, dissimilar, not alike
ums. *see* umsett
umsetjing: translation
umsett: translated
umvølt: translated, adapted
under medv. af *see* under medvirkning af
under medvirkning af: with the collaboration of
under trykken: in press
under udgivelse: in course of publication
underskønt: magnificent
underskrift: signature
undersnit: bottom edge
undersøgelse(r): investigation(s), study(ies)
undersøkelse(r): investigation(s), study(ies)
understr. *see* understreget, understregning
understreget: underlined

40

understregning(er): underlining(s)
understrek. *see* understrekning
understrekning(er): underlining(s)
undertitel: subtitle
undertrykt: suppressed
ungdomsudgave: juvenile edition
unumm. *see* unummereret
unummereret: unnumbered
uops. *see* uopskaaret
uopskaaret: unopened, uncut
uopskr. *see* uopskaaret
upag. *see* upagineret
upagineret: with pages unnumbered
upg. *see* upagineret
usedvanlig: unusual, unusually
usigneret: unsigned
utal: multitude
utarb. *see* utarbeidelse,
  utarbeidet
utarbeidelse: preparation,
  editing
utarbeidet: prepared, edited
utdrag: extract(s)
utg. *see* utgave, utgit, utgiver
utgave: edition
utgit: published, edited
utgitt: published, edited
utgiver: editor
utgjevi: edited
utgjevne: edited
utgjør: constitutes, comprises
utk. *see* utkommer
utklippsbok: scrapbook
utkommer: is (are) published
utrykt: unpublished
utsolgt: out-of-print
utstilling: exhibition
utvalg: selection
uundvaerlig: indispensable
uunnvaerlig: indispensable
uvurderlig: invaluable

våben: coat(s) of arms
våbenskjold(e): coat(s) of arms
vaelskbd. *see* vaelskbind
vaelskbind: half-sheepskin
  binding with corners

vaerdi: value
vaerdifuld: valuable
vaerdig: worthy
vaerk(er): work(s)
vakker: beautiful, handsome
vakkert: beautiful, handsome
vandmaerke: watermark
vandskjold(er): water stain(s)
vandskjoldet: stained by water
vannmerke: watermark
vannskjold(er): water stain(s)
vanskelig: difficult
vår: Spring
våren: Spring
variant(er): variant(s)
variation(er): variation(s)
vasket: washed
vedføjet: added, written in
vedhaengende: attached
vedlagt: accompanying, added,
  enclosed
vejledn. *see* vejledning
vejledning: introduction, direc-
  tions
velbev. *see* velbevaret
velbevaret: well-preserved
velbevart: well-preserved
velh. *see* velholdt
velholdt: well-preserved
velin. *see* velinpapir
velinpapir: vellum paper
venstre: left-hand
verdi: value
verdifull: valuable
verdifullt: valuable
verdiløs: worthless
verk(er): work(s)
versalbogstav(er): capital(s)
vetenskapelig: scientific,
  scholarly
videnskabelig: scientific,
  scholarly
vidner: witnesses
vidunderlig: marvelous
vign. *see* vignet
vignet(ter): vignette(s), head-
  piece(s)
vignetkobber: engraved vignette

41

vigtig: important
vigtigst(e): most important
vinrødt: wine-colored
vinter: Winter
vinteren: Winter
virkningsfuld: striking, impressive
vuggetryk: incunabulum(a)

vurdering: evaluation

xylograferet: woodcut

yderst: extremely
ydre: outer, external
ypperlig: outstanding
ytre: outer, external

DUTCH

aanbieding: offer
aangeb. *see* aangeboden
aangeboden: offered
aangekondigd: announced
aangevuld: increased,
  supplemented
aanhangsel: appendix,
  supplement, annex
aanhangselen: appendixes,
  supplements, annexes
aanhangsels: appendixes,
  supplements, annexes
aant. *see* aantekening
aantal: number
aantekening(en): annotation(s),
  note(s)
aantrekkelijk(e): attractive
aanvulling(en): addition(s),
  supplement(s)
aanwezig: extant, available
aanwinst: acquisition
ab. *see* abonnement
abonn. *see* abonnement
abonnement: subscription
acht(ste): eight(h)
achttien(de): eighteen(th)
achterplat(ten): back cover(s)
afb. *see* afbeelding
afbeelding(en): illustration(s)

afbestellen: cancel
afbn. *see* afbeeldingen
afd. *see* afdeling
afdeling(en): part(s)
afdruk: printing
afgebroken: broken off
afgeknaagd: gnawed
afgescheurd: torn off
afgesneden: trimmed, opened
afgeweekt: loose, unstuck
afkorting: abridgment,
  abbreviation
afl. *see* aflevering
aflev. *see* aflevering
aflevering(en): part(s), issue(s)
afmeting: size, format
afschr. *see* afschrift
afschrift(en): copy(ies)
afzonderlijk: separate(ly),
  detached
album: album
algemeen: general, generally
alleenverkoop: exclusive
  distribution
alles wat verscheen: all
  published
alles wat verschenen is: all
  published
almanak: almanac

als nieuw: as new
anastatisch: anastatic
ander: other, another
anders: otherwise
annotatie(s): annotation(s)
anoniem: anonymous
antiquaar: antiquarian bookseller
antiquariaat: antiquarian
  bookshop
aquarel: water color
aquatint: aquatint
arabesk: arabesque
archief: archives
art. *see* artikel
artikel: article, essay
artikelen: articles, essays
artikels: articles, essays
atlas: atlas
auteur: author
auteursrecht: copyright
authentiek: authentic
autobiographie: autobiography
autograaf(grafen): autograph(s)
autotypie: halftone engraving
azuurblauw: azure-colored

b.v. *see* bij voorbeeld
band(en): binding(s), cover(s),
  wrapper(s)
bandnummer: volume number
bandstempel: binder's tool
beginletter: initial
behalve: except, besides
bekrabbeld: disfigured by
  scribbling
bekroond: prize-winning
belangrijk: important,
  outstanding
bellettrie: fiction
ben. *see* benevens
benedenmarge: lower margin
benevens: together with,
  including
bep. *see* beperkt
beperkt: limited
beredeneerd: commented
bericht(en): report(s)

besch. *see* beschadigd
beschad. *see* beschadigd
beschadigd: damaged
beschreven: described
besmeurd: soiled
bestelformulier: order form
bestellen: to order, to place an
  order
bestelling: order
betaling: payment
betr. *see* betreffende
betreffende: concerning
bevat: contains
bevestigd: confirmed
bevestiging: confirmation
bew. *see* bewerkt
bewerker: editor
bewerking: version, adaptation
bewerkt: edited, arranged,
  adapted
bez. *see* bezorgd
bezaan: sheepskin
bezorgd: edited
bibl. *see* bibliotheek
bibl.-st. *see* bibliotheek-stempel
bibliografie: bibliography
bibliografisch: bibliographic
bibliothecaris: librarian
bibliotheek: library
bibliotheek-stempel: library
  mark, library stamp
bij elkaar: together
bij voorbeeld: for example
bijdr. *see* bijdrage
bijdrage(n): contribution(s)
bijeengezocht: collected
bijeenverzameld: collected
bijgeb. *see* bijgebonden
bijgebonden: bound in
bijgev. *see* bijgevoegd
bijgevoegd: added, appended
bijl. *see* bijlage
bijlage(n): appendix(es),
  supplement(s)
bijvoegsel: supplement, appendix
bijvoegselen: supplements,
  appendixes

bijvoegsels: supplements,
  appendixes
binder: bookbinder
binnenkort: shortly
binnenlands: domestic
binnenrand: inside margin
binnenspiegel: lining, *doublure*
blad(en): leaf(ves), page(s)
blad van het voorwerk: preliminary leaf
bladmotief: leafy scroll
bladnummering: foliation
bladwijzer: index, table of
  contents
bladz. *see* bladzijde
bladzijde(n): page(s)
blanco: blank
blauw: blue
blazoen: coat(s) of arms
blind: blank, unadorned
blinddr. *see* blinddruk
blinddruk(ken): blind tooling
blindgestempeld: blind-tooled
blindstempel: blind tooling
bloemenvignet(ten): floral
  vignette(s)
bloemlezing: anthology
bloemornament(en): floral
  ornament(s)
bloempje(s): small floral
  design(s)
bloemstempel: floral design used
  in tooling
blokboek: block book
blz. *see* bladzijde
blzz. *see* bladzijden
bnd. *see* band
boek(en): book(s)
boekband: binding
boekbinder: bookbinder
boekdeel(delen): volume(s)
boekdrukker: printer
boekenstalletje: small secondhand
  bookstore
boekhandel: bookshop, book trade
boekhandelaar: bookdealer
boekje(s): booklet(s), small
  book(s)

boekomslag: book jacket, dust
  wrapper
boeksneden: edges of a book
bont: multicolored
bordure: ornamental border
bovenaan: at the top
bovenrand: upper margin
brandgat: burn
breedte: width
breuk: break, crack
briefwisseling: correspondence
brochering: stitching, sewing
brochure(s): small book(s),
  brochure(s), pamphlet(s)
brokaat: brocade
bronnen: sources
bruin: brown
buckr. *see* buckram
buckram: buckram
buigzaam: flexible, limp
buiten de tekst plaat: not in the
  text
buitenlands: foreign
buitenrand: outside margin
bundel(s): collection(s),
  volume(s)

calicot: calico
caricatuur: caricature
cartographie: cartography
cartonnage: cased binding
cartouche: cartouche
cat. *see* catalogus
catalogus(sen): catalog(s)
censuur: censorship
chagrijnleder: shagreen
clandestiene uitgave: clandestine
  printing
col. *see* colophon
collatie: collation
collationeren: collate
collectie: collection
colophon: colophon
comment. *see* commentaar
commentaar: commentary
compendium: abridgment
compilatie: compilation
compilator: compiler

compl. *see* compleet
compleet: complete
concordantie: concordance
contributie: membership fee
copie: copy, imitation
couv. *see* couvert
couvert(en): cover(s)
cplt. *see* compleet
critisch: critical
cursief: in italics
custode: catchword

d. *see* deel
dagboek: diary
datum van verschijnen: date of
  publication
de meeste: the majority of, the
  greater part
deel: part, volume
deelnummer: volume number
deeltje: small volume
defect: defective
definitief: definitive
delen: parts, volumes
derde: third
dertien(de): thirteen(th)
dertig(ste): thirty(ieth)
devies: device, motto
diagr. *see* diagram
diagram(men): diagram(s)
dichtwerken: poems, poetical
  works
dikte: thickness
diss. *see* dissertatie
dissertatie(s): dissertation(s)
dln. *see* delen
dltje. *see* deeltje
dof: dull, lusterless
door bemiddeling van: through
  the intermediary of
doorgestreept: crossed out,
  canceled; effaced
doorlopend: continuous,
  consecutive
doorschieten: interleave
doorschoten: interleaved
doorstrepen: to cross out,
  cancel; to efface
doos: box

46

dr. *see* druk
drie: three
driemaandelijks: quarterly
droge naald: dry point
druk(ken): print(s), edition(s)
drukfout(en): misprint(s),
  printing error(s)
drukker: printer
drukkerij: printing firm
drukkersmerk: printer's mark
drukpers: press
drukvermelding: imprint
dubbelbl. *see* dubbelblad
dubbelblad: double page, double
  leaf
dubbelen: duplicates
duizend(ste): thousand(th)
dun: thin, of poor quality

e.a. *see* en andere
e.v.a. *see* en vele anderen
ed. *see* editie
editie: edition
een: one
eenjarig: yearly, of one year
eenkleurig: monochrome
eerste: first
eerste druk: first printing, first
  edition
eerste uitgave: first edition
eeuw: century
eeuwse: century
eigenh. *see* eigenhandig
eigenhandig: autograph, in one's
  own hand
eigennaam: proper name
einde: end
eindvignet: tailpiece
elf(de): eleven(th)
elk: each, every
en andere: and others, among
  others
en vele anderen: and many others
en zo voort: and so forth
enig bekende: only one known
enig exemplaar: unique copy
enigsz. *see* enigszins
enigszins: somewhat, a little
enkele: a few

enz. *see* en zo voort
epiloog: epilogue, postface
etiket: label
ets(en): etching(s)
ex. *see* exemplaar
ex.-l. *see* ex-libris
ex-libris: *ex libris*
exempl. *see* exemplaar
exemplaar(aren): copy(ies)
expl. *see* exemplaar
exx. *see* exemplaren
ezelsoor: dog-ear

facs. *see* facsimile
facsimile: facsimile
factuur: invoice
feestbundel: volume of tributes
fig. *see* figuur
figuren: figures, diagrams
figuur: figure, diagram
filet(en): fillet(s)
fluweel: velvet
fluwelig: velvet-like
foedraal: box, slipcase
fol. *see* folio
foliëring: foliation
folio: folio
formaat: format
foto(s): photograph(s)
fotocopie: photocopy, photostat
fotogr. *see* fotografie
fotografie: photograph
fotografisch: photographic
fotogravure: photogravure
fr. *see* fraai
fraai: handsome, handsomely
franco: postpaid, prepaid
fransetitel: half-title page
frisheid: freshness
front. *see* frontispies
frontisp. *see* frontispies
frontispies: frontispiece

gaaf: sound, in perfect condition
geannoteerd: annotated
geannuleerd: canceled
geaquareleerd: hand-colored
gearceerd: hatched
geb. *see* gebonden, gebied

gebied: area, subject
geblakerd: scorched
gebogen: curved
gebonden: bound
geborduurd: embroidered
gebr. *see* gebruikt
gebrek: defect
gebrekkig: defective, imperfect
gebrocheerd: sewed
gebroken: split
gebronsd: reddish-brown
gebruikssporen: traces of use
gebruikt: used, worn
gebruind: browned
gec. *see* gecartonneerd
gecart. *see* gecartonneerd
gecarton. *see* gecartonneerd
gecartonneerd: bound in boards
gecensuureerd: censored,
   suppressed
geciseleerd: chiseled, goffered
gecompleteerd: completed
geconserveerd: preserved
gecycl. *see* gecyclostileerd
gecyclostileerd: multigraphed
ged. *see* gedeelte, gedurende
gedat. *see* gedateerd
gedateerd: dated
gedeelte(n): part(s), section(s)
gedeeltelijk: part(ly)
gedenkboek: commemorative
   volume
gedenkschrift: commemorative
   volume
gedicht(en), poem(s)
gedr. *see* gedrukt
gedreven: embossed
gedrukt: printed
gedrukte omslag: printed cover
gedurende: during
geel: yellow
geëmailleerd: enamel(ed)
geëtst: etched
geëtste plaat: etching
gefacsimileerd: reproduced in
   facsimile
gefactureerd: invoiced
gefolieerd: foliated
gegevens: data

geglansd: calendered
gegr. *see* gegraveerd
gegrav. *see* gegraveerd
gegraveerd: engraved
geh. *see* geheel
geheel: full, whole, entirely
gehoogd: heightened
geill. *see* geillustreerd
geills. *see* geillustreerd
geillumineerd: illuminated
geillustr. *see* geillustreerd
geillustreerd: illustrated
geillustreerd omslag: illustrated
  cover
gejasperde sneden: sprinkled
  edges
gekl. *see* gekleurd
gekleurd: colored
geknaagd: gnawed
gekrast: scratched
gekreukeld: wrinkled
gekuist: expurgated
gel. *see* gelegenheid
gelegenheid: occasion,
  opportunity
gelezen: read
gelijke band: uniform binding
gelijkluidend: identical text
gelijktijdig: contemporary
gelijmd: glued
gelinieerd: ruled, lined
gelithografeerd: lithographed
gemarmerd: marbled
gemarmerde sneden: marbled
  edges
gemutileerd: mutilated
genumm. *see* genummerd
genummerd: numbered
geornamenteerd: decorated
gepagin. *see* gepagineerd
gepagineerd: paged
geparafeerd: initialed
geplakt: pasted, mounted
geplet: crushed
gepointilleerd: stippled
gepolijst: polished, burnished
gerangschikt: arranged,
  classified

geredigeerd: directed
geregleerd: ruled, lined
gerep. *see* gerepareerd
gerepareerd: repaired
gereserveerd: reserved
gerestaureerd: mended, repaired
geribd: ribbed, grained; bound
  with raised bands
gerubriceerd: rubricated
geruit: checkered
gesatineerd: glazed
gesch. *see* geschept
geschaafd: rubbed, scratched
geschat: esteemed
geschatte prijs: estimated price
gescheiden: separate, single
geschenkboek(en): gift book(s)
geschept: handmade
gescheurd: torn
geschilderd: painted
geschreven: written, composed
geschrift(en): pamphlet(s),
  paper(s)
gesign. *see* gesigneerd
gesigneerd: signed
gesleten: worn
gespikkeld: speckled
gestaakt: discontinued
gestempeld: stamped, tooled
gestenc. *see* gestencild
gestencild: mimeographed,
  duplicated
getal: number
getekend: drawn
getint: tinted
getiteld: entitled
gevl. *see* gevlekt
gevlamde zijde: watered silk
gevlekt: spotted
gevouwen: folded
gewaardeerd: esteemed
gewassen: washed
gewijd aan: dedicated to
gewijz. *see* gewijzigd
gewijzigd: altered
gewoon: ordinary
gezet: composed, set
gezocht: sought after, rare;

searched
gids: guide
glad: smooth
gladde snede: smooth edge
  trimmed edge
glossarium: glossary
glosse: gloss
goed: good
gothisch: gothic
goud: gold
gouden: gilt, decorated with gold
goudstempeling: gilt-stamped
gr. *see* gravure
grafiek(en): graph(s)
grafische-voorstelling(en): rep-
  resentation(s), graph(s)
graph. *see* graphiek
graphiek(en): graph(s)
grav. *see* gravure
gravure(s): engraving(s)
groen: green
groot papier: large paper
grootte: size
grotendeels: mostly
groteske: block letter

h. *see* half
half: half
halfband: half binding
halfjaarlijks: semiannual
halfleder: half leather, half calf
halfleer: half leather, half calf
halflinnen: half cloth
halfmarokijn: half morocco
halfperkament: half vellum
hand: hand
handboek: manual
handel: trade
handelaar: dealer
handeling(en): paper(s)
handgekleurd: hand-colored
handingekl. *see* handingekleurd
handingekleurd: hand-colored
handleiding: manual
handschr. *see* handschrift
handschrift(en): manuscript(s)
handt. *see* handtekening
handtekening(en): hand

drawing(s), signature(s)
helft: half
heliogravure: photogravure
herdr. *see* herdruk
herdruk(ken): reprint(s)
herdrukt: reprinted
herfst: Fall, Autumn
herinneringen: memoirs
herkomst: provenance
hersteld: repaired
herstelling: repair
hertenleer: buckskin, doeskin
herz. *see* herzien
herzien: revised
herziening: revision
hetz. *see* hetzelfde, hetzelve
hetzelfde: the same
hetzelve: the same
hier en daar: here and there,
  occasional
hierbij: herewith
hled. *see* halfleder
hlf. *see* half
hlflinn. *see* halflinnen
hlinn. *see* halflinnen
hln. *see* halflinnen
hoek(en): corner(s)
hoesje(s): dust wrapper(s)
honderd(en): hundred(s)
honderdste: hundredth
hoofd: superscription
hoofdje: rubric, heading
hoofdletter(s): capital(s)
hoofdstuk(ken): chapter(s)
hoogst: extremely
hoogte: height
houtblok: wood block
houten: wooden
houtgravs. *see* houtgravures
houtgravure(s): wood
  engraving(s), woodcut(s)
houtsn. *see* houtsnede
houtsnede(n): woodcut(s)
houtvrij: wood-free
H.S. *see* handschrift
hs. *see* handschrift
hss. *see* handschriften
huls: slipcase

i.d.t. *see* in de tekst
i.h.b. *see* in het boek
ieder: every
iets: somewhat
ill. *see* illustratie
illegaal: unauthorized
illuminatie: illumination
illust. *see* illustratie
illustr. *see* illustratie
illustratie(s): illustration(s)
impressum: imprint
in beslag genomen: confiscated
in de tekst: in the text
in het boek: in the book
in overeenstemming met: in
  agreement with
in samenwerking met: in
  collaboration with
in vellen: in sheets
in voorbereiding: in preparation
incompleet: incomplete, defective
incunabel(en): incunabulum(a)
ing. *see* ingebonden
ingebonden: bound in
ingekl. *see* ingekleurd
ingekleurd: in colors, colored
ingel. *see* ingeleid
ingelast: intercalated
ingelegd: laid in
ingeleid: introduced
ingelijmd: glued in, reglued
ingelijst: framed, bordered
ingen. *see* ingenaaid
ingenaaid: sewed
ingeperst: embossed
ingeplakt: pasted in
ingescheurd: torn
ingevoegd: inserted
inh. *see* inhoud
inhoud: contents
inhoudsopgave: table of contents
init. *see* initiaal
initiaal(en): initial letter(s),
  initial(s)
inkoop: purchase
inl. *see* inleiding
inlegblad: interleaved page,
  loose-leaf

inleid. *see* inleiding
inleidend: preliminary
inleiding: introduction
inlichting: inquiry
inschrift: inscription
inscriptie: inscription
inteken. *see* intekenaar
intekenaar: subscriber
intekenaarster: subscriber
intekenen: to subscribe
intekening: subscription
inwendig: internal, inner
inzage. *see* ter inzage
ivoorperk. *see* ivoorperkament
ivoorperkament: ivory vellum

jaar: year
jaarbericht(en): annal(s),
  transaction(s)
jaarboek: annual, yearbook
jaarboekje: yearbook
jaargang: year
jaarlijks: annual
jaartal: date
jaarverslag: annual report
jansenistenband: Jansenist
  binding
jrg. *see* jaargang
juchtleer: Russian leather

k. *see* kaart
kaart(en): map(s), chart(s)
kaartje(s): small map(s),
  chart(s)
kalfsleer: calf
kalfsleren band: calf binding
kant(en): margin(s)
kanttekening(en): marginal
  note(s)
kantwerk: lacework
kapitaal: capital letter
kapitaalband: headband
karton: cardboard, pasteboard
kartonnage(s): pasteboard
  binding(s)
kartonnen band: bound in boards
katern(s): quire(s)
katoen: cotton, cotton cloth

keerzijde: verso
kettingband: chained binding
keurig(e): exquisite, neat, clean
keus: selection
keuze(n): selection(s)
kinderboek: children's book
kl. *see* klein, kleur
klamp(en): clasp(s)
klein: small
klemband(en): clip binder(s),
  ring binder(s)
kleur(en): color(s)
kleuren-reproductie(s): color
  reproduction(s)
kleurendr. *see* kleurendruk
kleurendruk: color print
kleurenkaart(en): colored
  map(s)
klrn. *see* kleuren
kneep: joint
knop: boss(es)
kol. *see* kolom
kolom(men): column(s)
kolomtitel: headline
kop: top edge
kop verguld: gilt top
kopen: to buy
koper: copper
kopergr. *see* kopergravure
kopergrav. *see* kopergravure
kopergravure: copper engraving
koperlichtdruk: photoengraving
koptitel: heading, title
kopvignet: headpiece
kort: short, brief
korting: discount
kras: scar, scratch
kroniek(en): chronicle(s)
krt. *see* kaart
krtjes. *see* kaartjes
krtn. *see* kaarten
krulornament: arabesque
kunstdrukpapier: coated paper
kunstfoto(s): art photograph(s)
kunstled. *see* kunstleder
kunstleder: imitation leather
kunstmatig: artificial
kwart: quarter, one fourth

kwartaal: quarter(ly)
kwartaalblad: quarterly

l. *see* licht, linnen
laatst: last
lacune: gap
langw. *see* langwerpig
langwerpig: oblong
ldr. *see* leder
led. *see* leder
leder: leather
lederen: leather
leer: leather
leerboek: textbook
leerkapitaal: leather headband
leersnede: leather-cut
leesbaar: legible
leiding: direction
lelie: fleur-de-lys
lengte: length
lente: Spring
les(sen): lecture(s)
letter(en): letter(s)
letterkunde: literature
levensbeschrijving: biography
leverbaar: available, in stock
levering: delivery
levertijd: delivery date
lezing(en): lecture(s), reading(s)
licht: slightly
lichtdr. *see* lichtdruk
lichtdruk: photoengraving,
  phototype
lidmaatschap: membership
liefhebber: collector, amateur
lijn(en): line(s)
lijnenspel: pattern of lines
lijst: list; border
links: left
linn. *see* linnen
linnen: cloth
lint(en): tie(s)
literatuur: literature
litho. *see* lithografie
lithogr. *see* lithografie
lithografie: lithograph,
  lithography
lithografisch: lithographic

ln. *see* linnen
lnn. *see* linnen
loofwerk: leafy scroll decoration
lopende deel: current volume
los(se): loose; single (volume)
losbladig: loose-leaf
lr. *see* leder, leer
luchtfoto(s): aerial photo(s)
luxe: de luxe
luxe-editie: de luxe edition
luxe-uitgave: de luxe publication

m. *see* met
maandblad: monthly publication
maandelijks: monthly
maandschr. *see* maandschrift
maandschrift: monthly, monthly
  magazine
mager: thin, fine-faced
map(pen): portfolio(s), pocket(s)
marge(s): margin(s)
marmer: marbling, marbled
marmering: marbling
marokijn: morocco
marokijnleer: morocco
marokko. *see* marokijn
matig: mediocre
meander: lacelike pattern
medaillon: medallion
mede-auteur: joint author
mededeling(en): communi-
  cation(s)
medew. *see* medewerking
medewerker(s): collaborator(s),
  contributor(s)
medewerking: collaboration
meerdere: several
meertalig: polyglot
meestal: mostly, generally
meeste *see* de meeste
mengelwerk(en): miscellany(ies)
merend. *see* merendeels
merendeels: greater part
met: with
met inbegrip van: including
met verwijzing naar: with reference to
micro-foto(s): microphoto-
  graph(s)
52

middeleeuwen: Middle Ages
midden: center
mimeogr. *see* mimeographeerd
mimeographeerd: mimeographed
miniatuur: miniature
mod. *see* modern
mod. gec. *see* modern
  gecartonneerd
modern: modern
modern gecartonneerd: modern
  cased-board binding
moirézijde: watered silk
monografie: monograph
monster: pattern, specimen
mooi: fine, beautiful, handsome
motief: design, pattern
mozaïek: mosaic
muziek: music

n.v.v. *see* niet verder verschenen
naam: name
naamlijst: register, list of
  names
naamloos: anonymous
naar aanleiding van: with
  reference to
nabootsing: imitation, copy
nadruk(ken): reprint(s)
nagel. *see* nagelaten
nagelaten: posthumous
nagenoeg: almost
nagezien: examined, inspected
namaak: imitation, fake
namelijk: namely, viz.
naslagwerk: reference work
nauwkeurig: exact
nawoord: epilogue
negen: nine
negende: ninth
negentien(de): nineteen(th)
negentig(ste): ninety(ieth)
net: nice, neat
niet in de handel: not for general
  sale, privately printed
niet meer verschenen: no more
  published
niet verder verschenen: no more
  published
nieuw(e): new

nl. *see* namelijk
no. *see* nummer
noot: note
noten: notes
notulen: proceedings,
   transactions
nummer(s): number(s), item(s)
nummering: pagination
nummert door: continuous paging
nw. *see* nieuw

o. *see* origineel
o.a. *see* onder andere(n)
o.m. *see* onder meer
o/snee. *see* op snede
obl. *see* oblong
oblong: oblong
omgevouwen: folded
omgew. *see* omgewerkt
omgewerkt: revised, rewritten
omgezet: inverted
omlijst: framed, bordered
omlijsting: frame, border
omsl. *see* omslag
omslag: cover
omstreeks: circa, about
onafgesn. *see* onafgesneden
onafgesneden: uncut
onbed. *see* onbeduidend
onbedrukt: blank
onbeduidend: insignificant,
   insignificantly
onbeschr. *see* onbeschreven
onbeschreven: blank, unused
onder andere(n): among others
onder meer: among others
onder rembours: cash on
   delivery
onderaan: at the bottom
onderdrukt: suppressed
ondergrond: background
ondermarge: lower margin
onderschrift: legend, caption
ondersteuning: support
onderstreept: underlined
onderstrepen: to underline
onderstrept: underlined
onderstreping(en): underlining(s)

ondert. *see* ondertitel
ondertekend: signed
ondertekening: signature
ondertitel: subtitle
onderweg: in transit
onderwerp: subject
onderzocht: investigated
onderzoek: inquiry, investigation
onfr. *see* onfris
onfris: not fresh, worn
ongedr. *see* ongedrukt
ongedrukt: unprinted, unpublished
ongehecht: unstitched
ongekuist: unexpurgated
ongenummerd: unnumbered
ongeopend: unopened
ongeschonden: untouched,
   undamaged
ongeveer: approximately
ongewijzigd: unchanged
ongewoon: exceptional
onleesbar: illegible
onopengesneden: unopened, uncut
onrechtmatig: unauthorized,
   pirated
onregelmatig: irregular
ontbr. *see* ontbreekt
ontbreekt: lacking, missing
ontelb. *see* ontelbaar
ontelbaar: innumerable,
   numerous
ontst. *see* ontstaan
ontstaan: originate
ontw. *see* ontworpen
ontworpen: designed
onuitgeg. *see* onuitgegeven
onuitgegeven: unpublished
onv. *see* onveranderd
onveranderd: unchanged,
   unrevised
onverk. *see* onverkort
onverkort: unabridged
onverminkt: undamaged,
   unmutilated
onvolledig: defective, incomplete
oorkonde(n): document(s),
   charter(s)
oorspr. *see* oorspronkelijk

53

oorspronkelijk: original
oorspronkelijke uitgave: original
edition
op aanvraag: on request
op snede: on the edge
op zicht: on approval
opdr. *see* opdracht
opdracht: dedication
opdruk: tooling
opeenvolgend: consecutive,
successive
openbare les: inaugural address
opengesn. *see* opengesneden
opengesneden: cut open
opgehelderd: clarified
opgeplakt: pasted up, mounted
opgespoord: traced
opgezet: set up, mounted
opl. *see* oplaag
oplaag(lagen): edition(s)
opn. *see* opnieuw
opnieuw: again, anew
opschrift: inscription
opstellen: works, miscellanea
optie geven: to give the first
refusal
or. *see* origineel
origin. *see* origineel
origineel: original
ornament(en): ornament(s)
oud: old
overdr. *see* overdruk
overdruk: reprint, offprint
overgeb. *see* overgebonden
overgebonden: rebound
overgedrukt: reprinted
overgegaan in: continued as
overgeplakt: pasted over
overgezet: translated
overzetting: translation
overzicht: abstract, synopsis,
survey

p. *see* pagina
p.d. *see* per deel
p.dl. *see* per deel
paar: a few

pagina(e): page(s)
pagineerd: paged
paginering: pagination
pamflet(ten): pamphlet(s)
papier: paper
paraaf: paraph, flourish
particuliere uitgave: privately
printed
pennenaam: pseudonym
pentekening(en): pen and ink
drawing(s)
pentk. *see* pentekening
per deel: each part, volume
per kruisband: by book post
periodiek: periodical
perk. *see* perkament
perkament: parchment, vellum
pers: press
photogr. *see* photographie
photographie(s): photo(s)
pl. *see* plaat
plaat: plate
plaatje: small plate
plaatpapier: plate paper
plaats: place
plaats van herkomst: place of
origin
plaatsregister: list of places
plan: plan, project
plannen: plans, projects
plano: in sheets
plat(ten): side(s) of a book
platen: plates, illustrations
platenalbum: album of
illustrations
platenatlas: atlas of plates
platenregister: index to plates
platte ribben: flat bands
plattegr. *see* plattegrond
plattegrond(en): plan(s), map(s)
pltn. *see* platen
poezie: poetry
polychroom: multicolored
portef. *see* portefeuille
portefeuille: portfolio
porto: postage
portr. *see* portret

portret(ten): portrait(s)
portrn. *see* portretten
posthuum: posthumous
postpakket: postal parcel
potloodaant. *see* potloodaanteken-
 ing
potloodaantekening(en): pencil
 note(s)
potloodtekening: pencil drawing
pp. *see* pagine
prachtband: de luxe binding,
 ornamental binding
prachtig: splendid, magnificent
prachtuitgave: de luxe edition
preliminair: preliminary
prent(en): engraving(s), print(s)
prentenboek: picture book
prijs: price
prijsopgaaf: quotation
prijzen: prices
privédruk: privately printed
proefnummer(s): specimen
 copy(ies)
proefschrift: thesis
provisorisch: interim, temporary
pseudoniem: pseudonym
publicatie(s): publication(s)

rand(en): margin(s), border(s)
randglosse(n): marginal note(s)
randversiering(en): ornamental
 border(s)
randwerk: ornamental border
rankwerk: scrollwork
recht van terugzending: option of
 return
rechts: right
recto: recto, front side
red. *see* redactie
redact. *see* redactie
redacteur: editor
redactie: editorship
redactiecommissie: editorial
 committee
rede: speech, address
redelijk: reasonable
reeks: series, set
reg. *see* register

regel: line
regelnummers: line numbers
register: index
registerdeel: index volume
rekening: account, bill
repertorium: list, index;
 reference work
repr. *see* reproductie
reprod. *see* reproductie
reproductie(s): reproduction(s)
restauratie: repair
ribben: raised bands, edges
ribbenband(en): ribbed binding(s)
riemen: laces
rijk: rich, richly
roestvlek(ken): rust spot(s),
 foxing
roestvlekje(s): small rust spot(s)
roestvlekkig: foxed
roman: novel
romeins: roman type
ronde gotische letter: bastard
 type
rood: red
rose: pink
rubriceren: classify; rubricate
rubricering: classification;
 rubrication
rubriek(en): heading(s), section(s)
rug(gen): back(s)
rugschild: back label
rugschildje: small back label
rugtitel: back title piece
rugveld(en): panel(s) on spine
rugzijde: back of a book, spine
ruil: exchange
ruiling: exchange
ruim: more than; wide
ruiten: checkered pattern
ruitformig: lozenge-shaped
rustiek: rustic

samen: together
samengeb. met *see* samengebonden met
samengebonden met: bound with
samengebracht: compiled
samengesmolten: merged

samengest. *see* samengesteld
samengesteld: compiled
samengevoegd: merged
samensteller: compiler
samenvatting: summary
samenvoegen: to merge
samenw. *see* samenwerking
samenwerking: collaboration
schaafplek: scratch, chafed spot
schaal: scale
schaapleer: sheepskin
schaars: scarce, rare
scharn. *see* scharnier
scharnier: hinge, joint
schenking: gift
schets: sketch
schetskaart(en): sketch map(s),
  outline map(s)
scheur(en): crack(s), tear(s)
schild: medallion
schimmelvlek(ken): mildew
  spot(s)
schoon: clean
schotschrift: libelous pamphlet
schr. *see* schrijver
schram: scar, scratch
schrift: handwriting, hand
schrijver: author, writer
schrijver-uitgever: privately
  published
schroeivlek: burn
schuifdoos: slipcase
schuilnaam: pen name,
  pseudonym
schutbl. *see* schutblad
schutblad: end paper
serie: series
sierlijk: neat, elegant
sierlijst: ornamental border
sierrand: ornamental border
signat. *see* signatuur
signatuur(turen): signature(s)
simili. *see* similigravure
similigravure: halftone engraving
slappe band: flexible binding
slecht: bad, badly
slechts: only, merely
sleutelroman: *roman à clef*

slijtage: traces of wear
slordig: tattered
slot: end, conclusion
slot(en): clasp(s)
slotvignet: tailpiece
sluitornament: tailpiece
smaadschrift: lampoon
smal: narrow
smoezel. *see* smoezelig
smoezelig: dirty, smudged
snede(n): edge(s)
snee. *see* snede
soepel: limp, flexible
soepele band: flexible binding
sommige: some
soms: sometimes, in some
  instances
spec. *see* speciaal
speciaal: special, separate
spiraalband: spiral binding
spoed: rush, haste
sporen: traces, marks
spotprent(en): caricature(s)
spreukband: lettered scroll,
  legend
sprokkelingen: collectanea
st. *see* stempel, stuk
staalgr. *see* staalgravure
staalgravs. *see* staalgravures
staalgravure(s): steel
  engraving(s)
staat: condition, state
standaardwerk: standard work
steen(en): lithograph(s)
steendruk: lithography
steendrukkerij(en): lithograph(s)
stekig: wormholed
stempel: stamp, tool
stempelband: tooled binding
sterk: strong
sterrekaart: celestial chart
stichter: founder, founded by
stippel vergulding: gilt dots
stkn. *see* stukken
stn. *see* stukken
stof: cloth
stoffig: dusty
stofomsl. *see* stofomslag

stofomslag: cloth cover
strook: guard
stud. ab. *see* studenten
  abonnement
studenten abonnement: student
  subscription
stuk: piece, volume
stukje: small piece, pamphlet
stukken: pieces, volumes
stuks: pieces, volumes
suppl. *see* supplement
supplement: supplement
supra-exlibris: book stamp(s)

t. *see* tekst
t/m. *see* tot en met
taal: language
tab. *see* tabel
tabel(len): table(s), list(s)
tachtig(ste): eighty(ieth)
tal van: a great number of
talr. *see* talrijk
talrijk: numerous
tamelijk: rather
te koop: for sale
teek. *see* tekening
teekening: *see* tekening
tek. *see* tekening
teken. *see* tekening
tekening(en): drawing(s)
tekn. *see* tekening
tekst: text
tekstafb. *see* tekstafbeeldingen
tekstafbeeldingen: illustrations in
  the text
tekstfig. *see* tekstfiguren
tekstfiguren: illustrations in the
  text
tekstgravures: engravings in the
  text
tekstillustraties: illustrations in
  the text
tekstverlies: loss of text
telkens: each (every) time
ter ere: in honor
ter inzage: on approval
ter perse: in press
terugzending: return

tez. *see* tezamen
tezamen: together
tien(de): ten(th)
tijd: time
tijdelijk: temporarily
tijdschrift: periodical, journal
tit. *see* titel
titel(s): title(s), title page(s)
titel en inhoud niet verschenen:
  title page and index not done
titelafb. *see* titelafbeelding
titelafbeelding: illustrated title
titelblad: title page
titelgravure: engraved title
titelpagina: title page
titelpl. *see* titelplaat
titelplaat: frontispiece
titelpr. *see* titelprent
titelprent: frontispiece
titelvignet: headpiece
toegel. *see* toegelicht
toegelicht: explained
toegevoegd: added
toel. *see* toelichting
toelichting: explanation
toestand: condition
toestemming: permission
toezicht: supervision
toneelstuk: play
toongravure: chiaroscuro
tot en met: through, up to and
  including
totaal: total, in all
traktaat: treatise
tussen: between
tussentijdse verkoop voorbe-
  houden: subject to previous sale
twaalf(de): twelve (twelfth)
twee(de): two (second)
tweedehands: secondhand
tweemaandelijks: semimonthly
tweevoud: duplicate
twintig(ste): twenty(ieth)

uit de band: binding loose
uit de tijd: contemporary
uit dezelfde tijd: contemporary
uitdr. *see* uitdrukking

57

uitdrukking(en): expression(s)
uitg. *see* uitgegeven
uitgaaf: edition, publication
uitgave. *see* uitgaaf
uitgebreide: enlarged
uitgeg. *see* uitgegeven
uitgegeven: published
uitgekn. *see* uitgeknipt
uitgeknipt: cut out
uitgescheurd: torn out
uitgesneden: cut out, excised
uitgesteld: deferred
uitgever: publisher
uitgeversband(en): publisher's
  binding(s)
uitgevershuis: publishing firm
uitgevoerd: executed
uitgewerkt: elaborated, developed
uitkomen: to appear
uitlegging: commentary
uitsl. *see* uitslaand
uitslaand: unfolding
uitst. *see* uitstekend
uitstekend: excellent
uittreksel: excerpt
uitv. *see* uitverkocht
uitverk. *see* uitverkocht
uitverkocht: out of print
uitvoerig: detailed
uitvouwbaar: unfolding
unciaal: uncial
uniek: sole, unique
unif. *see* uniform
uniform: alike, in a uniform
  style

v.d.tijd. *see* van dezen tijd
vakken: sections
vals: false
van dezen tijd: contemporary
varia: miscellanies
varkensleer: pigskin
vaste bestelling: firm order
veel: many
veelkleurig: varicolored
veertien(de): fourteen(th)
veertig(ste): forty(ieth)
veiling: auction sale

veilingsvoorwaarden: conditions
  of sale
vel(len): leaf(ves), sheet(s),
  gathering(s)
veld(en): panel(s)
vele: many
velijnpapier: vellum
verb. *see* verbeterd
verbeterd: improved, corrected
verbetering: correction
verboden: suppressed
verder: further, otherwise
verfrommeld: crushed, crinkled
verg. *see* verguld, vergulding
vergeeld: yellowed
verguld: gilt, decorated with gold
vergulde binnenrand: inside
  dentelle
vergulde sneden: gilt edges
vergulding: decorations in gold
verhaal: narrative, story
verhalen: narratives, stories
verhandelingen: proceedings
verkl. *see* verkleurd
verklaard: explained
verklar. *see* verklarend
verklarend: explanatory
verklaring: commentary,
  explanation
verkleind: reduced
verkleurd: faded, discolored
verkocht: sold
verkoop: sale
verkoping: sale, auction
verkort: abridged
verkorte titel: short title
verkorting: abridgment
verkrijgbaar: available
verlucht: illuminated
verluchting: illumination
verm. *see* vermeerderd
vermeerderd: enlarged,
  augmented
vernieuwd: restored
verouderd: aged, obsolete
verpakking: packing
verplicht: under obligation
vers. *see* versierd

versch. *see* verscheen,
 verscheiden
verscheen: appeared, issued
verscheiden: several
verschenen: published
verschijnt binnenkort: to appear
 shortly
verschoten: faded
versierd: decorated
versiering: decoration
verslag: report
versleten: worn, tattered
verspreid: scattered
versterkt: reinforced
vert. *see* vertaling
vertaald: translated
vertaling: translation
vertolking: interpretation
vertraagd: delayed
vervallen: dilapidated, in poor
 condition
vervalsing: falsification, forgery
vervangen door: replaced by
vervolg: continuation
vervolgwerk: serial publication
verz. *see* verzameld
verzamelaar: collector
verzamelaarsband: three-quarter
 binding
verzameld: compiled, collected
verzameld werk: collective work
verzameling: collection,
 compilation
verzameltitel: collective title
verzamelwerk: collective work
verzen: verse, poems
verzonden: forwarded
verzorgd: produced
vier(de): four(th)
vierkant: square
vign. *see* vignet
vignet(ten): vignette(s)
vijf(de): five (fifth)
vijfig(ste): fifty(ieth)
vijftien(de): fifteen(th)
vl. *see* vlekkig
vlekje(s): small spot(s)
vlekkeloos: spotless, immaculate
vlekkig: foxed, spotted

vliegend blad: flyer, leaflet
vlugschrift: pamphlet
vocht: moisture
vochtigheit: humidity
vochtvlekkig: damp-stained
voet: bottom
volgwerk: serial publication
volksuitgave: popular edition
voll. *see* volledig
volled. *see* volledig
volledig: complete, completely
volrandig: with margins uncut
voor rekening van: charged to,
 for account of
voorbereiding: preparation
voorbericht: foreword, preface
voordracht(en): talk(s),
 speech(es), lecture(s)
voorhanden: available
voorjaar: Spring
voorlopig: interim, temporary
voornamelijk: mainly
voorplad: front cover
voorraad: stock
voorrede: introduction, preface
voorsnede: fore edge
voorst. *see* voorstelling
voorste: foremost
voorstel. *see* voorstelling
voorstelling(en): represen-
 tation(s), illustration(s)
voortgezet door: continued by
voortitel: half title
voortreff. *see* voortreffelijk
voortreffelijk: excellent
voortzetting: continuation
vooruitbetaald: prepaid
voorw. *see* voorwoord
voorwaarde(n): condition(s)
voorwerk: preliminary pages,
 front matter
voorwoord: foreword, preface
voorzijde: recto, front side
vouw: fold
vracht: freight
vrij van rechten: duty free
vrijblijvend: without commitment
vrnl. *see* voornamelijk
vuil: soiled, dirty

59

waarde: value
waardevol: valuable
waaronder: among which
waarop: on which
waarvan: of which
wapen: arms
wapenboek: book of arms
wapencartouche: cartouche containing a coat of arms
wapenpl. *see* wapenplaten
wapenplaten: plates of coats of arms
wapenschild: coat of arms
wat: somewhat, slightly
watermerk: watermark
watervl. *see* watervlekken, watervlekkig
watervlekken: water stains
watervlekkig: stained by water
weekblad: weekly
weervl. *see* weervlekkig
weervlekkig: weather-stained
weggeschrapt: effaced, erased
weinig: a little, little
wekelijks: weekly
werk(en): work(s)
werkje: opuscule, pamphlet
wetenschappelijk: scientific
wiegedruk(ken): incunabulum(a)
winter: Winter
wit(te): blank, white
woord vooraf: preface
woordenboek: dictionary
woordenlijst(en): vocabulary(ies)
worm(en): worm(s), wormed
wormgaatje(s): small wormhole(s)
wormstekig: wormed

z.j. *see* zonder jaartal
z.p.&j. *see* zonder plaats en jaar
z.pl. *see* zonder plaats
zaak- en plaatsregister: index of subjects and places
zaakregister: subject index
zamen. *see* tezamen
zeer: very, exceedingly
zegel: seal
zeldz. *see* zeldzaam
zeldzaam: rare
zelfd(e): same
zending: shipment
zes(de): six(th)
zestien(de): sixteen(th)
zestig(ste): sixty(ieth)
zeven(de): seven(th)
zeventien(de): seventeen(th)
zeventig(ste): seventy(ieth)
zijde: side; silk
zincographisch: zincographic
zoekgeraakt: lost, mislaid
zojuist verschenen: just published
zomer: Summer
zonder band: unsewn
zonder jaartal: without date of publication
zonder plaats: without place of publication
zonder plaats en jaar: without place or date
zonder titel: without title page
zw. *see* zwart
zwaar: heavy, severely
zwak: weak
zwart: black
zwarte kunst: mezzotint
zwijnsleer: pigskin

FRENCH

à: to, with
a. *see* acier, année, avec
à coins: with corners, cornerpieces
à comp. *see* à compartiments
à compartiments: in squared
patterns
à décor linéaire: with linear-
design decoration
à dent. *see* à dentelle
à dentelle: in dentelle design
à fermoirs: with clasps
à fond: thoroughly
à fond criblée: with dotted
background
à fr. *see* à froid
à froid: blind tooling
à grain écrasé: crushed grain
à grain long: straight-grained
à la grotesque: in grotesque
style
à la main: by hand
à lanières: with laces, ties
à long grain: straight-grained
à paraître: to appear
à part: aside, separate
à pleine page: full-page
à toutes marges: with full
margins, untrimmed
ab. *see* abîmé

abîmé: damaged, in poor condition
abond. *see* abondamment
abondamment: abundantly
abonn. *see* abonnement
abonné: subscriber
abonnement: subscription
abrégé: abridged
abréviation: abbreviation
abt. *see* abonnement
accroc. tear
achevé *see* achevé d'imprimer
achevé d'imprimer: completion
of printing note
acier: steel
adapt. *see* adaptation, adapté
adaptation: adaptation
adapté: adapted
addenda: addenda
additif: additional
adr. *see* adresse
adresse: address
agrémenté: ornamented,
decorated
airain: brass, bronze
ais: binder's board(s)
ais de bois: wood board(s)
ajouté: added
alb. *see* album
album: album
alfa: esparto paper

alinéa: paragraph
allongé: long, elongated
almanach: almanac
amande: almond-colored
amarante: amaranthe, a soft
  reddish-purple color
amateur: collector
amphore(s): vase(s), design
  representing vase(s)
an. *see* ancien, année
anc. *see* ancien
ancien: old, former
angle: angle
annales: annals
année: year
annexe: attached supplement
annot. *see* annotation, annoté
annotation: annotation
annoté: annotated
annuaire: annual, yearbook
annuel: annual, once a year
anon. *see* anonyme
anonyme: anonymous
ant. *see* antiqué
anthologie: anthology
antiqué: tooled
app. *see* appendice
apparition: appearance
append. *see* appendice
appendice: appendix
apprêté: polished, calendered
approximatif: approximate
aqu. *see* aquarelle
aquarelle: water color
aquarellé: painted in water colors
aquatinte: aquatint, water color
arabesque: arabesque
archives: archives, records
ardoise: slate, color of slate
ardoisé: slate-colored
argenté: silvered
armes: armorial designs
armoiries: heraldic designs
armorié: decorated in heraldic
  designs
arraché: torn off, torn out
aritificiel: artificial
atlas: atlas

attaches: ties
atteinte: damaged
au comptant: for cash
au pointillé: stippled
aubergine: eggplant-colored
augm. *see* augmenté
augmenté: enlarged
aut. *see* auteur, autographe,
  autour
auteur: author
autobiographie: autobiography
autog. *see* autographe
autogr. *see* autographe
autographe: autograph
autographié: autographed
autor. *see* autorisé
autorisé: authorized
autour: around
aux armes: with armorial designs
aux petits fers: with small,
  fine-designed tooling
av. *see* avec
avant-propos: preface, introduction
avec: with
avec témoins: with witnesses
avertissement: notice
azuré: azured, tooled in close
  parallel lines

b. *see* bois, broché
balafre: scar, scoring
bande: band, strip pattern
bandeau(x): border strip(s)
banderole: ornamental band,
  scroll
barbes: deckled edge
bariolé: variegated
barré: canceled
bas. *see* basane
bas de page: foot of the page
basane: sheepskin
bâtarde: bastard type
beau: fine, beautiful
beige: beige-colored
bel: beautiful, fine
belle: beautiful, fine
bibl. *see* bibliothèque

bibliographie: bibliography
bibliographique: bibliographical
bibliophile: booklover
biblioth. *see* bibliothèque
bibliothécaire: librarian
bibliothèque: library
biffé: lined through, erased
bigarré: variegated
biographie: biography
bistre: dark brown, sepia
bl. *see* blanc
blanc: blank, white
blas. *see* blason
blason: armorial shield
bleu: blue
bleu lavande: lavender blue
bleuté: blued
bois: wood block, woodcut
boîte: box
boîtier: slipcase
bon: good
bon état: in good condition
bord: edge
bord. *see* bordure
bordeau: border design
bordure: ornamental border
bouquin: used book of small
  value
bouquinerie: secondhand bookstore
bouton(s): knob(s), boss(es)
br. *see* bradel, broché
brad. *see* bradel
bradel: bradel, a cased binding
brique: brick-colored
brisé: broken
bristol: bristol board
broch. *see* broché
brochage: stitching, stitched
  binding
broché: stitched, sewed
brochure, pamphlet, pamphlet-
  style binding
brodé: embroidered
brûlure: burn
brun: brown
brunâtre: brownish
bruni: browned, burnished

bulletin: bulletin
burin: steel engraving tool

c. *see* cassé, coins
cabochon(s): knob(s), boss(es)
cachet: stamp, seal
cachet de bibliothèque: library
  stamp
cadre: frame, design forming a
  frame
cahier: quire, signature; notebook
caissons: line designs forming
  square or oblong frames
calligraphié: handwritten, in
  fine style
calque: tracing
camaieu: chiaroscuro
capsule: slipcase, container
car. *see* caractère, carré
caractère(s): letter(s), type
carnet: notebook
carré: square
cart. *see* carton, cartonnage,
  cartonné
cart-croq. *see* carte-croquis
cart. d'éd. *see* cartonnage de
  l'éditeur
cartable: cardboard cover,
  carrying case
carte: map
carte-croquis: sketch map
cartographie: cartography
carton: cardboard, pasteboard
carton. *see* cartonnage, cartonné
cartonn. *see* cartonnage
cartonnage: board binding, cardboard covers
cartonnage de l'éditeur: publisher's binding
cartonnage de protection: protective cover
cartonné: bound in boards
cartouche: ornamental oval frame,
  cartouche; inset map
cassé: broken
cassure: break
cdé. *see* cordé
censure: censorship

63

cent: one hundred
cent. *see* centimètre
centimètre(s): centimeter(s)
centre: center
cerne: ring, circle
ch. *see* chaque, chiffré
chacun: each
chag. *see* chagrin
chagr. *see* chagrin
chagrin: shagreen
chagriné: made to resemble
  shagreen
chaînette: chainlike design used
  in decorating bindings
chamois: chamois
chansonnier: songbook
chapitre: chapter
chaque: each
charn. *see* charnière
charnière: hinge, joint
chef-d'oeuvre: masterpiece
chemise: wrapper, usually of
  cloth or paper
chemise à cordonnets: wrapper
  with ties
chemise-étui: slipcase
chevrette: kidskin
chg. *see* chagrin
chgr. *see* chagrin
chif. *see* chiffré
chiffon: rag, rag paper
chiffré: numbered
chiffres en manchette: marginal
  numbers
chrestomathie: anthology
chromo. *see* chromolithographie
chromol. *see* chromolithographie
chromolithographie: lithograph
  in color
chronique(s): chronicle(s)
cinq(ième): five(fifth)
cinquante(ième): fifty(ieth)
cis. *see* ciselé
ciselé: chiseled
citron: citron, lemon-colored
clair: clear, light-colored
clair-obscur: chiaroscuro
clef: key

co-auteur: coauthor
codex: codex
coiffe(s): headband(s), leather
  roll-over at top and bottom of
  spine
coins: corners, corner designs
col. *see* colonne, coloré
coll. *see* collection
collation: collation
collé: glued
collection: collection
colonne: column
colophon: completion of printing
  note
color. *see* coloré, colorié
coloré: colored
colorié: colored
coloris: coloring
com. *see* commerce
comm. *see* commentaire, commenté
commande: order
commentaire: commentary
commenté: annotated
commerce: trade
comp. *see* compartiments,
  complet
compart. *see* compartiments
compartiments: panel sections
compilateur: compiler
compilation: compilation
compl. *see* complet
complet: complete
comportant: comprising
comporter: comprise, include
comprenant: including
comptant *see* au comptant
compte: account
compte-rendu: proceedings
concordance: concordance
cons. *see* conservé
conserv. *see* conservé
conservation: preservation
conservé: preserved
considérablement: considerably
consolidé: reinforced, strengthened
cont. *see* contenant

conte: tale
contemp. *see* contemporain
contemporain: contemporary
contenant: containing
contenu: content
continuation: continuation
contre-garde: page opposite
  flyleaf
contrefaçon: counterfeit, pirated
  edition
copie: copy
coquille: misprint
cordé: with bands
cordonnets: ties, cords
corr. *see* corrigé
corrigé: corrected
corrigenda: corrigenda
couché. *see* papier couché
coul. *see* couleur
couleur: color
coupe(s): cut(s)
coupé: cut, opened
coupure: cut
cour. *see* courant
courant: running
couronne: crown
couronné: approved, awarded a
  prize or some special honor
court de marges: narrow margins
couv. *see* couvert, couverture
couvert: covered
couverture: cover
couverture de protection: protective cover
couverture(s) muette(s): blank
  cover(s)
cramoisi: deep red
crayonnage: pencil marks
crème: cream-colored
crétonne: cretonne
criblé: dotted
croq. *see* croquis
croquis: sketch
cuir: leather
cuir de Russie: Russian leather
cuivre: copper, copper engraving
cul-de-lampe: tailpiece

d. *see* dans, date, demi, doré, dos
d. et c. *see* dos et coins
d.l.t. *see* dans le texte
d.-r. *see* demi-reliure
d.-rel. *see* demi-reliure
d.s.t. *see* doré sur tranches
dactylographié: typewritten
daim: buckskin, doeskin
damassé: linen damask
damiers: checkered designs
dans: in
dans le texte: in the text
date: date
de: of, from, with
de l'époque: contemporary
de luxe: de luxe
de prochaine publication: soon to
  be published
de relai: alternative, substitute
déboîté: loosened in the joints
débroché: unstitched
déch. *see* déchiré, déchirure
déchir. *see* déchiré, déchirure
déchiré: torn
déchirure: tear, torn place
décollé: unglued
décoloré: discolored
décor: decoration, design
décoré: decorated
découpé: cut off, cut out
découpure: cut
décousu: unsewn
dédicace: dedication note
dédicacé: with dedication note
dédicatoire: dedicatory
déf. *see* défectueux, défectuosité
défaut: defect
défect. *see* défectueux
défectueux: defective, damaged
défectuosité(s): defect(s)
définitif: definitive
défr. *see* défraîchi
défraîchi: shopworn, faded
délié: with binding loosened
demandé: sought, wanted
demi: half
demi-chagrin: half-shagreen
  binding

demi-reliure: half binding
dent. *see* dentelle
dentelle: lacelike design used in
  tooling bindings
dentelle de pampres: leafy vine
  design
dentelle intérieure: inside lace
  design
dép. *see* dépliant
dépl. *see* dépliant
dépliant: unfolding, folding
déplier: to unfold
dérel. *see* dérelié
dérelié: with binding gone
dern. *see* dernier
dernier: last
des. *see* dessin
dess. *see* dessin
dessin: drawing, design
dessiné: designed, drawn
détaché: detached, loose
déteint: faded, discolored
détérioré: deteriorated
deux(ième): two (second)
devise: motto, inscription
diagr. *see* diagramme
diagramme: diagram
diff. *see* différent
différent: different
dim. *see* dimension
dimension: dimension, size
disloqué: disjointed
disponible: available
dissert. *see* dissertation
dissertation: dissertation
dix(ième): ten(th)
dix-huit(ième): eighteen(th)
dix-neuf: nineteen
dix-neuvième: nineteenth
dix-sept(ième): seventeen(th)
doc. *see* document
docum. *see* document
document: document
dor. *see* doré, dorure
doré: gilt, decorated with gold
doré sur témoins: with gilt on
  uncut edges
doré sur tranches: with gilt edges

dorure: gilding, decoration in gold
dos: back of a book
dos à compartiments: back with
  sections
dos à nerfs: back with raised
  bands
dos et coins: back and corners
dos refait: rebacked
doubl. *see* doublure
double: double
doublé: lined
double-couronne: double crown
double emboîtage: double slipcase
double page: double page
doubles gardes: double end papers
doublure: lining
douze(ième): twelve(twelfth)
droit: straight
ds. *see* dans

é. *see* état
eau-f. *see* eau-forte
eau-forte: etching
éb. *see* ébarbé
ébarb. *see* ébarbé
ébarbé: trimmed
éc. *see* écaille
écaille: scalelike design, mottled
échelle: scale
écoinçon(s): corner design(s)
écorchures: skinned spots
écorné: with corners broken
écrasé: crushed
écriture: writing
écru: natural-colored
écusson: armorial shield
écusson de tomaison: volume-
  number label
éd. *see* éditeur, édition
édit. *see* éditeur, édition
éditeur: publisher, editor
édition: edition
édition collective: anthology,
  collected works
édition princeps: *editio princeps*
effacé: effaced
égratignure: scratch
él. *see* élégant

élég. *see* élégant
élégant: elegant
éliminé: eliminated
ém. *see* émail
émail: enamel
émargé: trimmed, margins cut
  down
émaux: enamels
emb. *see* emboîtage
emboît. *see* emboîtage
emboîtage: case
emboîté: cased, bound
émeraude: emerald-colored
émoussé: dulled, rounded
en: in
en double: duplicated, repeated
en fasc. *see* en fascicules
en fascicules: in fascicules
en feuilles: in sheets
en ff. *see* en feuilles
en pleine page: in full page
en regard: opposite, facing
en réimpression: being reprinted
en simile: in facsimile
en souscription: on subscription
en sus: additional, above
en-tête: heading, headpiece
enc. *see* encadrement
encadr. *see* encadrement
encadré: framed
encadrem. *see* encadrement
encadrement: frame, border
encart. *see* encartage
encartage: insertion
encastré: inset
enchères: auction
encollé: pasted, mounted
end. *see* endommagé
endomm. *see* endommagé
endommagé: damaged
enfoncé: embossed
enlevé: missing, removed
enluminé: illuminated, decorated
  with colors by hand
enluminure: illumination
ens. *see* ensemble
ensemble: together, group
ent. *see* entièrement

entamé: slightly damaged
entièr. *see* entièrement
entièrement: entirely
entredeux: space between two
  designs, design used to fill that
  space
entrelacs: interlaced fillets,
  interlacings
entrenerfs: panels between raised
  bands
env. *see* environ, envoi
envir. *see* environ
environ: about
envoi: dedicatory note or inscription
ép. *see* époque
épaisseur: thickness
épid. *see* épidermé, épidermure
épidermé: with surface of skin
  scraped off
épidermure: place where skin
  has been scraped
épigraphe: epigraph
épis: grain, design representing
  grain
époq. *see* époque
époque: time, period, contemporary
épr. *see* épreuve
épreuve: proof
épuisé: exhausted, out-of-print
érafl. *see* éraflure
éraflé: scraped
éraflure: scraped spot
escarboucle: carbuncle
esquisse: sketch
essai: essay
est. *see* estampe
estampe: print, engraving
estampé: stamped, embossed
estampille: stamp
estimé: esteemed
ét. *see* état, étude
état: condition, stage
état de conservation: condition
état de neuf: as new
étiq. *see* étiquette
étiquette: label

fleurdelisé: decorated with fleur-de-lys
fleurette: small floral design
fleuronné: having a floral design
fleurons: large floral design
fleurons d'angle: corner floral designs
fleurons de titre: floral design included in a title page
fol. *see* folio
folio: folio
folioté: foliated
foncé: deep, dark
format: format
fort: thick, strong
fort estimé: highly esteemed
fr. *see* français, à froid
fraîcheur: freshness
français: French
franco: prepaid, costs of carriage paid
frappé: stamped, tooled
frappé à froid: blind-tooled
froissé: wrinkled
froissures: wrinkles, wrinkling
front. *see* frontispice
frontisp. *see* frontispice
frontispice: frontispiece
frott. *see* frotté
frotté: scraped, roughened
frottis: light discoloration, smear
fusains: charcoal drawings
fx. titre: *see* faux-titre

g. *see* gravé
gaine: slip cover
gainé: slip-covered
garde(s): end paper(s)
gauf. *see* gaufré
gaufré: goffered
gaufrure: goffering
gd. *see* grand
genre: type
glacé: glazed, coated
glands: acorns, designs representing acorns
glose: gloss

glossaire: glossary
goth. *see* gothique
gothique: gothic
gouaché: painted in gouache
gouttière: fore edge
gr. *see* grain, grand, gravé, gravure
gr. au trait. *see* gravure au trait
gr.s.bois. *see* gravure sur bois
grain: grain
grain écrasé: crushed grain
grand: large
grand de marges: large margins
grandeur: size
granit. *see* granité
granité: colored to resemble granite
granulé: small-grained
graphique: line design, line drawing
gras: thick, heavy
grattage: scratch
gratté: scratched
grav. *see* gravé, gravure
gravé: engraved
graveur: engraver
gravure: engraving, print
gravure au trait: line engraving
gravure sur bois: wood engraving, woodcut
grd. *see* grand
grecque: ornamental border design
grenat: pomegranate-colored
griffé: scratched
griffonné: with scribblings
gris: gray
gros: large, thick
grotesque: grotesque
guilloché: with a chequered pattern
guillochures: chequered patterns
guirl. *see* guirlande
guirlande: garland

h. *see* hors
h.c. *see* hors commerce
h.com. *see* hors commerce

h.t. *see* hors-texte
hachure: hatching, shading
haut: top, upper part
haut. *see* hauteur
hauteur: height
hebdomadaire: weekly
hectographié: hectographed
hélio. *see* héliogravure
héliochromie: color engraving
héliogr. *see* héliogravure
héliogravé: photoengraved
héliogravure: photoengraving
héliotypie: photoprinting
historié: historiated, ornamented
Hol. *see* Hollande
Hollande: Holland
hors: outside
hors commerce: not for sale,
  privately printed
hors-texte: not in the text
huit(ième): eight(h)
humidité: moisture

ident. *see* identique
identique: uniform, identical
ill. *see* illustration, illustré
illisible: illegible
illustr. *see* illustration, illustré
illustrateur: illustrator
illustration: illustration
illustré: illustrated
immaculé: immaculate
imp. *see* imprimé, imprimerie,
  imprimeur
impeccable: impeccable
impr. *see* imprimé, imprimerie,
  imprimeur
impression: printing
imprim. *see* imprimé, imprimerie
imprimé: printed, printed matter
imprimerie: printing, printing
  firm
imprimeur: printer
in-fol. *see* in-folio
in-folio: folio
in-plano: in sheets; broadside
in-t. *see* in-texte

in-texte: in the text
inclus: inclusive, enclosed
incunable: incunabulum
inéd. *see* inédit
inédit: unpublished
inégalable: unmatched
inexpurgé: unexpurgated
inf. *see* inférieur
infér. *see* inférieur
inférieur: lower
infime: very small, minute
init. *see* initiale
initiale(s): initial letter(s)
inscr. *see* inscription
inscript. *see* inscription
inscription: inscription
insign. *see* insignifiant
insignif. *see* insignifiant
insignifiant: insignificant
int. *see* intérieur
intégral: complete
intér. *see* intérieur
interc. *see* intercalé
intercalé: intercalated
interfolié: interleaved
intérieur: interior, inner
interligné: interlinear
interversion: transposition
interverti: transposed
intitulé: entitled
intr. *see* introduction
introduction: introduction
introuvable: impossible to find
italique: italics
ivoire: ivory-colored

j. *see* japon
jans. *see* janséniste
jansén. *see* janséniste
janséniste: Jansenist, an unorna-
  mented style of binding
japon: Japan paper
jaquette: book jacket, wrappers
jasp. *see* jaspé
jaspé: marbled, sprinkled
jaune: yellow
jauni: yellowed

jaunissures: yellowed marks, foxing
jésus: paper of approximately superroyal size
jeu de filets: line pattern
joints: joints
jonquille: jonquil-colored, pale yellow
journal: newspaper, periodical
jouxte: next to
jumelés: paired, reinforced
justifié: justified

l. see largeur, lettre, lieu
l.a. see lettre autographe
lâche: weak
lanières: laces
larg. see largeur
largeur: width
lav. see lavallière
lavable: washable
lavall. see lavallière
lavallière: russet-colored
lavé: washed
lavis: wash, wash drawing
lég. see léger, légèrement
légende: legend, caption
léger: slight, light
légèrement: slightly
lettre: letter
lettre autographe: autograph letter
lettres bâtardes: slanting type letters
lettres rondes: round type letters
lettrine: reference letter, decorated initial letter
lexique: lexicon
lib. see libraire, librairie
libelle: lampoon, small libelous work
libr. see libraire, librairie
libraire: bookseller
librairie: bookstore
lie de vin: purplish-red
lieu: place
ligne: line
ligné: lined

lilas: lilac
lim. see liminaire, limité
limin. see liminaire
liminaire: preliminary, prefatory
limité: limited
lin: linen
linéaire: line pattern, linear
lisible: legible
lisse: smooth, trimmed
listel: a border fillet
lith. see lithographie, lithographié
litho. see lithographie, lithographié
lithogr. see lithographie, lithographié
lithographie: lithograph
lithographié: lithographed
livr. see livraison
livraison: part, issue
livre: book
livre d'heures: Book of Hours
livre d'occasion: secondhand book
long: long, the long way
longueur: length
losange: diamond-shaped pattern
losangé: tooled in a diamond-shaped pattern
lourd: heavy
luxe: de luxe

m. see marbré, maroquin
mac. see maculé
maculature: mackle, waste sheet
maculé: spotted, soiled
maigre: thin
majuscules: capital letters
man. see manuscrit
manchette(s): marginal note(s)
manq. see manquant
manquant: lacking
manque: lacks, is missing
manuscrit(s): manuscript(s)
maquette: specimen volume
mar. see maroquin
marb. see marbré, marbrure
marbré: marbled
marbrure: marbling
marge(s): margin(s)

71

margin. *see* marginal
marginal: marginal
maroq. *see* maroquin
maroquin: morocco
maroquiné: made to resemble morocco, with morocco finish
marque d'imprimeur: printer's mark
marron: maroon, chestnut-colored
mastique: mastic
mat: with mat finish
mauv. *see* mauvais
mauvais: bad
médaillon: medallion, inset
médiocre: mediocre
mélange: miscellany
mém. *see* mémoire
mémoire(s): memoir(s), report(s)
mensuel: monthly
meurtri: damaged, bruised
mi-marges: half margins
mi-maroquin: half morocco
mi-page: half page, near center of page
mi-souple: semiflexible
milieu: center
mille: thousand
mince: thin
minime: extremely small in quantity
minuscule: extremely small in size
mis à jour: brought up to date, revised
mise en page: layout of printed page
mobile: movable
mod. *see* moderne
moderne: modern
moire: moire, a watered fabric, usually silk
moisissure: mildew
monogr. *see* monogramme
monogramme: monogram
monographie: monograph
monté: mounted

morceau(x): piece(s), selection(s)
mordoré: bronzed
mors: joint
mosaïqué: decorated in mosaic patterns
mosaïque(s): mosaic(s), mosaic pattern(s)
motif: design, pattern
mouch. *see* moucheté
moucheté: speckled, spotted
mouil. *see* mouillé, mouillure
mouill. *see* mouillé, mouillure
mouillé: stained by dampness, moisture
mouillure: stain caused by moisture
mouton: sheepskin
mq. *see* manque
mque. *see* manque
ms. *see* **manuscrit**
mss. *see* **manuscrits**
mst. *see* **manuscrit**
muet: blank, undecorated
muette: blank, undecorated
mutilé: mutilated

n. *see* nom
n.c. *see* non chiffré
n.ch. *see* non chiffré
n.é. *see* non ébarbé
n.r. *see* non rogné
n.s. *see* nouvelle série
nacré: colored in mother-of-pearl
nch. *see* non chiffré
nerfs: raised bands, cords
nerfs plats: flat bands
neuf: new
neuf: nine
neuve: nine
neuvième: ninth
ni: neither
no. *see* numéro
nom: name
nom de plume: pen name, pseudonym
nomb. *see* nombreux
nombr. *see* nombreux
nombre: number

nombreux: numerous
non chiffré: unnumbered
non coupé: uncut
non ébarbé: untrimmed
non numéroté: unnumbered
non rogné: untrimmed
not. *see* notice
notice(s): note(s)
nouv. *see* nouveau
nouveau: new
nouvelle: new
nouvelle série: new series
num. *see* numéro, numéroté
numér. *see* numéroté
numéro: number
numérotation: numbering
numéroté: numbered

o. *see* original
obl. *see* oblong
oblong: oblong
occ. *see* occasion
occasion: bargain
ocre: ocher
oeuvre: work, opus
oeuvres choisies: selected works
olive: olive-colored
ombré: shaded
onciales: uncial letters
ondulé: wavy
onglets: tabs, binding strips
onze(ième): eleven(th)
opuscule: small work
or. *see* original
orange: orange-colored
ordin. *see* ordinaire
ordinaire: common, ordinary
orig. *see* original
origin. *see* original
original: original
orn. *see* orné
orné: decorated
ornem. *see* ornementé
ornement: ornament
ornementé: decorated
os: bone
ouv. *see* ouvrage
ouvr. *see* ouvrage

ouvrage: work

p. *see* page, pièce
p. de t. *see* pièce de titre
p. de tomaison *see* pièce de
  tomaison
p. de tr. *see* peau de truie
p.f. *see* petits fers
page(s): page(s)
page de garde: end paper
pages non chiffrées: unnumbered
  pages
pagination: pagination
pagination suivie: continuous
  pagination
paille: straw-colored
pailleté: spangled
paillettes: spangles
pâle: pale
pâli: paled, faded
pallette(s): small T-shaped
  design(s)
palmette: palm-leaf design
pampres: leafy vine design
pap. *see* papier
papier: paper
papier bible: Bible paper
papier couché: laid paper
papier de couleur: colored paper
papier(s) de garde: lining paper(s),
  end paper(s)
papier de riz: rice paper
papier glacé: coated paper,
  glazed paper
papier Japon: Japan paper
papier pailleté: spangled paper
papier vergé: laid paper
par places: in places
parafé: initialed
paragraphe: paragraph
paraître: appear
parch. *see* parchemin
parchem. *see* parchemin
parchemin: parchment, vellum
parcheminé: made to resemble
  parchment
parf. *see* parfait
parfait: perfect

part *see* à part
particulier: individual
partie: part
paru: appeared, published
parution: appearance, publication
passé: worn, faded
pastiche: imitation, copy
peau: leather, skin
peau de chamois: chamois skin
peau de chèvre: goatskin
peau de truie: pigskin
peau de vélin: vellum
peigne: combed edges
peigné: grained
peint: painted
perc. *see* percaline
percal. *see* percaline
percale: percale
percaline: book cloth, buckram
périodique: periodical
perlé: ornamented with small
  vignettes
perte de texte: loss of text
pet. *see* petit
petit: small
petits fers: small pattern designs
peu: little, few
phot. *see* photographie, photographique
photo *see* photographie
photocopie: photocopy
photog. *see* photographie,
  photographique
photogr. *see* photographie,
  photographique
photographie: photograph,
  photographic illustration
photographique: photographic
photograv. *see* photogravure
photogravure: photoengraving
phototypie: phototype
pièce: piece, part
pièce d'armes: armorial piece
pièce de milieu: centerpiece
pièce de titre: title label
pièce de tomaison: volume label
pièces: volume and title labels
piq. *see* piqué, piqûre
piqq. *see* piqûres
74

piqué: with small holes
piqué de vers: wormholed
piqûre(s): hole(s)
piqûre de vers: wormhole
pl. *see* planche
plaisant: attractive
plan: map, chart
planche(s): plate(s), illustration(s)
plaq. *see* plaquette
plaque: medallion, shield bearing
  a design
plaquette: booklet, pamphlet
plat(s): side(s) of a book, flat
  surface(s)
plat(s) de couverture: side(s) of
  the cover
plat inférieur: back cover
plat supérieur: front cover
platiné: decorated in platinum
plchs. *see* planches
plein: full
pli: fold
plié: folded
pll. *see* planches
plus. *see* plusieurs
plusieurs: several
pochette: pocket, strong envelope
pochoir: stencil
pointe: point
pointe sèche: dry point
pointillé *see* au pointillé
poli: polished, burnished
polych. *see* polychrome
polychrome: multicolored
porc: pigskin
porph. *see* porphyre
porphyre: porphyry
port: costs of carriage
port. *see* portrait
port.-front. *see* portrait-
  frontispice
portef. *see* portefeuille
portefeuille: portfolio
porto: costs of carriage
portr. *see* portrait
portrait: portrait
portrait-frontispice: frontispiece
  portrait
post. *see* postérieur

postér. *see* postérieur
postérieur: of a later date; back
postface: epilogue
posthume: posthumous
poussiéreux: dusty
pp. *see* pages
pp.n.ch. *see* pages non chiffrées
précieux: precious
précis: summary
préf. *see* préface
préface: preface, foreword
prél. *see* préliminaire
prélim. *see* préliminaire
préliminaire: preliminary
premier: first
prép. *see* préparation
préparation: preparation
prés. *see* présentation
présentation: presentation
presse: press
prisé: prized
privilège: privilege, permit to
  publish
prix: price
prochainement: soon
propre: clean
propriété littéraire: copyright
provenance: provenance, source
pseudonyme: pseudonym
pt. *see* petit
pub. *see* publication, publié
publication: publication
publié: published
pur: pure
pur chiffon: pure rag

qq. *see* quelques
quarante(ième): forty(ieth)
quatorze(ième): fourteen(th)
quatre(ième): four(th)
quatre-vingt(ième): eighty(ieth)
quatre-vingt-dix(ième):
  ninety(ieth)
quelq. *see* quelques
quelques: some, a few
queue du dos: foot of the back
quinze(ième): fifteen(th)

r. *see* relié
rabais: discount
rabat: flap
rac. *see* raccommodage
raccommodage(s): repair(s)
raciné: tooled in a design
  resembling tree roots
raisin: paper approximately
  royal size
raisonné: systematic
ramages: branch and flower
  design
rapiécé: mended
rappel: recall, repetition
rapport: report
rare: rare
rarissime: extremely rare
recherché: in great demand
récit: tale
recollé: reglued
rectification: correction
recto: recto, front side
recueil: collection
rédacteur: editor
rédaction: editorship
rédigé: compiled, edited
réduit: reduced
réédition: new edition
refait: remade, made over
refondu: reorganized, recast
réglé: ruled, lined
reh. *see* rehaussé
rehaussé: decorated, enhanced
réimp. *see* réimpression,
  réimprimé
réimposé: reimposed
réimpr. *see* réimpression
réimpres. *see* réimpression
réimpression: reprint, reprinting
réimprimé: reprinted
rel. *see* relié, reliure
relai *see* de relai
relevé: set off
relié: bound
relieur: binder
reliure: binding
reliure amateur: half binding
  with corners

reliure de l'époque: contemporary binding
reliure enchaînée: chained binding
reliure romantique: binding tooled in the romantic style
remanié: rearranged, revised
remboîté: rebound, recased
remonté: renewed
rempl. *see* remplié
remplié: folded on itself
renf. *see* renforcé
renforcé: reinforced
renouvelé: renewed
rép. *see* réparé
répar. *see* réparation
réparation: repair(s)
réparé: repaired, mended
répertoire: list, index
replié: folded on itself
repoussé: stamped in by hand, embossed
repr. *see* reproduction
reprod. *see* reproduction
reproduction: reproduction
rest. *see* restauré
restaurable: repairable
restauré: restored
résumé: summary
rev. *see* revu
révisé: revised
revu: revised
revue: periodical, review
richem. *see* richement
richement: richly
rinceau: branchlike design, foliated scroll
r° *see* recto
rocaille: encrusted pattern
rog. *see* rogné
rogn. *see* rogné
rogné: trimmed, cut
rom. *see* romantique
roman: novel
romant. *see* romantique
romantique *see* reliure romantique
rongé: gnawed, eaten

rosace: ornament resembling a rose, rosette
rosacé: decorated with rosettes
rouge: red
rouge et noir: printed in black, partly in red, rubricated
rouille: rust
roul. *see* roulette
roulette: circular design, fillet
rouss. *see* rousseurs
rousseurs: red spots, foxing
roussi: foxed, browned
ruban: ribbon, bookmark
rubrique: rubric
rubriqué: rubricated
rustique: rustic, unpolished

s. *see* sans, siècle, sur
s.a. *see* sans année
s.b. *see* sur bois
s.c. *see* sans couverture, sur cuivre
s.d. *see* sans date
s.éd. *see* sans éditeur
s.l. *see* sans lieu
s.l.n.d. *see* sans lieu ni date
s.p. *see* sans prix
sain: in good condition
saleux: dirty
sali: dirtied
salissures: dirty spots
sans: without
sans année: without year
sans couverture: without cover
sans date: without date
sans éditeur: without publisher
sans gravité: unimportant
sans lieu: without place of publication
sans lieu ni date: without place or date of publication
sans perte de texte: without loss of text
sans prix: without price
satin: satin
satinette: sateen
saumon: salmon-colored
sceau(x): seal(s)

étoffe: cloth
étr. *see* étranger
étranger: foreign
étroit: narrow
étude: study
étui: case, container
étui gainé: closed slipcase
étui-reliure: binding with case
ex. *see* exemplaire
ex-libris: bookplate
exceptionnellement: unusually
exemp. *see* exemplaire
exempl. *see* exemplaire
exemplaire(s): copy(ies)
exemplaire d'auteur: author's
  copy
exemplaire nominatif: copy
  designated for a person
explic. *see* explication
explicatif: explanatory
explication: explanation
exposé: summary
extr. *see* extrait
extrait: extract
exx. *see* exemplaire(s)

f. *see* faux, feuille, filets
f.-t. *see* faux-titre
fac. *see* faculté
facs. *see* facsimile
facsim. *see* facsimile
facsimile: facsimile
fact. *see* factice
factice: artificial, imitation
faculté: faculty
faible: feeble, weak
fané: faded
fantaisie: fancy, imaginative
fasc. *see* fascicule
fascic. *see* fascicule
fascicule: fascicule, part
fat. *see* fatigué
fatig. *see* fatigué
fatigué: worn
fauve: fawn-colored
faux: false, imitation
faux nerfs: imitation cords
faux-titre: half or bastard title

fc. *see* franco
fco. *see* franco
fend. *see* fendu
fendu: split
fente: break, split
fer: tool
ferm. *see* fermoirs
fermoir(s): clasp(s)
feuillages: foliage-like patterns
feuille(s): sheet(s)
feuille de garde: end paper
feuille volante: broadside
feuillet(s): sheet(s), leaf(ves)
feuillet d'errata: errata sheet,
  leaf
feuillet(s) de garde: end paper(s)
feuillet(s) mobile(s): loose-leaf
  sheet(s)
feuillets chiffrés: numbered
  sheets, leaves
feuillets non chiffrés: unnumbered
  sheets
ff. *see* feuilles, feuillets
ff. ch. *see* feuillets chiffrés
ff. nch. *see* feuillets non chiffrés
ficelles: laces
fig. *see* figure
figg. *see* figures
figure(s): illustration(s), dia-
  gram(s)
figuré: figured
fil. *see* filets
fileté: decorated with fillets
filets: fillets, line or band
  decorations
filets brisés: broken lines
filets courbes: curved line pattern
filets droits: straight line pattern
filets gras: heavy, thick fillets
filets maigres: thin fillets
filets ondulés: wavy line pattern
filigrane: watermark
fin de chapitre: ornamental
  design at end of chapter
finesse: fineness, high quality
fl.d.l. *see* fleur-de-lys
fleur. *see* fleurons
fleur-de-lys: lily design

scolies: critical notes
seize(ième): sixteen(th)
semestriel: semiannual
semis: scattering
séparé: separated, detached
sépia: sepia
sept(ième): seven(th)
sér. *see* série
série: series
seul. *see* seulement
seulement: only
siècle: century
signat. *see* signature
signature: signature
signé: signed
simili: facsimile, imitation
simili-cuir: imitation leather
simili-grav. *see* simili-gravure
simili-gravure: halftone engraving
simulé: simulated
six(ième): six(th)
soigné: carefully done
soixante(ième): sixty(ieth)
soixante-dix(ième): seventy(ieth)
souffert: injured, damaged
souillures: soil marks
souligné: underlined
soulignure: underlining
souple: flexible
sous: in, under
sous couverture: in covers
sous emboîtage: in container
sous portefeuille: in portfolio
sous presse: in press
sous-titre: subtitle
souscripteur: subscriber
souscription: subscription
sp. *see* spécial
spéc. *see* spécial
spécial: special
spécimen: sample, specimen
spirale: spiral
ss. *see* sous
suite: series
sup. *see* supérieur, supplément
supér. *see* supérieur
super-ex-libris: ownership mark

on outside cover
superfin: superfine
supérieur: top, upper
suppl. *see* supplément
supplément: supplement
supprimé: suppressed, censored
supralibros: property stamp
sur: on
sur bois: on wood
sur cuivre: on copper
surfin: superfine

t. *see* tête, texte, titre, tome
t.d. *see* taille-douce
tabis: watered silk, tabby
tabl. *see* tableau
table: index, table
tableau: picture, table
tache: spot, stain
taches d'humidité: damp spots
tacheté: spotted
taille-douce: copperplate
taupe: taupe
teinte: tint
teinté: tinted
tellière: paper, approximately
  foolscap size
témoins: witnesses, untrimmed
  edges
terni: tarnished
tête: head of a book, top edge
tête-de-chapitre: chapter head
tête-de-nègre: dark brown
tête-de-page: head of page
tête de série: first of series
tétrachromie: four-color print
texte: text
thèse: thesis
timb. *see* timbré
timbré: stamped
tir. *see* tirage
tirage: edition, printing
tirage à part: separate, reprint
tirage restreint: limited edition
tiré: printed
tissu: woven material
tit. *see* titre
titre: title, title page

77

titre courant: running title
titre-frontispice: title frontispiece
toile: cloth
toilé: cloth-covered
toile de lin: linen cloth
toile de soie: silk
toile écrue: unbleached cloth
tom. *see* tomaison
tomaison: volume numbering
tome: tome, volume
ton(s): shade(s)
torsade: spiral or cable-like
  design
touché: lightly damaged
toute toile: full cloth
tr. *see* traduction, traduit,
  tranche
traces: marks, traces
traces d'usure: traces of wear
trad. *see* traduction, traduit
traducteur: translator
traduction: translation
traduit: translated
trait: line
traité: treatise
tranche: trench, hollow edge
travail de vers: signs of worms
treize(ième): thirteen(th)
trente(ième): thirty(ieth)
très: very
trimestriel: quarterly
triple: triple
trois(ième): three(third)
trou(s) de vers: wormhole(s)
truie: pigskin
typ. *see* typographique

typographique: typographic

un: one
une: one
uni: smooth, even
uniformément: uniformly
unique: unique, sole
us. *see* usagé, usé
usag. *see* usagé
usagé: worn
usé: worn
usure: worn spot

v. *see* veau, vélin
variante(s): variant(s)
veau: calf
vél. *see* vélin
vélin: vellum
velours: velvet
velouté: velvet-like, with velvet
  surface
vendu: sold
vente: sale
verdâtre: greenish
vers: worms
verso: verso, back side
vient de paraître: just published,
  just out
vign. *see* vignette
vignette: vignette
vingt(ième): twenty(ieth)
viol. *see* violet
violet: violet
v° *see* verso
volume: volume

zincotypie: zinc engraving

GERMAN

A. *see* Auflage, Ausschnitt
a.d.Zt. *see* aus der Zeit
Abb. *see* Abbildung
Abbild. *see* Abbildung
Abbildgn. *see* Abbildungen
Abbildung(en): illustration(s)
Abbr. *see* Abbreviatur
Abbreviatur(en): abbreviation(s)
Abdr. *see* Abdruck
Abdruck(e): copy(ies), offprint(s)
abgebildet: reproduced
abgeblättert: come off
abgedr. *see* abgedruckt
abgedruckt: printed, reprinted
abgegriffen: worn
abgelöst: detached
abgen. *see* abgenutzt
abgenutzt: worn
abgerissen: torn off
abgeschabt: scraped
abgeschn. *see* abgeschnitten
abgeschnitten: cut away
abgesetzt: sold
abgew. *see* abgewetzt
abgewetzt: chafed
Abh. *see* Abhandlung
Abhandlung(en): transaction(s),
  treatise(s)
Abkürzung(en): abbreviation(s)
Abnahmeverpflichtung: subscribers must contract for the
  entire series
Abonnement: subscription
Abriss: synopsis
Abschn. *see* Abschnitt
Abschnitt(e): section(s)
Abschürfung(en): abrasure(s)
Abt. *see* Abteilung
Abteilung(en): part(s)
Abtl. *see* Abteilung
abweichend: different, differing
  from
Abzug(züge): copy(ies)
acht(e): eight(h)
achtzehn(te): eighteen(th)
achtzig(ste): eighty(ieth)
A.d.W. *see* Akademie der
  Wissenschaften
Ahnentafel(n): genealogical
  table(s)
Akad. *see* Akademie
Akad.W. *see* Akademie der
  Wissenschaften
Akademie: academy
Akademie der Wissenschaften:
  Academy of Science(s)
Alben: albums
Album: album
alles Erschienene: all published
alles was erschien(en): all that

was (were) published
allg. verst. *see* allgemeinverständlich
allgemeinverständlich: popular,
   easy to understand
alphabetisch: alphabetical(ly)
als Handschrift gedruckt: privately printed
als Manuskript gedruckt: privately printed
alt: old
Altersspur(en): trace(s) of aging
altkol. *see* altkoloriert
altkoloriert: colored long ago
Altkolorit: old coloring
amtl. *see* amtlich
amtlich: official
anast. *see* anastatisch
anastatisch: anastatic
Anf. *see* Anfang
Anfang: beginning
Anfrage: inquiry, request
angeb. *see* angebunden
angebd. *see* angebunden
angebunden: bound with
angefleckt: slightly spotted
angefressen: gnawed
angegilbt: slightly yellowed
anger. *see* angerissen
angerändert: slightly spotty
   along margins
angerandet: with beginnings of
   staining on edges
angerissen: slightly torn
angeschlagen: slightly bruised
angeschlg. *see* angeschlagen
angeschm. *see* angeschmutzt
angeschmutzt: slightly soiled
angeschnitten: slightly damaged
   by cutting
angestaubt: slightly dusty
Anh. *see* Anhang
Anhang: appendix
Anhänge: appendixes
ankol. *see* ankoloriert
ankolor. *see* ankoloriert
ankoloriert: slightly colored
Anl. *see* Anlage

Anlage(n): enclosure(s)
Anm. *see* Anmerkung
Anmerk. *see* Anmerkung
Anmerkg. *see* Anmerkung
Anmerkung(en): note(s)
Annalen: annals
anon. *see* anonym
anonym: anonymous(ly)
Anrandung(en): beginning(s) of
   stains along the edges
Ans. *see* Ansicht
anscheinend: apparently
Ansicht(en): view(s)
anspruchsvoll: pretentious
anstelle: instead of
Anstreich. *see* Anstreichungen
Anstreichungen: marks
Anthologie: anthology
Antiqua: roman letters, roman
   type
Antiquar: rare-book dealer
Antiquariat: secondhand bookshop,
   secondhand dealer; rare-book
   dealer
Anzahl: number
App. *see* Appendix
Appendix: appendix
Aquarell: water color
Aquatinta: aquatint
Arabeskenstempel: arabesque
   stamping(s)
Arbeit(en): work(s), study(ies)
Archiv: archives
Atlanten: atlases
Atlas: atlas
aufgeklebt: mounted, pasted on
aufgelegt: edited
aufges. *see* aufgesetzt
aufgeschnitten: opened with paper
   knife
aufgesetzt: patched, mounted
aufgewalzt: rolled on under
   pressure, laminated
aufgez. *see* aufgezogen
aufgezeichnet: recorded
aufgezogen: mounted
Aufl. *see* Auflage
Auflage: edition

Auflagenvermerk: note concerning edition
Auflg. *see* Auflage
Aufnahmen: photographs
Aufsätze: essays, papers
aus der Zeit: of that time
Ausbess. *see* Ausbesserung
Ausbesserung: repair
ausführl. *see* ausführlich
ausführlich: *in extenso*, detailed
Ausg. *see* Ausgabe
Ausgabe: printing, edition
Ausgabe letzter Hand: definitive edition
ausgeb. *see* ausgebessert
ausgebess. *see* ausgebessert
ausgebessert: repaired
ausgebrochen: broken loose
ausgemalt: illuminated
ausgeprägt: stamped, raised
ausgeschlagen: lined
ausgeschn. *see* ausgeschnitten
ausgeschnitt. *see* ausgeschnitten
ausgeschnitten: cut out, excised
ausgew. *see* ausgewählt
ausgewählt: selected
ausgezeichn: *see* ausgezeichnet
ausgezeichnet: excellent, in excellent state
Ausklapptafel(n): folding plate(s)
Ausland: foreign countries
ausnahmslos: without exception
ausradiert: erased, scratched out
ausschlagbar: fold-out
Ausschn. *see* Ausschnitt
Ausschnitt: excision, clipping
aussen: externally
ausser: except, besides
äusserst: outermost, utmost, lowest (price)
Ausw. *see* Auswahl
Auswahl: selection
Auszug: excerpt
Auszüge: excerpts
auszugsweise: in excerpts
Autogr. *see* Autograph
Autograph: autograph

autographiert: autographed
autographisch: handwritten
autor. *see* autorisiert
autoris. *see* autorisiert
autorisiert: authorized
Autotypien: illustrations in autotype

Ballonleinen: balloon cloth
Band: ribbon, band, tie; volume
Bände: volumes
Bändchen: small volume(s), pamphlet(s)
Bänder: ribbons, bands, ties
Banderole(n): narrow band(s)
Bandzahl(en): volume number(s)
Barverkauf: cash sale
Bastardschrift: bastard type
Bd. *see* Band
Bdch. *see* Bändchen
Bdchn. *see* Bändchen
Bde. *see* Bände
Bdn. *see* Bände
bdr. *see* bedruckt
bearb. *see* bearbeitet
Bearb. *see* Bearbeiter, Bearbeitung
Bearbeiter: reviser(s)
bearbeitet: reworked, revised
Bearbeitung: revision
bed. verm. *see* bedeutend vermehrt
bedeutend vermehrt: considerably enlarged
bedruckt: printed
begr. *see* begründet
begründet: founded
beh. *see* behandelt
behandelt: deals with
beiderseitig *see* beidseitig
beidseit. *see* beidseitig
beidseitig: on both sides
Beifügung: addition
beigeb. *see* beigebunden
beigebunden: bound with
beigedr. *see* beigedruckt
beigedruckt: bound together, issued with

81

Beiheft: supplementary issue
Beil. *see* Beilage
Beilage: appendix, supplement
beiliegt: added
Beitr. *see* Beitrag
Beitrag(träge): contribution(s)
bekleistert: pasted over, covered
  with glue
bekritzelt: scribbled on
Belletristik: belles-lettres,
  fiction
bemerkenswert: noteworthy
ben. *see* benutzt
benutzt: used, with traces of use
Benutzungsspuren: traces of use
ber. *see* berieben
berechnet: planned, calculated,
  estimated
berechtigt: authorized
bereinigt: expurgated
Bericht(e): bulletin(s)
Berichtigung(en): correction(s)
berieben: scraped
berühmt(est): (most) famous
bes. *see* besonders
besch. *see* beschädigt
beschabt: scraped
beschäd. *see* beschädigt
beschädigt: damaged
Beschädigung(en): defect(s)
bescheuert: chafed
Beschlag: mounting, decoration
Beschläge: mountings, decorations
beschmutzt: soiled
beschn. *see* beschnitten
beschnitten: cut, trimmed
beschränkt: limited
beschrieben: inscribed, covered
  with writing
Besitzeintragung(en): note(s)
  concerning ownership
Besitzverm. *see* Besitzvermerk
Besitzvermerk: notation of
  ownership
besonders: special, separate
besorgt: edited, prepared
best. *see* bestossen

Bestellung(en): order(s)
bestoss. *see* bestossen
bestossen: bruised, injured
beweglich: movable, mobile
bez. *see* bezeichnet, bezogen
bezeichnet: designated
bezogen: covered
bezügl. *see* bezüglich
bezüglich: concerning
Bibl. *see* Bibliographie
bibliogr. *see* bibliographisch
Bibliograph(en): bibliographer(s)
Bibliographie(n): bibliography(ies)
bibliographisch: bibliographic
Bibliothekar(e): librarian(s)
Bibliotheksausgabe: library
  edition
Bibliotheksband(bände): ex-library
  volume(s)
Bibliotheksstempel: library stamp
biegs. *see* biegsam
biegsam: flexible
Bild(er): picture(s)
Bildbeigaben: plates
Bilderwerk: volume of plates
Bildinitialen: illustrated initial
  letters
Bildn. *see* Bildnis
Bildnis(se): portrait(s)
Bildseiten: plates
Bildtaf. *see* Bildtafel
Bildtafel(n): illustrated plate(s)
Bildteil: picture section
Bindg. *see* Bindung
Bindung: binding
biogr. *see* biographisch
biographisch: biographical
bisher: up to now
bitte anfordern: please request
Bl. *see* Blatt
blassblau: pale blue
Blatt: leaf, page
Blättchen: small leaf(ves), page(s),
  leaflet(s)
Blätter: leaves, pages
blattgr. *see* blattgross
blattgross: full page
Blattrand(ränder): margin(s)

Blattweiser: list(s) of catchwords
Blattzahl: number of sheets
Blattzählung: numbering of leaves
blau: blue
Bld. see Bild
Bleianm. see Bleianmerkungen
Bleianmerkungen: pencil notes
Bleistiftanmerkungen: pencil notes
Bleistiftanstrich(e): pencil mark(s)
Bleistiftmarginalien: marginal pencil notes
Bleistiftnotiz(en): penciled note(s)
Bleistiftstriche: pencil lines
Bleistiftunterstreichungen: pencil underlining
Bleistiftvermerke: pencil marks
blindgepr. see blindgeprägt
blindgeprägt: blind-tooled
Blindpressung: blind tooling
Bll. see Blätter
Blumenrankenornament: interlaced floral ornamentation
Blumenstempel: floral stamping(s)
Blütenlese(n): anthology(ies)
blütenweiss: immaculately white
Blz. see Blattzahl
Bog. see Bogen
Bogen: sheet
Bögen: sheets
Bord. see Bordüre
Bordüre(n): border(s), ornamental frame(s)
br. see broschiert
Br. see Broschur
Brandschaden: damage caused by burning
Braunanmalung: coloration in brown
Bräunung(en): browning(s), browned spot(s)
breit: wide
Breite: width
breitrandig: with wide margin(s)
Brief(e): letter(s)

Brief-Faksimile: facsimile letter
Briefbeil. see Briefbeilage
Briefbeilage(n): supplement(s) of letter(s)
Briefwechsel: correspondence
Brokatpapier: brocaded paper
bronziert: lustrous dark brown
brosch. see broschiert
broschiert: stitched in paper covers
Broschur: brochure binding
Broschüre(n): pamphlet(s), brochure(s)
brsch. see broschiert
Bruch: fold
brüchig: brittle
Bruchspuren: traces of cracking
Buchausgabe: edition in book form
Buchbinder: bookbinder(s)
Buchbinderpreis: binding cost
Buchdeckel: cover(s) of book(s)
Buchdr. see Buchdrucker, Buchdruckerei
Buchdrucker: printer(s)
Buchdruckerei: printer, print shop
Buchdruckpapierüberzug: cover of printing paper
Bücherliebhaber: bibliophile(s)
Büchersammler: book collector(s)
Buchh. see Buchhandlung
Buchhandel: book trade, bookstore
Buchhändler: bookdealer(s)
Buchhandlung: bookdealer, bookstore
Buchschmuck: book decoration
Buckram-Leinen: buckram
Bund: band
Bünde: bands
Bunt- und Schwarzdruck: color and black and white
Buntbilder: colored illustrations
Buntpapier: multicolored paper
Bütten: handmade paper

chromolith. see chromolithographiert
chromolithographiert: chromolithographed

Chronik(en): chronicle(s)

D. *see* Deckel
d.i. *see* das ist
d.Z. *see* der Zeit
d.Zt. *see* der Zeit
dabei: including, attached
dafür: in contrast
Damast: damask
dargest. *see* dargestellt
dargestellt: represented
Darst. *see* Darstellung
darstellend: representing
Darstellung(en): representation(s)
das ist: that is
dass. *see* dasselbe
dasselbe: the same
Dat. *see* Datum
datiert: dated
Datierung: dating, date
Datum: date
dazugeh. *see* dazugehörig
dazugehörend: accompanying,
   matching
dazugehörig: accompanying,
   matching
dazwischen: in between
Deckbl. *see* Deckblatt
Deckblatt: cover sheet
Decke: cover
Deckel: cover(s)
Deckelbezug(bezüge): cover-
   ing(s) of cover(s)
Deckelvergoldung: gilding on
   side
Deckname(n): pseudonym(s)
Ded. *see* Dedikation
Dedikation: dedication note
def. *see* defekt
defekt: damaged, incomplete
Defekt(e): deficiency(ies), flaw(s)
dekorativ: decorative, sumptuous
demnächst: in the near future
Denkschrift(en): memoir(s),
   memorandum(a); commemorative volume(s)
der Zeit: of that time
ders. *see* derselbe

derselbe: the same
dess. *see* desselben
desselben: of the same
Detailaufnahme(n): photograph(s)
   of details
Di. *see* Dissertation
Diagramme: diagrams
Dicke: thickness
dies. *see* dieselbe
dieselbe(n): the same
Diss. *see* Dissertation
Dissertation: dissertation
Dokumentenpapier: parchment
   paper
doppelblattgross: double-page
   size
Doppeldruck(e): double impres-
   sion(s)
doppels. *see* doppelseitig
doppelseitig: double page
doppelt: duplicated, double
Doppeltafeln: double plates
Dr. *see* Druck, Drucker
Drama: play(s)
drei: three
dreissig(ste): thirty(ieth)
dreizehn(te): thirteen(th)
dritte: third
Drittel: third(s)
Druck(e): print(s)
Drucker: printer(s)
Druckerm. *see* Druckermarke
Druckermarke(n): printer's
   mark(s)
Druckersignet: printer's device
Druckerzeichen: printer's mark(s)
Druckfehlerverzeichnis(se):
   errata list(s)
Druckvermerk: colophon
Dublettenstempel: stamp(s)
   designating duplicate copy(ies)
dunkelrot: dark red
Dünndr.-Pap. *see* Dünndruck-
   papier
Dünndruck: thin paper, India
   paper
Dünndruckausgabe: thin-paper
   edition

Dünndruckpapier: thin paper,
  India paper
Dupl. *see* Duplikat
Duplikat(e): duplicate(s)
durchg. *see* durchgesehen
durchgearb. *see* durchgearbeitet
durchgearbeitet: revised
durchgeh. *see* durchgehend
durchgehend: throughout
durchges. *see* durchgesehen
durchgesehen: verified, reviewed
durchgestrichen: crossed out
durchgez. Bünde. *see* durchgezogene Bünde
durchgezogene Bünde: raised
  bands
durchlaufd. *see* durchlaufend
durchlaufend: consecutive,
  consecutively numbered
durchlocht: perforated
durchsch. *see* durchschossen
durchschossen: interleaved
durchstrichen: crossed out
durchweg: throughout
durchwegs: throughout

ebd. *see* ebenda
Ebd. *see* Einband
ebda. *see* ebenda
ebenda: same place
ebendaselbst: same place
ebendazu: for the same
ebenf. *see* ebenfalls
ebenfalls: also
Ecke(n): corner(s)
Eckfleuron(s): corner floral
  motif(s)
Eckkartusche(n): corner
  cartouche(s)
Eckstück(e): cornerpiece(s)
eigenh. *see* eigenhändig
eigenhändig: autograph, handwritten
eigent. *see* eigentümlich
eigentümlich: characteristic;
  queer
eighd. *see* eigenhändig
ein: one

ein paar: a few, some
Einb. *see* Einband
Einband: binding
Einbanddecke(n): cover(s) for
  binding
Einbanddeckel: cover(s)
Einbandrücken: spine
Einbandzeichnung: binding design
Einbd. *see* Einband
Einbddecke. *see* Einbanddecke
Einblattdr. *see* Einblattdruck
Einblattdruck: broadside
Einf. *see* Einführung
einfach: simple
einfarbig: single color
Einfassung: frame, border
Einfassungsleiste: frame
Einführung: introduction
eingeb. *see* eingebunden
eingebunden: bound in
eingedr. *see* eingedruckt
eingedruckt: printed in text
eingef. *see* eingeführt
eingeführt: introduced, prefaced
eingegangen: no longer published,
  ceased publication
eingehängt: cased in, inserted
eingeklebt: pasted in
eingel. *see* eingeleitet
eingelassen: recessed, set in
eingelegt: inserted loosely, laid in
eingeleitet: with introduction
eingem. *see* eingemalt
eingemalt: painted in
eingeprägt: stamped in
einger. *see* eingerissen
eingerissen: torn
eingerückt: aligned
eingeschaltet: inserted, intercalated
eingestampft: destroyed, pulped
eingraviert: engraved
Einl. *see* Einleitung
Einlegetabelle(n): tipped-in
  chart(s)
einleit. *see* einleitend
einleitend: introductory
Einleitung: introduction

einmalig: one-time, unique
Einriss: small tear
eins: one
Einschaltblatt(blätter): inserted leaf(ves)
einschl. *see* einschliesslich
einschliesslich: including, inclusive
Einschluss: inclusion
Einschub(schübe): insertion(s)
einseitig bedruckt: printed on one side only
einseitig gedruckt: printed on one side only
Eintrag. *see* Eintragung
Eintragung: entry, note
einz. *see* einzeln
Einzelausgabe: separate (edition)
Einzelband(bände): separate volume(s)
Einzeldarstellung(en): monograph(s)
Einzelheft(e): separate issue(s)
Einzeljahrgang(gänge): separate annual volume(s)
einzeln: separate, separately
einzelne: several
Einzelnummer: single number
Einzelpr. *see* Einzelpreis
Einzelpreis: price for each part
Einzeltitel: separate item(s)
einzusetzen: to be inserted
elf(te): eleven(th)
Empf. *see* Empfänger
Empfänger: recipient
Endblätter: end papers
enth. *see* enthält, enthalten
enthält: contains
enthalten(d): contain(ing)
Entwurf(würfe): draft(s), plan(s), sketch(es)
entzückend: attractive, charming
erg. *see* ergänzt
Erg. *see* Ergänzung
Erg.-Bd. *see* Ergänzungsband
Erg.-H. *see* Ergänzungsheft
ergänzt: supplemented, complemented

Ergänzung(en): supplement(s)
Ergänzungsband: supplementary volume
Ergänzungsheft: supplementary issue
Erhaltung: state of preservation
Erinnerungen: memoirs
erkl. *see* erklärend, erklärt
erklär. *see* erklärend
erklärend: explanatory
erklärt: explained, clarified
Erklärung: explanation
erl. *see* erläuternd, erläutert
Erl. *see* Erläuterung
erläuternd: explanatory
erläutert: annotated
Erläuterung(en): explanation(s)
Ermässigung: reduction
erneuert: renewed, replaced
ersch. *see* erschienen
erscheint demnächst: to appear in the near future
erschienen: published
ersetzt: replaced
erst: not until, only
Erstausgabe: first edition
Erstdruck: first printing
erste Ausgabe: first edition
erstmalig: original, for the first time
erstmals: for the first time
erw. *see* erweitert
erweitert: enlarged
Erz. *see* Erzählung
Erzählung: story
Eselsohren: dog-ears
Etikett(e): label(s)
Etui(s): case(s), box(es)
etw. *see* etwas
etwa: approximately
etwas: rather, somewhat
Ex. *see* Exemplar
Exempl. *see* Exemplar
Exemplar(e): copy(ies)
Exkurs(e): insertion(s), supplementary paper(s)
Expl. *see* Exemplar
Exx. *see* Exemplare

f. *see* fehlen, fehlt, folio
F. *see* Folge
Fächerstempel: fan-shaped
  stamp(s)
Faks. *see* Faksimile
Faksim. *see* Faksimile
Faksimile: facsimile(s)
Faksimiledruck: facsimile
  reprint
faksimiliert: copied in facsimile
fälschlich: erroneously
Fälschung: forgery, fake
Faltblatt: folding leaf
Faltkarte: folded map
Faltkupf. *see* Faltkupfer
Faltkupfer: folding copper-
  plate(s)
Falttaf. *see* Falttafel
Falttafel(n): folding plate(s)
Falttfln. *see* Falttafeln
Falz: fold, joint
Familienwappen: coat of arms
farb. *see* farbig
Farbendr. *see* Farbendruck
Farbendruck: color print
Farbentafeln: colored plates
Farbentafln. *see* Farbentafeln
farbig: colored
Farblichtdruck(e): photographic
  color reproduction(s)
Farbtaf. *see* Farbtafel
Farbtafel(n): colored plate(s)
Fassung: version
fast: almost
Fbdr. *see* Farbendruck
Feder: pen
Federornament: feather-like
  ornamental design
Federzeichnungen: pen and ink
  drawings
fehlen: lacking
fehlerhaft: erroneous, deficient
Fehlstelle(n): deficiency(ies),
  defective spot(s)
fehlt: lacks, is missing
fein: fine, delicate
Feinleinen: fine cloth
feinst: most delicate(ly)

Feld(er): panel(s)
ferner: further, furthermore
fest: firm, solid
Festschrift: commemorative
  volume
Feucht.-Sp. *see* Feuchtigkeitsspuren
Feuchtigkeit: moisture
Feuchtigkeitsschäden: damage,
  imperfections caused by moisture
Feuchtigkeitsspuren: traces of
  moisture
ff. *see* folgende
Fig. *see* Figur
Figur(en): figure(s), diagram(s)
figürl. *see* figürlich
figürlich: figured
Fil. *see* Fileten
Fileten: fillets
fingerfl. *see* fingerfleckig
fingerfleckig: finger-marked
Fingerspuren: fingerprints, traces
  of handling
Fl. *see* Fleck
fl. *see* fleckig
flach: flat
Flechtband: lace-ribbon ornamental design
Fleck(e): spot(s), stain(s)
Fleckchen: small spot(s)
fleckenfrei: spotless
fleckenlos: spotless
fleckig: spotted
flex. *see* flexibel
flexibel: flexible
fliegender Vorsatz: flyleaf
fliegendes Blatt: broadside
Florilegium: anthology
Flugblatt(blätter): broadsheet(s),
  handbill(s)
Flugschrift(en): pamphlet(s)
Fol. *see* Foliant
fol. *see* folio
Folge: series
folgend(e): following, and following
  pages
Foliant(en): folio volume(s)
foliiert: foliated

Foliierung: foliation
folio: folio, sheet
Format: size, format
Formatangabe: designation of
  size
fortgef. *see* fortgeführt
fortgeführt: continued
fortges. *see* fortgesetzt
fortgesetzt: continued
fortlaufend: consecutive
Forts. *see* Fortsetzung
Fortsetzung: continuation
Fotogr. *see* Fotografie
fotogr. *see* fotografiert
Fotografie(n): photo(s)
fotografiert: photographed
Fraktur: black-letter type
franz. *see* französisch
Franzband: leather binding,
  usually calf
französisch: in French style,
  French
frisch: fresh
Frische: freshness
Front. *see* Frontispiz
Frontispiz: frontispiece
Frühdruck: early print, near
  incunabulum
Frühjahr: Spring
Frzbd. *see* Franzband
fünf(te): five (fifth)
fünfzehn(te): fifteen(th)
fünfzig(ste): fifty(ieth)
Fussnote(n): footnote(s)

G. *see* Goldschnitt
galant: risqué, erotic
ganz: entire(ly), quite
ganz wenig: very little
Ganzgoldschnitt: all edges gilt
gänzl. umgearb. *see* gänzlich
  umgearbeitet
Ganzleder: full leather
Ganzleinen: full cloth
Ganzleinwand: full cloth
gänzlich umgearbeitet: entirely
  revised
ganzs. *see* ganzseitig

ganzseit. *see* ganzseitig
ganzseitig: full page
Ganztafeln: full-page plates
geb. *see* gebunden
gebdn. *see* gebunden
gebr. *see* gebrochen
Gebr.-Sp. *see* Gebrauchsspur
Gebr.-Spur. *see* Gebrauchsspur
gebrauchsfleckig: stained through
  use
Gebrauchsspur(en): mark(s) of use
gebräunt: foxed, browned
gebrochen: broken
gebunden: bound
Gedenkschrift: commemorative
  publication
gediegen: solid(ly), strong(ly)
gedr. *see* gedruckt
gedruckt: printed
gefalt. *see* gefaltet
gefaltet: folded
geflickt: patched
gefranst: worn
gegen bar: cash
gegenüber: facing, opposite
gegenübergest. *see* gegenübergestellt
gegenübergestellt: facing
Gegenwart: present
gegilbt: yellowed
geglättet: smoothed, burnished
geh. *see* geheftet
geheftet: stitched, bound in
  pamphlet style
gehöht: heightened
gekl. *see* geklebt
geklebt: pasted, pasted together
geknickt: dog-eared, cracked, bent
gekr. *see* gekrönt
gekrönt: prize-winning
gekürzt: shortened, condensed
gelbfleckig: with yellow spots,
  foxed
Geleitwort: introduction, introductory note
Gelenk(e): joint(s)
gelitten: suffered, damaged
gelockert: loosened

88

gelöscht: canceled
gem. *see* gemalt
gemalt: hand-colored
Gemeinschaft: collaboration,
 co-operation
gemeinverst. *see* gemeinverständlich
gemeinverständlich: popular
gen. *see* genannt
genannt: mentioned
genarbt: grained
gepl. *see* geplant, geplatzt
geplant: planned, scheduled
geplatzt: burst, cracked
gepr. *see* geprägt, gepresst
geprägt: embossed
gepresst: stamped, tooled
gepunzt: punched out, embossed
ger. *see* gering
gerade Bandzahlen: even volume
 numbers
gering: unimportant, inferior,
 cheap
geringfügig: insignificant, slight
gerippt: ribbed
gerissen: torn
ges. *see* gesammelt
gesammelt: collected
Gesamtaufl. *see* Gesamtauflage
Gesamtauflage: entire edition
Gesamtausgabe: complete edition
Gesamtreg. *see* Gesamtregister
Gesamtregister: general index
Gesamtwerk: collected work,
 entire work
geschätzt: highly valued, estimated
Geschenkausgabe: gift edition
Geschenkband: gift volume
Geschenkeinband: gift binding
Geschenkexemplar: gift copy
geschichtl. *see* geschichtlich
geschichtlich: historical
geschickt: clever, skillful
geschn. *see* geschnitten
geschnitten: engraved, cut
geschrotet: dotted, sprinkled
gesprenkelt: sprinkled

gesprungen: cracked, broken
gest. *see* gestempelt, gestochen
gestempelt: stamped, marked
 with a stamp
gestickt: embroidered
gestochen: engraved
gesucht: sought after, in demand
getönt: toned, tinted
getr.Z. *see* getrennte Zählung
getrennte Zählung: separate
 numbering
getuscht: tinted
gewaschen: washed
geweisst: whitened
gewidmet: dedicated to
gewöhnlich: usual(ly)
gez.S. *see* gezählte Seiten
gezählte Seiten: numbered pages
gilbfleckig: with yellow spots,
 foxed
Glanzpapier: glossy paper
glatt: smooth
gleichmässig: uniform
gleichnamig: with the same name,
 title
Glossar: glossary
Glwd. *see* Ganzleinwand
golddurchwirkt: gold-brocaded
Goldfil. *see* Goldfileten
Goldfileten: gold fillets
Goldfolienumschlag: gold-leaf
 decorated covers
goldgedr. *see* goldgedruckt
goldgedruckt: printed with gold
goldgehöht: heightened with gold
goldgeprägt: gold-stamped
Goldornament(e): gilt decoration(s)
Goldprägung: gold stamping
Goldpressung: gold stamping
Goldschmuck: gilding
Goldschn. *see* Goldschnitt
Goldschnitt: gilt edge(s)
goldverz. *see* goldverziert
goldverziert: decorated with gold
Goldverzierung: gold decoration
got. *see* gotisch
gotisch: gothic type
Gr.-Ausg. *see* Gross-Ausgabe

graph. *see* graphisch
graphisch: graphic, graphical
graphische Darstellung(en):
  graph(s)
grav. *see* graviert
Grav. *see* Gravüre
graviert: engraved
Gravüre(n): engraving(s),
  etching(s)
Gross-Ausgabe: large edition
Grösse(n): size(s)
grösstenteils: mostly, largely
Groteskschrift: block letter(s)
grün: green
Grund: background
grundlegend: basic, fundamental
Grundr. *see* Grundriss
Grundriss(e): outline(s), com-
  pendium(ia), primer(s)
Gummistempel: rubber stamp(s)
Gutachten: expert attestation(s)
Gzld. *see* Ganzleder
Gzln. *see* Ganzleinen
gzstg. *see* ganzseitig

H. *see* Hälfte, Heft
Habilitationsschrift: thesis re-
  quired for the induction of
  lecturers at state universities
Hadernpapier: rag paper
Halbband: half volume, divided
  volume
Halbfranz: half calf
Halbfranzband: half-calf binding
Halbjahrsband: semiannual
  volume
Halbkalbsleder: half calf
Halbleder: half leather
Halbleinen: half cloth
Halbleinwand: half cloth
Halbmaroquin: half morocco
Halbmonatsschrift: fortnightly
  publication
Halbperg. *see* Halbpergament
Halbpergament: half vellum
Halbschweinsleder: half pigskin
Hälfte(n): half, half volume(s)
Hand: scribe

Hände: scribes
Handel: trade
Handexemplar: personal copy,
  reference copy
handgeb. *see* handgebunden
handgebunden: hand-bound
handgemalt: hand-painted
handgeschöpft: handmade
handgestickt: embroidered
handkol. *see* handkoloriert
handkoloriert: hand-colored
Handschr. *see* Handschrift
Handschrift: manuscript, autograph
handschriftl. *see* handschriftlich
handschriftlich: handwritten
hauchdünn: ultra thin
Hauptwerk: main work
Heft(e): part(s), issue(s), num-
  ber(s)
Heften: parts, issues, numbers
Heftkante(n): edge(s) on binding
  side
Heftung: stitching
hektogr. *see* hektografiert
hektografiert: hectographed
Heliograv. *see* Heliogravüre
Heliogravüre: photoengraving
hell: light-colored, bright
hellblau: light blue
Helldunkelschnitt: chiaroscuro
heller: lighter colored
Herausgabe: editing
Herausgeber: editor(s)
herausgegeben: published, edited
herausgeschnitten: cut out,
  excised
Herbst: Autumn, Fall
hergestellt: produced
herrlich: magnificent
hervorrag. *see* hervorragend
hervorragend: outstanding
Hfranzbd. *see* Halbfranzband
Hfrz. *see* Halbfranzband
Hfte. *see* Hefte
Hftn. *see* Heften
Hfz. *see* Halbfranzband
Hfzbd. *see* Halbfranzband

hie und da: occasionally, in some
  places
hier und da: occasionally, in
  some places
Hilfstabellen: auxiliary tables
hinterlegt: mounted, strengthened
Hl. *see* Halbleinen
Hldr. *see* Halbleder
Hled. *see* Halbleder
Hln. *see* Halbleinen
Hlwd. *see* Halbleinwand
Hlz. *see* Holzschnitt
hohl: hollow, curved
hohler Schnitt: hollow edge,
  fore edge
Holzdeck. *see* Holzdeckel
Holzdeckel: wooden board(s)
Holzdeckelband: binding with
  wooden boards
Holzdeckeleinband: binding with
  wooden boards
holzfleckig: foxed
holzfr. *see* holzfrei
holzfrei: free of wood, pure rag
  (paper)
Holzschn. *see* Holzschnitt
Holzschnitt(e): woodcut(s)
Holzschnitt-Bordüre(n): woodcut
  border(s)
Holzschnitt-Porträt(e): woodcut
  portrait(s)
Holzschnittfleuron(s): woodcut
  fleuron(s)
Holzschnittmarke: woodcut mark
Holzschnittumrahmung: woodcut
  border, frame
Holzstich(e): woodcut(s), wood
  engraving(s)
Holzstock(stöcke): wood block(s)
Hpergt. *see* Halbpergament
Hpgt. *see* Halbpergament
Hprgt. *see* Halbpergament
Hrsg. *see* Herausgeber
hrsg. *see* herausgegeben
Hs. *see* Handschrift
hs. *see* handschriftlich
Hschwldr. *see* Halbschweinsleder
Hschwsldr. *see* Halbschweinsleder

hübsch: handsome
hundert(ste): hundred(th)

i.H. *see* in Heften
i.J. *see* im Jahr
Ill. *see* Illustration, Illustrator
ill. *see* illustriert
illuminiert: illuminated
illust. *see* illustriert
Illustrat. *see* Illustration
Illustration(en): illustration(s)
Illustrator: illustrator
illustriert: illustrated
im Druck: in press
im Erscheinen: in progress
im Erscheinen begriffen: in
  process of publication
im Innern: inside
im Jahr: in the year
im Text: in the text
im übrigen: otherwise
imit. *see* imitiert
imitiert: imitated, artificial
Impr. *see* Impressum
Impressum: imprint
in Heften: in parts
in sich selbständig: complete in
  itself
in Vorbereitung: in preparation
Inh.-Verz. *see* Inhaltsverzeichnis
Inhalt: contents
Inhaltsverzeichnis: table of contents
Init. *see* Initialen
Initialen: initial letters
inkl. *see* inklusive
inklusive: inclusive, including
Inkun. *see* Inkunabel
Inkunabel(n): incunabulum(a)
Innenkantenvergoldung: gilding on
  inner margins of covers
Innenspiegel: *doublure*, lining
Innere(s): interior, inside
Inschrift: inscription
insges. *see* insgesamt
insgesamt: all together
intakt: intact, complete
Intarsia: inlay, mosaic

Intarsie: inlay, mosaic
Interimsausgabe: provisional
　edition
irrtümlich: erroneous(ly),
　wrong(ly)

J. *see* Jahr
Jahr: year
Jahresabonnement: annual sub-
　scription
Jahresbezugspreis: cost per year
Jahresg. *see* Jahresgabe
Jahresgabe: New Year's
　publication
Jahrg. *see* Jahrgang
Jahrgang: year, volume
Jahrgänge: years, volumes
Jahrh. *see* Jahrhundert
Jahrhundert: century
jährl. *see* jährlich
jährlich: annual(ly)
Jansenisteneinband: Jansenist
　binding
je: per volume, per item
jeder: each
Jg. *see* Jahrgang
Jgge. *see* Jahrgänge
Jh. *see* Jahrhundert
Jhdt. *see* Jahrhundert
Juchten: Russian leather
Jungfern-Pergament: virgin
　parchment

K. *see* Kustode
Kalbdrbd. *see* Kalblederband
Kalblederband: full-calf binding
kalligr. *see* kalligraphisch
kalligraphisch: calligraphic
Kaltnadel: dry point
Kante(n): edge(s) of cover
Kantenvergoldung: gilding on
　edges of cover
Kap. *see* Kapitel
Kapital(e): headband(s), head-
　cap(s)
Kapitel: chapter(s)
kart. *see* kartoniert
Karte(n): map(s), chart(s)

Kartensk. *see* Kartenskizze(n)
Kartenskizze(n): sketch map(s)
Kartographie: cartography
Karton: pasteboard, cardboard;
　cancel
Kartonhülle: pasteboard slipcase
kartoniert: bound in boards
Kartonumschlag: pasteboard case
Kartusche(n): cartouche(s)
Kassette: box, slipcase
käuflich: for sale
Kaufpreis: purchase price
kaum: scarcely, hardly
kenntlich: recognizable, charac-
　terized
Kette(n): chain(s)
Ketteneinband: chained binding
Kinderbuch(bücher): children's
　book(s)
Kinderlesebuch(bücher): horn-
　book(s), primer(s)
kl. *see* klein
klar: clear, distinct
Klbldbd. *see* Kalblederband
Kldr. *see* Kunstleder
klein: small
knapp: narrow(ly)
Knick: folding
Knickfalte(n): bent fold(s)
Kniff(e): fold(s)
Kodex: codex
Kohlezeich. *see* Kohlezeichnung
Kohlezeichnung(en): charcoal
　drawing(s)
Kol. *see* Kolophon
kol. *see* koloriert
Kol.-titel: *see* Kolumnentitel
Kollat. *see* Kollation
Kollation: collation
kollationiert: collated
Kolophon: colophon
kolor. *see* koloriert
kolorierfähig: suitable for coloring
koloriert: colored
Kolorit: coloring
Kolumnentitel: running title
Komm. *see* Kommentar
komm. *see* kommentiert

Komment. *see* Kommentar
Kommentar: commentary
kommentiert: commented
Komödie(n): comedy(ies)
komp. *see* komponiert
Komp. *see* Komponist
Kompilationswerk: compiled
  work
Kompilator: compiler
kompl. *see* komplett
komplett: complete
komponiert: composed
Komponist: composer
konform: alike, uniform
Konkordanz: concordance
Konvolut: lot
Kopf: head, top
Köpfe: heads, tops
Kopfgoldschnitt: gilt top edge
Kopfleiste(n): headpiece(s)
Kopfsteg: headstick, head
  margin
Kopft. *see* Kopftitel
Kopftitel: headline, running title
korr. *see* korrigiert
Korrektur(en): correction(s)
korrigiert: corrected
kostbar: expensive, precious
Kpfrst. *see* Kupferstich
Kpfrtaf. *see* Kupfertafel
kplt. *see* komplett
Kpr. *see* Kupferstich
Kprt. *see* Kupfertitel
kräftig: strong
Kratzer: scratch(es)
krit. *see* kritisch
kritisch: critical, critically
Kritzel: doodling(s)
Krt. *see* Karte
Kt. *see* Karte
kt. *see* kartoniert
Kte. *see* Karte
Ktn. *see* Karten
Kunstbeil. *see* Kunstbeilage
Kunstbeilage(n): supplementary
  art plate(s)
Kunstblatt(blätter): art print(s),
  reproduction(s)

Kunstdruck: art print
Kunstdruckanhang: supplement of
  art prints
Kunstdruckbeilagen: supplementary
  printed art plates
Kunstdruckpapier: art paper,
  fine-coated glossy paper
Kunstdrucktafel(n): art plate(s)
Kunstleder: artificial leather,
  leatherette
Künstler: artist(s), illustrator(s)
künstlich: artificial
Kupf. *see* Kupferstich
Kupf.-Tfln. *see* Kupfertafeln
Kupfer: copper, copper engrav-
  ing(s)
Kupferplatte(n): copperplate(s)
Kupferstecher: copperplate
  engraver
Kupferstich(e): copper engrav-
  ing(s), etching(s)
Kupfert. *see* Kupfertitel
Kupfertafel(n): copper engrav-
  ing(s), engraved plate(s)
Kupfertiefdruck: copper engraving
Kupfertiefdruckreproduktion(en):
  copper-engraved reproduction(s)
Kupfertitel: engraved title page
Kursive: italics
Kursivschrift: italics
kurzrandig: with small margins
Kurztitel: short title
Kust. *see* Kustode
Kustode(n): signature marking(s)
Kustoden: catchwords
Kustos: catchword
Kvergold. *see* Kantenvergoldung

L. *see* Lage
l. *see* letzt, links
l.fl. *see* leicht fleckig
Lackeinband: lacquered binding
läd. *see* lädiert
Ladenpr. *see* Ladenpreis
Ladenpreis: list price
lädiert: slightly damaged
Lage(n): quire(s), signature(s)
Lagebezeichnung: designation of

quires, signatures
Landkarte(n): map(s)
langnarbig: long-grained
laufende Kolumnentitel: running titles
Ldnpr. *see* Ladenpreis
Ldr. *see* Leder
Ldrbd. *see* Lederband
Ldrecke. *see* Lederecke
Lebensbeschreibung: biography
Led. *see* Leder
Leder: leather
Lederband: leather binding
Lederecke(n): leather corner(s)
Lederetui: leather case
Lederintarsie: leather mosaic
Lederkanten: leather edges
Lederrücken: leather back
Lederschl. *see* Lederschliesse
Lederschlaufe(n): leather loop(s)
Lederschliesse(n): leather clasp(s), tie(s)
Lederschnittornamentik: leather-cut decoration
Lederstreifen: leather strip(s)
leer: blank, empty
Lehrbuch: textbook
leicht: a little, slightly
leicht fleckig: slightly spotted
leimfleckig: glue-spotted
Leinen: cloth
Leinenband: cloth binding
Leinendecke(n): linen cover(s)
Leinenstreifen: linen strips, tapes
Leinw. *see* Leinwand
Leinwand: cloth
Leinwandband: cloth binding
Leinwdbd. *see* Leinwandband
Leiste(n): border(s)
Leporello-Album: album of fold-out pages in panorama form
Leporello-Form: fold-out, panorama form
Lesart(en): reading(s), interpretation(s)
lesbar: legible
Letter(n): letter(s)

letzt: last
Lex. *see* Lexikon
Lexika: dictionaries
Lexikon: dictionary
Lfg. *see* Lieferung
Lfgn. *see* Lieferungen
Lgebez. *see* Lagebezeichnung
Lgebzg. *see* Lagebezeichnung
Lichtdr. *see* Lichtdruck
Lichtdruck: photoengraving
Lichtdrucktafel(n): photographic plate(s)
Liebhaber: amateur(s), collector(s)
Liebhaberausg. *see* Liebhaberausgabe
Liebhaberausgabe: collector's edition
Liebhaberdruck: collector's printing
Liebhabereinband: three-quarter binding
Liederanhang(hänge): appendix(es) of songs
Liederbuch: songbook
Lief. *see* Lieferung
lieferbar: available
Lieferg. *see* Lieferung
Lieferung(en): number(s), part(s), fascicle(s)
Lieff. *see* Lieferungen
Liefg. *see* Lieferung
liegt bei: is included, laid in
Lilie(n): fleur(s)-de-lys
Linie(n): line(s)
liniiert: ruled
link: left-hand
links: to the left
Lit.-Verz. *see* Literatur-Verzeichnis
Literatur-Verzeichnis: list of references, bibliography
Literaturangabe(n): reference(s)
Lith. *see* Lithografie
lith. *see* lithografiert
Lithogr. *see* Lithografie
Lithograf. *see* Lithografie
Lithografie(n): lithograph(s),

lithography
lithografiert: lithographed
Ln. *see* Leinen
Lnb. *see* Leinenband
Loch: hole
löcherig: with holes, wormholed
Löchlein: small hole(s)
Lochung: wormholing, perforation
locker: loose
los: loose
Löschen: erasing
lose Bogen: loose-leaf
lose im Einband: loose in binding
Lustspiel(e): comedy(ies)
Luxusausgabe: de luxe edition
Lw. *see* Leinwand
Lwb. *see* Leinwandband
Lwd. *see* Leinwand
Lwdbd. *see* Leinwandband

M-A. *see* Miniaturausgabe
MA. *see* Mittelalter
mager: thin, narrow
Maiblumeninitiale(n): initial(s) decorated with lilies of the valley
Maj. *see* Majuskel
Majuskel: upper-case letter
makellos: immaculate, perfect
makuliert: damaged, pulped
manch: some, a few
Manuskr. *see* Manuskript
Manuskript: manuscript, type-script
Mäppchen: little portfolio(s)
Mappe(n): portfolio(s)
Mar. *see* Maroquin
Märchen: folk tale(s), tale(s), fairy tale(s)
Marginalie(n): marginal note(s)
marmor. *see* marmoriert
marmoriert: marbled
Maroq. *see* Maroquin
Maroquin: morocco
Maroquinécraséband: bound in crushed morocco
Maroquinlederband: bound in morocco

maschinschriftlich: typewritten
massgeblich: standard, recognized
mässig: poor, moderate
Massstab: scale
matt: dull, pale
Mäusefrass: gnawing of mice
Medaillon: medallion
mehr. *see* mehrere
mehr nicht erschienen: no more published
mehrere: several
mehrf. *see* mehrfach
mehrfach: multiple, in several places, several copies
mehrfarbig: varicolored
meist: mostly
Memoiren: memoirs
Menge: a great many
merklich: noticeable
merkw. *see* merkwürdig
merkwürdig: unusual, remarkable
Messingschliessen: brass clasps
Metallbuckel: metal boss(es), knob(s)
Metallecke(n): metal corner(s)
Metallschliesse(n): metal clasp(s)
Metallschnitt: metal cut
Min. *see* Miniatur, Minuskel
Miniatur(en): miniature(s)
Miniaturausgabe: miniature edition
Minuskel(n): minuscule(s), lower-case letter(s)
Mitarb. *see* Mitarbeit
Mitarbeit: collaboration
Mitarbeiter: collaborator(s)
mitgebunden: bound with
mitgenommen: not fresh
mitsamt: together with
Mitteilung(en): communication(s)
Mittelalter: Middle Ages
mittelalterlich: medieval
mittelmässig: moderate
Mittelstück: centerpiece
Mitverfasser: joint author(s)
Mitw. *see* Mitwirkung
Mitwirkung: co-operation
MNE. *see* mehr nicht erschienen
Moiréseide: moire silk

95

Monatsschr. *see* Monatsschrift
Monatsschrift: monthly publication
Monogr. *see* Monographie, Monogramm
Monogramm: monogram
Monogrammstempel: stamped initials
Monographie(n): monograph(s)
montiert(e): mounted
Motiv: pattern, design
Ms. *see* Manuskript
Muschelverzierung: shell-like decoration
Musikbeilage(n): music supplement(s)
Muster: pattern(s)
Musterbeispiel: choice sample, pattern

n. *see* netto, neu
N.a.T. *see* Name auf Titelblatt
n.F. *see* neue Folge
n.i.H. *see* nicht im Handel
n.R. *see* neue Reihe
n.S. *see* neue Serie
Nachahmung: imitation
Nachbildung(en): reproduction(s)
Nachdr. *see* Nachdruck
Nachdruck: reprint, pirated edition
Nachdruckrecht: copyright
Nachf. *see* Nachfolger
Nachfolger: successor(s)
nachgeklebt: reglued
nachgelassen: posthumous
nachgeliefert: furnished later
nachgeschnitten: recut
nachgestochen: re-engraved
nachgewiesen: traced, documented
nachgezogen: retraced, freshened
Nachlass: literary remains
Nachschlagewerk(e): reference work(s)
Nachschrift: postscript, postface
Nachstich(e): re-engraving(s)

Nachtr. *see* Nachtrag
Nachtrag(träge): appendix(es)
Nachw. *see* Nachwort
Nachwort: postscript
Nagelschaden: damaged by nailing
Nagelspur(en): trace(s) of nailing
nahezu: nearly
Name auf Titelblatt: name on the title page
Narbe(n): grain(s)
Nebent. *see* Nebentitel
Nebentitel: subtitle, subhead
nett: nice
netto: net
neu: new
Neuauflage: new edition
Neuausg. *see* Neuausgabe
Neuausgabe: new edition, reprint
neubearb. *see* neubearbeitet
neubearbeitet: revised
Neudruck: reprint
neue Folge: new series
neue Reihe: new series
neue Serie: new series
neuer: newer
Neuerscheinung(en): recent publication(s)
neuest: newest
neun(te): nine(th)
neunzehn(te): nineteen(th)
neunzig(ste): ninety(ieth)
neuw. *see* neuwertig
neuwertig: as good as new
ng. *see* nicht gezählt
nicht gezählt: not counted, unnumbered
nicht im Handel: not for general sale, privately printed
no. *see* netto
No. *see* Nummer
Notenanhang: music appendix
Notenanhg. *see* Notenanhang
Notenbeil. *see* Notenbeilage
Notenbeilage(n): supplement(s) of music
Notenbeisp: *see* Notenbeispiel
Notenbeispiel(e): musical illustration(s)

Notizen: notes
Novelle(n): long short story(ies)
Nr. *see* Nummer
num. *see* numeriert
numer. *see* numeriert
numeriert: numbered
Numerierung: numbering,
  pagination
Nummer: number
Nummernschildchen: small
  numbered label(s)
nur an Bibliotheken: only to
  libraries

o. *see* ohne
O. *see* Original
o.Dr. *see* ohne Drucker
o.Ersch.Verm. *see* ohne
  Erscheinungsvermerk
o.J. *see* ohne Jahr
o.O. *see* ohne Ort
o.O.Dr.u.J. *see* ohne Ort,
  Drucker und Jahr
o.O.u.J. *see* ohne Ort und Jahr
o.O.u.Verl. *see* ohne Ort und
  Verleger
o.O.u.Vlg. *see* ohne Ort und
  Verlag
o.U. *see* ohne Umschlag
oben: on top
Oberrand: top margin
Oberschnitt: top edge
Obr. *see* Originalbroschur
Offizin: print shop, printing office
Offsetdruck: offset printing
öfters: fairly frequently
Ohfranz. *see* Originalhalbfranz
Ohfrz. *see* Originalhalbfranz
Ohldr. *see* Originalhalbleder
Ohlwd. *see* Originalhalbleinwand
ohne: without
ohne Drucker: without printer
ohne Erscheinungsvermerk:
  without imprint
ohne Jahr: without year, without
  date
ohne Jahresangabe: without date
  of publication

ohne Ort: without place of publication
ohne Ort, Drucker und Jahr:
  without place, publisher, and date
ohne Ort und Jahr: without place
  and date
ohne Ort und Verlag: without place
  and publisher
ohne Ort und Verleger: without
  place and publisher
ohne Umschlag: without covers
Ohprgt. *see* Originalhalbperga-
  ment
Old. *see* Originalleinwand
Oldr. *see* Originalleder
olivgrün: olive green
Olw. *see* Originalleinwand
Olwd. *see* Originalleinwand
Opappbd. *see* Originalpappband
Opbd. *see* Originalpappband
Opp. *see* Originalpappband
Oppbd. *see* Originalpappband
Or. *see* Original
ordentl. *see* ordentlich
ordentlich: regular
Orhfranz. *see* Originalhalbfranz
Orig. *see* Original
Origbd. *see* Originalband
Orighleinen. *see* Original-
  halbleinen
Original: original, original binding
Originalband: original binding
Originalbroschur: original bro-
  chure binding
Originaleinband: original binding
originalgetreu: authentic
originalgross: original size
Originalhalbfranz: original half
  calf
Originalhalbleder: original half
  leather
Originalhalbleinen: original half
  cloth
Originalhalbleinwand: original
  half cloth
Originalhalbpergament: original
  half vellum
Originalleder: original leather

Originalleinen: original cloth
Originalleinwand: original cloth
Originalleinwandband: original
　cloth binding
Originalmappe: original portfolio
Originalpappband: original boards
Originalumschlag: original
　wrapper
Origleinen: *see* Originalleinen
Origlwd. *see* Originalleinwand
Origumschlag. *see* Original-
　umschlag
Orlwd. *see* Originalleinwand
Ormappe. *see* Originalmappe

P. *see* Papier
Pag. *see* Paginierung
paginiert: paginated
Paginierung: page numbering
Pamphlet(e): pamphlet(s)
Pap. *see* Papier
Papier: paper
Papierbeschädigung(en): dam-
　age(s) in the paper
Papierfehler: defect(s) in the
　paper
Pappband: bound in pasteboard
　covers
Pappe: pasteboard
paraphiert: initialed
Partie(n): section(s)
Partiturbeilage(n): supplement(s)
　of music scores
Pb. *see* Pappband
Pbd. *see* Pappband
Perg. *see* Pergament
Pergament: parchment, vellum
Pergament-Schale: parchment
　cover
Pergamentartig: imitation vellum
Pergamentband: vellum binding
Pergamentbezug: vellum covering
Pergamentpapierumschlag: vel-
　lum paper covers
Pergt. *see* Pergament
Perkal: calico
Perkalin: buckram
Pers.u.Ortsreg. *see* Personen-

　und Ortsregister
Personen- und Ortsregister: per-
　son and place index
Personenverz. *see* Personen-
　verzeichnis
Personenverzeichnis: index of
　persons
Pg. *see* Pergament
Pgt. *see* Pergament
Pgtbd. *see* Pergamentband
Phot. *see* Photographie
Photogr. *see* Photographie
Photographie(n): photo(s)
Photogravüre: photogravure
Pl. *see* Plan
Plan: plan, design
Pläne: plans, designs
Plansk. *see* Planskizze
Planskizze(n): sketch plan(s)
Platte(n): plate(s)
poliert: burnished
Portf. *see* Portfolio
Portfolio: portfolio
Porto: costs of carriage, postage
Portr. *see* Porträt, Portrait
Portrait: portrait
Portraite: portraits
Portraits: portraits
Porträt: portrait
Porträte: portraits
Porträts: portraits
Postgebühren: costs of mailing
posthum: posthumous
postum: posthumous
Pp. *see* Pappband, Pappe
Ppbd. *see* Pappband
Pr. *see* Preis
Pr.-A. *see* Prachtausgabe
Prachtausg. *see* Prachtausgabe
Prachtausgabe: de luxe edition
prächtig: marvelous
prachtv. *see* prachtvoll
prachtvoll: wonderful, magnificent
Prägestempel: embossed stamp
Prägung: goffering
Preis: price
Preis auf Anfrage: price on
　request

Preis pro komplett: price for the entire work
preisgekrönt: prize-winning
Preisschrift: prize-winning publication
Prgt. *see* Pergament
Privatdruck: privately printed
Privileg: privilege, permit to publish
pro Jahr: per year, each year
pro komplett: price for the entire work
Probeseiten: specimen pages, sample pages
Progr. *see* Programmschrift
Programmschrift: school publication
Prospekt: prospectus
prunkvoll: sumptuous
Pseudonym(e): pseudonym(s)
punktiert: dotted, stippled
Punktstempel: dot stamping(s)

qu. *see* quer
Qu.-Fol. *see* Querfolio
quadratisch: square
Quart: quarto
Quartal(e): quarter(s)
Quartausgabe: quarto edition
Quartband: quarto
Quelle(n): source(s)
Quellenangabe(n): source reference(s)
quer: oblong
Querfolio: oblong folio
Querformat: oblong format

r. *see* recto
R. *see* Reihe
R.-Tit. *see* Rückentitel
Rabatt: discount
rad. *see* radiert
Rad. *see* Radierung
Radg. *see* Radierung
radiert: erased with knife or eraser
Radierung: etching
Rahmenstempel: framelike

stamping(s)
Randanmerkungen: marginal notes
Randbemerkungen: marginal notes
Randecke(n): corner(s) of margin
Randeinriss: tear in margin
Ränder: margins
Randleiste(n): border(s), frame(s)
Randnoten: marginal notes
Randnotizen: marginal notes
Randschrift(en): marginal note(s)
Randwasserfleck(e): marginal water stain(s)
Randwurmstich(e): marginal wormhole(s)
Ranken: scrollwork
Ratenzahlung: on the installment plan
Raubdruck: pirated edition
rautenförmig: lozenge-shaped
Rautenwappen: lozenged coat of arms
rcks. *see* rückseitig
re. *see* rechts
recht: right-hand
rechteckig: right-angled, square or rectangular
rechtmässig: authorized
rechts: to the right
recto: recto, front side
Red. *see* Redaktion
red. *see* redigiert
Redaktion: editorship
Rede(n): speech(es), address(es)
redigiert: edited
Reg. *see* Register
Register: index, table of contents
Registerband: index volume
Registerbd. *see* Registerband
Registerbl. *see* Registerblatt
Registerblatt(blätter): index page(s)
reichst: very rich(ly), abundant(ly)
reichvergold. *see* reichvergoldet
reichvergoldet: richly gilt
reichverziert: richly decorated
Reihe: series
Reihenfolge: order, sequence
Reinschrift: fair copy

reizend: attractive
reizvoll: charming
Rekto: front side
Reliefkarte: relief map
Reliefprägung: raised stamping
rep. *see* repariert
repar. *see* repariert
repariert: repaired
Repertorium: list, index
Reprod. *see* Reproduktion
Reproduktion(en): reproduction(s)
resp. *see* respektive
respektive: respectively
Rest(e): remainder, remnant(s)
Restauflage: remainder
restauriert: restored
rev. *see* revidiert
revidiert: revised
Richtigstellung(en): correction(s), corrigendum(da)
Riemen: leather tie(s)
Riss(e): tear(s)
Risse: plans, sketches
Rocaille(n): shell-like design(s)
rohe Bogen: unbound and unfolded sheets
Rohleinen: raw linen
Rollenstempel: roll stamp(s)
Roman(e): novel(s)
rose: pink
Rosette(n): rosette(s)
rostflecktig: rust-stained, foxed
rot: red
rotbraun: brick-red
Rötelzeichnung(en): sanguine drawing(s)
rotgedr. *see* rotgedruckt
rotgedruckt: printed in red
rötlich: reddish
Rotschnitt: red edge(s)
Rotstiftmarginalien: red pencil notes
Rsch. *see* Rückenschild, Rückenschildchen
Rschild. *see* Rückenschild
Rubr. *see* Rubrik, Rubrizierung
rubr. *see* rubriziert
Rubrik(en): column(s)

Rubrikator(en): rubricator(s)
rubriz. *see* rubriziert
rubriziert: rubricated
Rubrizierung: rubrication
Rückblatt: back sheet
Rückdeckel: back cover
Rücken: back, spine
Rückenfeld(er): panel(s) on spine
Rückengoldpressung: gold tooling on back
Rückenschild: back label
Rückenschildchen: small back label
Rückentitel: title on spine
Rückenvergold. *see* Rückenvergoldung
Rückenvergoldung: back gilding
rückseitig: on the verso
Rückvergoldg. *see* Rückenvergoldung
rückw. *see* rückwärtig
rückwärtig: back, rear
rückwärts: at the rear
rund: approximately, roughly
Rundblick(e): panorama(s)
Rv. *see* Rückenvergoldung
Rverg. *see* Rückenvergoldung
Rvg. *see* Rückenvergoldung

s. *see* siehe
S. *see* Seite
SA. *see* Separatabdruck
S.-A. *see* Separatabdruck
Sachregister: subject index
Saff. *see* Saffian
Saffian: morocco
Saffianband: morocco binding
Sammelband(bände): collected volume(s)
Sammeltitel: collective title
Sammelwerk: collective work
Sammetband: velvet binding
Samml. *see* Sammlung
Sammlg. *see* Sammlung
Sammlgn. *see* Sammlungen
Sammlung(en): collection(s)
Samt: velvet
sämt. *see* sämtliche

sämtl. *see* sämtliche
sämtliche: all
Sars. *see* Sarsenetteinband
Sarsenetteinband: cloth binding
satiniert: coated
saub. *see* sauber
sauber: clean
Schabblatt(blätter): mezzotint(s)
Schabspur: trace of rubbing
Schabstelle(n): chafed spot(s)
Schachbrettmuster: checkered
  design
Schaden: damage, defect
Schäden: damages, defects
schadh. *see* schadhaft
schadhaft: damaged
Schafleder: sheepskin
Schaflederüberzug: covering of
  sheepskin
Scharniere: hinges, joints
Schatulle: box
Schaubild(er): illustration(s)
Schauspiel(e): play(s)
Schemata: diagrams
Scherenschnitt(s): silhouette(s)
Schild: label
Schildchen: small label(s)
Schildpattleder: mottled calf
Schl. *see* Schliesse
Schl.-B. *see* Schlussblatt
Schlagwort: subject heading;
  key word, catchword
schlecht: bad, defective
Schliessband(bänder): tie(s)
Schliesse(n): clasp(s)
Schliessenrest(e): remnant(s)
  of clasps
Schlussband: end volume
Schlussblatt: end leaf
Schlüsselroman: *roman à clef*
Schlussschr. *see* Schlussschrift
Schlussschrift: colophon
Schlusst. *see* Schlusstitel
Schlusstitel: colophon
Schlussvermerk: concluding
  note, colophon
Schlussvignette: tailpiece
Schmähschrift(en): lampoon(s)

Schmaloktav: narrow octavo
schmiegsam: flexible, limp
schmuck: nice
Schmuckstück(e): decorative
  device(s)
schmutzig: soiled, dirty
Schmutztit. *see* Schmutztitel
Schmutztitel: half title
Schnitt(e): edge(s) of a book;
  cut(s), engraving(s)
Schnörkel: flourish(es), scroll(s),
  paraph(s)
Scholie(n): critical note(s)
schön: beautiful, handsome
schraffiert: azure-tooled,
  hatched
Schraffierung: hatching
Schrifttum: literature
Schriftwiedergab. *see* Schrift-
  wiedergabe
Schriftwiedergabe(n): reproduc-
  tion(s) of handwriting
Schuber: protective case, slipcase
Schutzhülle: protective cover,
  covering
Schutzumschlag: jacket, paper
  wrapper
schw. *see* schwarz
schwarz: black
schwarzweiss: black and white
Schweinsleder: pigskin
Schweinslederbezug: pigskin
  covering
Schwldr. *see* Schweinsleder
Schwsldr. *see* Schweinsleder
Sd. *see* Sonderdruck
sechs(te): six(th)
sechzehn(te): sixteen(th)
sechzig(ste): sixty(ieth)
sehr selten: very rare
Seide: silk
Seidenp. *see* Seidenpapier
Seidenpapier: tissue paper
Seidenspiegel: silk *doublure(s)*
Seidenüberzug: silk covering
Seite(n): page(s)
seitengross(e): full page
Seitenwand(wände): side(s)

Seitenzahl: number of pages
Seitenzählung: pagination
selbständige Buchausgabe: separate issue in book form
Selbstbiographie: autobiography
Selbstverl. *see* Selbstverlag
Selbstverlag: published by the author
selten: rare, scarce
Seltenheit: rarity
seltenst: rarest
Sengschaden: scorch damage
Separatabdruck: separate, reprint, offprint
Separatdruck: separate, reprint, offprint
Separattafel(n): separate plate(s)
Ser. *see* Serie
Serie(n): series
sieben(te): seven(th)
siebzehn(te): seventeen(th)
siebzig(ste): seventy(ieth)
Siegel: seal(s)
siehe: see
sign. *see* signiert
Signet: printer's or publisher's device
signiert: signed
Silberdruck: silver printing
Silberdurchbruch: silver filigree
silbergetrieben: silver-chased
silbern: silver
Silberornament(e): silver decoration(s)
Sitzungsberichte: proceedings
Sk. *see* Skizze
Skizze(n): sketch(es)
Slg. *see* Sammlung
soeben erschienen: just out
Sommer: Summer
Sonderabdr. *see* Sonderabdruck
Sonderabdruck: separate printing, offprint
Sonderausgabe: special edition
Sonderdruck: separate printing, offprint
Sonderh. *see* Sonderheft
Sonderheft(e): special issue(s),

special number(s)
sonst: otherwise
soweit erschienen: as far as published
soweit festzustellen: as far as can be ascertained
Sp. *see* Spalte(n)
sp. *see* spaltig
Spalte(n): column(s)
spaltig: columned
Spiegel: *doublure(s)*
Spitzenbordüre(n): lacelike border design(s)
Spitzenmuster: lacelike pattern(s)
Spottschrift(en): lampoon(s)
Spruchband(bänder): legend(s), lettered scroll(s)
Sprung: crack
Sprünge: cracks
SS. *see* Seiten
St. *see* Stempel, Stich
St.a.T. *see* Stempel auf dem Titelblatt
St.a.Tr. *see* Stempel rückseitig auf Titelblatt
stach: engraved
Stahlst. *see* Stahlstich
Stahlstich(e): steel engraving(s)
Stammbaum: genealogical tree
Stammbuch(bücher): *album (alba) amicorum*
Stammtafel(n): genealogical table(s)
stark: strong, heavy
stärker: stronger, heavier, relatively extensive
statt: instead of
Stehkante(n): edge(s) of cover
Stehkantenfilet(en): fillet(s) on edge of cover
Stehkantenvergoldung: gilding on edge of cover
steif: stiff
steifbr. *see* steifbroschiert
steifbroschiert: bound in stiff paper covers
stellenw. *see* stellenweise
stellenweise: partly, occasionally

Stempel: stamp
Stempel auf dem Titelblatt:
    stamp on the title page
Stempel rückseitig auf Titelblatt:
    stamp on verso of title page
Ster.-Aufl. *see* Stereotyp-Auflage
Stereotyp-Auflage: reprint edi-
    tion from stereotype plates
stereotypiert: stereotyped
Stich(e): engraving(s)
Stichwort: key word; subject
    heading
Stil: style
Stockfl. *see* Stockfleck
stockfl. *see* stockfleckig
Stockfleck(en): spot(s) caused
    by dampness
stockfleckig: foxed, spotted by
    dampness
stockig: molded
Streitschrift(en): pamphlet(s)
Strichätzung: line etching
Striche: lines
Stricheisen: tool for line engrav-
    ing
Stück(e): piece(s)
Studienführer: study guide(s)
Stundenbuch(bücher): Book(s)
    of Hours
Subskr. *see* Subskription
Subskription: subscription
Subskriptionspreis: subscription
    price
Super-Exlibris: book stamp(s)
Superlibros: book stamp(s)
Suppl. *see* Supplement
Supplement: supplement
Supplementband: supplementary
    volume
Sz. *see* Seitenzahl

T. *see* Tafel, Teil, Titel
T.-A. *see* Taschenausgabe
Tab. *see* Tabelle
Tabelle(n): chart(s), table(s)
tadellos: irreproachable, perfect
Taf. *see* Tafel
Tafel(n): plate(s)

Tafelband: volume of plates
Tafelserie: series of tables
Tafelwerk(e): work(s) of plates
Tageb. *see* Tagebuch
Tagebuch: diary, journal
Taschenausgabe: pocket edition
Taschenformat: pocket-size
Tausend(e): thousand(s)
Teil(e): part(s)
teils: partly
teilw. *see* teilweise
teilweise: partly, in part
tekt. *see* tektiert
tektiert: blotted out
Textabb. *see* Textabbildung
Textabbildung(en): illustration(s)
    in the text
Textband: volume of text
Textbeschäd. *see* Textbeschädi-
    gungen
Textbeschädigungen: damage done
    to text, loss of text
Textbilder: illustrations in the
    text
Textfiguren: figures in the text
Textholzschn. *see* Textholzschnitt
Textholzschnitt(e): woodcut(s) in
    the text
Textill. *see* Textillustration
Textillustration(en): illustration(s)
    in the text
textlich: textual
Textrevision: revision of text
Textspalte(n): column(s) of text
Textteil: textual portion
Textunterschrift(en): caption(s)
    under text
Textverlust: loss of text
Textvignetten: vignettes in the
    text
Textzeichn. *see* Textzeichnung
Textzeichnung(en): drawing(s)
    in the text
Tfl. *see* Tafel
Tfln. *see* Tafeln
Theil *see* Teil
tief: deep(ly)
Tiefdruck: photogravure

Tiefdruckabbildung(en): photo-
gravure illustration(s)
Tiefdruckbild(er): photogravure
picture(s)
Tiefdrucktafel(n): photogravure
plate(s)
Tintenfl. *see* Tintenfleck
Tintenfleck(e): ink stain(s)
Tintenschrift: writing in ink
Tit. *see* Titel
Titel: title(s)
Titelaufkleber: label(s) on title
page
Titelb. *see* Titelbild
Titelbild: frontispiece
Titelbl. *see* Titelblatt
Titelblatt: title page
Titelblattrückseite: verso of
title page
Titelbordüre: border on title
page
Titeldecke: title cover
Titeleinf. *see* Titeleinfassung
Titeleinfass. *see* Titeleinfassung
Titeleinfassung: border on title
page
Titelholzschnitt(e): woodcut on
title page(s)
Titelkupfer: engraving on title
page
Titelradierung: etching on title
page
Titelrückseite: verso of title
page
Titelschnitt: engraving on title
page
Titelüberschrift(en): title
heading(s)
Titelvignette: vignette on title
page
Tl. *see* Teil
Tle. *see* Teile
tls. *see* teils
Tondruck: chiaroscuro
Trachtenkupfer: copperplate
illustration(s) of costumes
Tragödie(n): tragedy(ies)
Traktat(e): tract(s), treatise(s)

Trauerspiel(e): tragedy(ies)
Trockenstempel: dry stamp
Ts. *see* Tausend
Tsd. *see* Tausend
Type(n): font(s) of type
typograph. *see* typographisch
typographisch: typographic

U. *see* Umschlag
u.a. *see* und andere, unter anderem
u.d.T. *see* unter dem Titel
u.ff. *see* und folgende
u.s.w. *see* und so weiter
ub. *see* unbeschnitten
überarb. *see* überarbeitet
überarbeitet: revised
überklebt: pasted over
Übers. *see* Übersetzer, Übersetzung
übers. *see* übersetzt
Überschrift(en): heading(s),
caption(s)
Übersetzer: translator(s)
übersetzt: translated
Übersetzung: translation
Übersicht: synopsis
Übersichtstabelle(n): synoptic
table(s)
übert. *see* übertragen
übertr. *see* übertragen
übertragen: translated
Übertragung: translation, version
übrig: remaining
übs. *see* übersetzt
Übs. *see* Übersetzung
uff. *see* und folgende
Umfang: in all
umfangr. *see* umfangreich
umfangreich: comprehensive
umfasst: comprises, contains
umgearb. *see* umgearbeitet
umgearbeitet: revised
umrahmt: framed
Umrahmung: frame, border
Umschl. *see* Umschlag
Umschlag: wrapper, jacket
Umschlagbild: cover design
Umschlagblatt(blätter): cover

sheet(s), paper cover(s)
Umschläge beigebunden: wrappers bound in
Umschlagt. *see* Umschlagtitel
Umschlagtitel: external title, title on wrapper (cover)
Umschrift(en): transcription(s)
unaufgeschn. *see* unaufgeschnitten
unaufgeschnitten: uncut, unopened
unaufgezogen: unmounted
unbedeut. *see* unbedeutend
unbedeutend: slight(ly); insignificant(ly)
unbedruckt: plain, without printed text
unbek. *see* unbekannt
unbekannt: unknown
unbereinigt: unexpurgated
unberührt: perfect, untouched
unbeschn. *see* unbeschnitten
unbeschnitten: untrimmed
unbestimmt: not established, indefinite
und andere: and others
und folgende: and the following
und so weiter: and so forth
unfrisch: not fresh, shopworn
ungebunden: unbound
ungedruckt: unpublished
ungefähr: approximately
ungeheftet: in loose sheets
ungenau: inexact, erroneous
ungerade Bandzahlen: odd volume numbers
ungez.Bll. *see* ungezählte Blätter
ungezählte Blätter: unnumbered leaves
Unicum: unique item
unleserl. *see* unleserlich
unleserlich: illegible
unn. *see* unnumeriert
unnumeriert: unnumbered
unpag. *see* unpaginiert
unpaginiert: unpaginated
unregelmässig: irregularly
unsauber: soiled, dirty

unt. *see* unten, unter
unten: at the bottom
unter: lower, under
unter anderem: among others
unter anderen: among others
unter dem Titel: under the title
unter Mitwirkung: with the collaboration
unterdrückt: suppressed, prohibited
Unterkante: bottom edge of cover
unterlegt: repaired; mounted
Unterrand: bottom margin
Unterschrift(en): signature(s)
Unterstr. *see* Unterstreichung
Unterstreich. *see* Unterstreichung
Unterstreichgn. *see* Unterstreichungen
Unterstreichung(en): underlining(s)
Unterstriche: underlinings
unterstrichen: underlined
Untertitel: subtitle(s)
unver. *see* unverändert
unveränd. *see* unverändert
unverändert: unchanged, unaltered
unvergl. *see* unvergleichlich
unvergleichlich: incomparable
unverkürzt: unabridged
unveröff. *see* unveröffentlicht
unveröffentlicht: unpublished
unvollständig: incomplete
Unziale: uncial
Urausgabe: original edition
Urheberrecht: copyright
urheberrechtlich: copyright
Urkunde(n): document(s)
Urkundennachweis: references to documents
Ursprung: origin
Urtext: original text
usw. *see* und so weiter

Variante(n): variant(s)
vb. *see* verbessert
Velinpapier: vellum paper
Velp. *see* Velinpapier
veränd. *see* verändert
verändert: revised

verb. *see* verbessert
verbessert: improved
verbilligt: reduced in price
verbl. *see* verblichen
verblasst: faded, paled
verblichen: faded
verbunden: misbound
vereinz. *see* vereinzelt
vereinzelt: here and there
Verf. *see* Verfasser
verf. *see* verfasst
verfärbt: discolored
Verfasser: author(s)
verfasst: composed, written
verfügbar: available
verg. *see* vergilbt
vergilbt: yellowed, faded
vergleiche: see, compare
vergoldet: gilt, decorated with gold
Vergoldung: gilding, decoration in gold
vergr. *see* vergriffen
vergriffen: out-of-print
Verh. *see* Verhandlungen
Verhandlungen: proceedings
verk. *see* verkauft
Verkauf: sale
verkauft: sold
verkleinert: reduced
Verl. *see* Verlag, Verlust
Verl. Anst. *see* Verlagsanstalt
Verl. Ges. *see* Verlagsgesellschaft
Verlag: publishing firm
Verlagsanstalt: publishing firm
Verlagseinband: publisher's binding
Verlagsgesellschaft: publishing firm
verlängert: elongated
Verlegereinband: publisher's binding
Verlegermarke: publisher's device
verloren: lost
Verlust: loss
verm. *see* vermehrt
vermehrt: enlarged

Vermerk: remark, note
vermischt: mixed, miscellaneous
veröff. *see* veröffentlicht
Veröff. *see* Veröffentlichung
veröffentlicht: published
Veröffentlichung: publication
vers. *see* versehen
Versalien: capital letters
verschieden: different, varying
verschlungen: interlaced
verschm. *see* verschmutzt
verschmutzt: soiled
Verschnürung: cording, interlacing
verschollen: disappeared without trace
verschossen: paled
versehen: furnished
versehentlich: mistakenly
verso: verso
verst. *see* verständlich
verständlich: comprehensible
verstärkt: strengthened, reinforced
Verstärkung: strengthening, support
verstaubt: dusty
versteigert: sold at auction
Versteigerung(en): auction(s)
Verstkg. *see* Verstärkung
verstümmelt: mutilated
vertieft: sunken, recessed
vervielf. *see* vervielfältigt
vervielfältigt: multigraphed
vervollst. *see* vervollständigt
vervollständigt: completed, supplemented
verwischt: blurred
Verz. *see* Verzeichnis
verz. *see* verziert
Verzeichnis: list, listing, index
verziert: decorated, adorned
Vf. *see* Verfasser
vgl. *see* vergleiche
viele: many
vier(te): four(th)
viertel: quarter(s), fourth(s)
vierteljährlich: quarterly
Vierteljahrsschrift: quarterly pub-

lication
vierzehn(te): fourteen(th)
vierzig(ste): forty(ieth)
Vign. *see* Vignette
Vignette(n): vignette(s)
violett: violet, mauve
Vlg. *see* Verlag
Vokab. *see* Vokabularium
Vokabularium: word list
Volksausgabe: popular edition
Vollbilder: full-page illustrations
völlig: wholly, entirely
vollst. *see* vollständig
vollst. umgearb. *see* vollständig
  umgearbeitet
vollständig: complete
vollständig umgearbeitet: completely revised
Vollständigkeit: completeness
von alter Hand: by an old hand
vor allem: above all, principally
vor kurzem erschienen: recently
  published, just out
vorauss. *see* voraussichtlich
voraussichtlich: expected to
  appear
Vorbereitung: preparation
Vorbertg. *see* Vorbereitung
Vorbes. *see* Vorbesitzer
Vorbesitzer: previous owner
Vorblatt(blätter): flyleaf(ves)
Vorder- und Rückdeckel: front
  and back covers
Vorderdeckel: front cover
Vordergrund: foreground
Vorderseite(n): front page(s)
vorgbdn. *see* vorgebunden
vorgeb. *see* vorgebunden
vorgebunden: bound in front of
vorhanden: present, available
Vorlage(n): model(s), pattern(s)
vorläufig: temporary, interim
Vorlesung(en): academic lec-
  ture(s)
Vorr. *see* Vorrede, Vorredner
vorrätig: in stock
Vorrede: preface
Vorredner: author of preface

Vors. *see* Vorsatz
Vorsatz(sätze): end paper(s)
Vorsatzbl. *see* Vorsatzblatt
Vorsatzblatt: end paper
Vorsatzpapier: end paper(s)
Vorst. *see* Vorstücke
Vorstücke: preliminary matter
Vort. *see* Vortitel, Vortrag
Vortitel: half title
Vortrag(träge): lecture(s)
Vorw. *see* Vorwort
Vorwort: preface
Vorz.-Ex. *see* Vorzugsexemplar
vorzügl. *see* vorzüglich
vorzüglich: pre-eminent
Vorzugsausgabe: special edition
Vorzugsexemplar(e): preferential
  copy(ies)

Wappen: coat of arms
Wappenbild: reproduction of coats
  of arms
Wappenprägung: coats of arms in
  blind tooling
Wappensupralibros: coat of arms
  used as book stamp
wasserbesch. *see* wasserbeschädigt
wasserbeschädigt: damaged by
  water
wasserfl. *see* wasserfleckig
Wasserfleck(en): water stain(s)
wasserfleckig: stained by water
wassergewellt: crinkled by water
Wasserrand(ränder): water
  stain(s)
wasserrandig: water-stained
Wassersch. *see* Wasserschäden
Wasserschäden: water-damaged
  in several places
wasserw. *see* wasserwellig
wasserwellig: crinkled by water
weggerissen: torn off
weggeschnitten: cut off
weitere: additional
wen. *see* wenig
wenig: little
wenige: few

Werk(e): work(s)
wichtig: important
Widm. *see* Widmung
Widmung: dedication note
wie neu: as new
Wiedergabe(n): reproduction(s)
Wiegendruck(e): incunabulum(a)
Wildld. *see* Wildleder
Wildleder: chamois leather
Wildlederband: chamois binding
Winter: Winter
winzig: minute
Wiss. *see* Wissenschaft
wiss. *see* wissenschaftlich
Wissenschaft(en): field(s) of
  learning, science(s)
wissenschaftlich: scholarly
Wochenschrift: weekly publication
wöchentlich: weekly
wohlerhalten: well-preserved
wohlfeil: inexpensive
Wörterbuch: dictionary, word
  list
Wortlaut: wording, text
wurmfrass: worm-eaten
Wurmgang(gänge): wormhole(s)
wurml. *see* wurmlöcherig
Wurmlöcher: wormholes
wurmlöcherig: wormholed
Wurmspur(en): trace(s) of
  worms
wurmst. *see* wurmstichig
Wurmstich(e): wormhole(s)
wurmstichig: with wormholes
Wurmstichspur(en): trace(s) of
  worms

Z. *see* Zeile
z.T. *see* zum Teil
z.Zt. *see* zur Zeit
Zahlentafeln: tables of figures
zahllos: innumerable
zahlr. *see* zahlreich
zahlreich: numerous
zart: delicate, delicately
zehn(te): ten(th)
Zeichen: sign(s), mark(s)

Zeichn. *see* Zeichnung
Zeichnung(en): drawing(s)
Zeile(n): line(s)
Zeilenzählung: line numbering
Zeit: time
Zeitgen. *see* Zeitgenosse
zeitgenöss. *see* zeitgenössisch
Zeitgenosse: contemporary
zeitgenössisch: contemporary
Zeitschrift: journal
Zeittaf. *see* Zeittafel
Zeittafel(n): chronological
  table(s)
Zensur: censorship
zerbrochen: cracked
zerknittert: crinkled
ziemlich: rather, fairly
Zierleiste(n): decorative
  border(s)
Zinkotypie(n): zincograph(s)
zirka: approximately
zis. *see* ziseliert
zisel. *see* ziseliert
ziseliert: chased, chiseled
zitiert: cited
Zs. *see* Zeitschrift
zsgest. *see* zusammengestellt
Zt. *see* Zeit
Ztsch. *see* Zeitschrift
zugeschrieben: attributed
zugleich: simultaneously
zuletzt erschien: last published
zum Teil: partly
zur Subskription gestellt: offered
  for subscription
zur Subkription stellen: to offer
  for subscription
zur Zeit: now, at present
zus. *see* zusammen
zusammen: together
Zusammenfassung: résumé
zusammengebunden: bound together
zusammengest. *see* zusammengestellt
zusammengestellt: collected,
  chosen, compiled
Zusatz(sätze): addendum(a)

Zustand: condition, state
zuverl. *see* zuverlässig
zuverlässig: reliable, authentic
zwanzig(ste): twenty(ieth)
zwei(te): two (second)

zweifarbig: two-color
zweisprachig: bilingual
zwischen: between
Zwischentitel: inserted title(s)
zwölf(te): twelve (twelfth)

ITALIAN

a. *see* autore
a carico di: at the expense of
a colori: in colors
a contanti: cash
a cordoni: with bands
a cura di: edited by
a doppia colonna: double column
a doppia facciata: double page
a doppia pagina: double page
a fianco: alongside
a fogli chiusi: uncut
a fogli dispari: leaves of varying sizes
a fogli sciolti: loose leaves
a freddo: blind tooling
a fronte: opposite
a grana lunga: straight-grained
a grandi margini: with wide margins
a mano: by hand
a mezza pagina: half page
a nervi: with raised bands
a.p.pag. *see* a piena pagina
a piccoli ferri: tooled in small designs
a piena pagina: full page
a pieni margini: with full margins
a richiesta: upon request
a secco: blind tooling

a spese dell'autore: at the author's expense
a spese dell'editore: at the publisher's expense
abb. *see* abbonamento
abbastanza: rather, sufficiently
abbon. *see* abbonamento
abbonam. *see* abbonamento
abbonamento: subscription
abbreviatura(e): abbreviation(s)
abbreviazione(i): abbreviation(s)
abbrunito: browned
abile: able, skillful
abilissimo: most skillful
abilmente: ably
abrasionato: abraded
abrasione(i): abrasion(s)
acc. *see* accresciuto
acciaio: steel
accomodato: mended, repaired
accresc. *see* accresciuto
accresciuto: enlarged
accuratezza: accuracy
acquaforte: etching
acquatinta: acquatint
acquerellato: water-colored
acquerello: water color
adattato: adapted
adorno: decorated, adorned
agg. *see* aggiunte

aggiorn. *see* aggiornato
aggiornato: brought up to date,
  modernized
aggiunte: additions, addenda
aggiunto: added
al principio: at the front
al retro: on the back
alla fine: at the end, at the back
alleg. *see* allegato
allegati: attached items
allegato: attached
allungato: elongated
almanacco: almanac
alquanto: somewhat
alt. *see* altezza
altezza: height
altrove: elsewhere
amatore: amateur
ampl. *see* ampliato
ampliato: enlarged
anastatico: anastatic
ancora: still, yet
angolo(i): corner(s)
ann. *see* annata, anno
annali: annals
annata: year
annesso(i): annex(es)
anno: year
annot. *see* annotazione
annotato: annotated
annotaz. *see* annotazione
annotazione(i): annotation(s)
annuale: annual
annuario: yearbook
annunzio: announcement
annuo: annual
anonimo: anonymous
ant. *see* anteriore, antico
anter. *see* anteriore
anteriore: front, anterior
antico: old
antip. *see* antiporta
antiporta: frontispiece
antologia: anthology
append. *see* appendice
appendice: appendix
applicato: applied, fastened to
arancione: orange-colored

archivio: archives
argento: silver
armi: arms
arricchito: enriched
arross. *see* arrossato
arrossato: with reddish spots
arrossature: reddish spots
arrotondato: rounded
asport. *see* asportato
asportato: carried away, gone
ass. *see* assicelle
assai: rather
assi: boards
assicelle: boards
assicelle di legno: wood boards
ast. *see* astuccio
astuccio: slipcase, box
atl. *see* atlante
atlante: atlas
attaccato: attached
atti: transactions
attraente: attractive
attualità: timeliness, quality of
  being up to date
aum. *see* aumentato
aumentato: enlarged, increased
aut. *see* autografo
autobiografia: autobiography
autogr. *see* autografo
autografo: autograph
autore: author
autoritratto: self-portrait
autorizzato: authorized
avaria: damage
avorio: ivory
avvertimento: notice
avviso: notice
azz. *see* azzurro
azzurrigno: bluish
azzurro: blue

b. *see* bianco, brossura
basso: lower
bastardi: bastard type
baz. *see* bazzana
bazzana: sheepskin
belliss. *see* bellissimo
bellissimo: most beautiful

ben tenuto: well-kept
bianco: white, blank
bianconero: black and white
bibliofilo: bibliophile
bibliografia: bibliography
bibliografico: bibliographical
bibliot. *see* biblioteca
biblioteca: library
bibliotecario: librarian
bicol. *see* bicolore
bicolore: bicolored
bicr. *see* bicromia
bicromia: bichrome
bimestrale: bimonthly
biografia: biography
blasone: blazon
blocco *see* in blocco
blu: blue
bod. *see* bodoniana
bodon. *see* bodoniana
bodoniana: in the style of Bodoni
bollettino: bulletin
borchie: bosses, knobs
bordo: edge
bordura: border
br. *see* brossura
bradel: bradel, a cased binding
broccato: brocaded
bross. *see* brossura
brossura: stitched, paper-cover
  binding
brossurato: stitched, in paper
  covers
bruciato: burned
bruciature: burned spots
brunito: burnished
brunitura(e): burnishing(s)
brutto: coarse
bucherello: little hole
busta: case

c. *see* carta
c.b. *see* carta bianca
c.s. *see* come sopra
ca. *see* carta
cad. *see* cadauno
cadauno: each
calce *see* in calce

calcografia: brass engraving
calico: calico
calligrafia: fine handwriting
calligraficamente: in fine handwriting
camicia(e): wrapper(s)
cancellato: canceled, crossed out
cancellatura(e): canceled, crossed-
  out area(s), erasure(s)
canzoniere: songbook
capil. *see* capilettera
capilett. *see* capilettera
capilettera(e): initial letter(s)
capit. *see* capitolo
capitale(i): capital letter(s)
capitello: headband
capitolo(i): chapter(s)
capolavoro: masterpiece
car. *see* carattere
carat. *see* carattere
caratt. *see* carattere
carattere: letters, type
carattere corsivo: cursive type,
  italics
carattere grecia: Greek type
carattere rom. *see* carattere
  romano
carattere romano: roman type
carattere rotondo: roman type
carattere tondo: roman type
caricatura: caricature
cart. *see* cartonato, cartone
carta: paper, map
carta a mano: handmade paper
carta bianca: blank page
carta bibbia: Bible paper
carta forte: heavy paper
carta geografica: map
carta grave: heavy paper
carta india: India paper
carta lucida: glazed paper
carta patinata: coated paper
carta pesante: heavy paper
carta topografica: topographic map
carta vergata: laid paper
carte: pages
carte non numerate: unnumbered
  pages

carte vedute: pictorial illustrations
cartella: portfolio; label, cartouche
cartellino: label
cartiglio: small map
cartina: small map
cartografia: cartography
carton. *see* cartonato
cartonaggio: board binding, boards
cartonato: bound in boards
cartonatura: board binding
cartoncino: thin cardboard
cartone: cardboard; bound in boards
cattivo: very bad
cc. *see* carte
ccnn. *see* carte non numerate
celebre: celebrated, notable
cellophan: cellophane
censura: censorship
censurato: censored
centesimo: hundredth
cento: hundred
centro: center
cerniera: joint, hinge
cesell. *see* cesellato
cesellato: chiseled, goffered
chiarezza: clearness, clarity
chiarissimo: very clear
chiaro: clear
chiaroscuro: chiaroscuro
chiave: key
chiodo: nail
chiosa: gloss
chiuso: closed, uncut
chiusura(e): catch(es), clasp(s)
ciasc. *see* ciascuno
ciascuno: each
cinquanta: fifty
cinquantesimo: fiftieth
cinque: five
circondato: surrounded by
cit. *see* citato
citato: cited
citazione(i): citation(s)
clandestino: clandestine

co-autore: coauthor
codice: codex
coevo: contemporary
col. *see* colore
collana: series
collaz. *see* collazione
collazione: collation
collez. *see* collezione
collezione: collection
colonna(e): column(s)
color. *see* colorato
colorato: colored
colore: color
colorito: coloring, colored
coloritura: coloring
come nuovo: as new
come sopra: as above
comm. *see* commercio
commentato: commented
commercio: trade
compartimento(i): section(s), panel(s)
compendio: compendium
compilato: compiled
compilatore: compiler
compilazione: compilation
compiuto: complete, perfect
compl. *see* complessivo, completo
compless. *see* complessivo
complessivo: including, inclusive
complesso: set, group
completo: complete
composto a mano: hand set
compr. *see* compreso
compreso: including
comune: ordinary
con: with
concordanza: concordance
cond. *see* condizione
condiz. *see* condizione
condizione: condition
confezione: make-up, fabrication
conosciuto: known
cons. *see* conservato, conservazione
conserv. *see* conservazione
conservato: in good condition, well-preserved

conservazione: state of preservation, condition
consunto: worn out, consumed
contemp. *see* contemporaneo
contemporaneo: contemporary
contenuto: contents
contin. *see* continuo
continuazione: continuation
continuo: continuous
conto: account
contornato: outlined, encircled
contorno: outline, frame
contraff. *see* contraffazione
contraffazione: pirated edition, counterfeit
cop. *see* coperta, copertina
copert. *see* copertina
coperta: covered, cover
copertina: cover
copertina conservata: wrapper preserved
copertina muta: blank cover
copia: copy
copia da prova: proof copy
copioso: copious
cord. *see* cordoni
cordonato: with bands
cordoncini: small, thin bands
cordoni: bands
corn. *see* cornice
cornice: border
corr. *see* corretto
corredato: furnished with
correttezza: correctness
corretto: corrected
correzzione(i): correction(s), amendment(s)
corroso: eaten, corroded
cors. *see* corsivo
corsivo: cursive, italic
corso: course
corto: short
corto di margine: narrow margins
costa: side, edge
cp. *see* copertina
crestomazia: anthology
crom. *see* cromolitografia

cromolitografia: chromolithography
cromolitografiche: chromolithographic
cromotipografia: chromotypography
cronaca(che): chronicle(s)
cronica(che): chronicle(s)
cros. *see* crostoso
crostoso: rough-grained
cucitura: sewing, stitching
cuffia(e): rolled edge(s) at top or bottom of spine
cuoio: leather
cuoio di Russia: Russian leather
cupo: dark
cura *see* a cura di
curato: edited
curatore: editor
curioso: unusual
cust. *see* custodia
custod. *see* custodia
custodia: slipcase

d. *see* dorso
da rilegare: needing binding
da tempo: long since
danneggiato: damaged
danno: damage
data: date
dattilografato: typewritten
debole: weak
dec. *see* decorazione
decimo: tenth
decor. *see* decorazione
decoratissimo: profusely decorated
decorato: decorated
decorazione: decoration
ded. *see* dedica
dedica: dedicatory note
definitivo: definitive
del rimanente: for the remainder
del tempo: of the time, contemporary
delizioso: delightful
dell'epoca: of the time
dentelle: dentelle

descr. *see* descrizione
descritto: described
descrizione: description
destro: right-hand
deterior. *see* deteriorato
deteriorato: deteriorated
dettagliato: detailed
deturpato: stained, spoiled,
  damaged
di lusso: de luxe
di pregio: prized
di prossima pubblicazione: to be
  published soon
diagramma(i): diagram(s)
diario: diary; daily journal
diciannove: nineteen
diciannovesimo: nineteenth
diciasette: seventeen
diciasettesimo: seventeenth
diciottesimo: eighteenth
diciotto: eighteen
dieci: ten
difetto: defect
difettoso: defective
dim. *see* dimensione, diminutivo
dimens. *see* dimensione
dimensione(i): dimension(s)
diminutivo: very small
dipinto: represented, painted
diritti d'autore: author's rights
dis. *see* disegnato, disegno
discreto: fair, moderate
disegnato: designed
disegno: design
dispari: disparate; odd-numbered
dispensa: quire, part
disponibile: available
dissertazione: dissertation
dist. *see* distinto
distinto: special, outstanding
diverso: varied
documentazione: documentation
documento(i): document(s)
dodicesimo: twelfth
dodici: twelve
domanda: request, demand
doppio: double
dor. *see* dorato

dorato: gilt
doratura(e): gilt design(s), gilding
dorso: back, spine
due: two
duplice: double

ecc. *see* eccetera, eccezionale
eccess. *see* eccessivo
eccessivo: excessive
eccetera: et cetera
eccetto: except
eccezionale: exceptional
ed. *see* edito
edit. *see* editore, editoriale
edito: edited, published
editor. *see* editoriale
editore: editor, publisher
editoriale: publisher's
ediz. *see* edizione
edizioncina: small edition
edizione: edition
edizione definitiva: definitive
  edition
edizione limitata: limited edition
edizione principe: first edition,
  editio princeps
effige: effigy
elenco: list
eliogravure: photoengraving
eliotip. *see* eliotipia
eliotipia: phototype
emendato: amended
entrambi: together, both
entro: in, within
ep. *see* epoca
epigrafe: epigraph
epoca: time, of the time
erroneam. *see* erroneamente
erroneamente: erroneously
errore: error
es. *see* esemplare
esattamente: exactly
esaur. *see* esaurito
esauritissimo: extremely hard to
  find
esaurito: exhausted, out-of-print
escluso: excluding, except for
escoriazione: excoriation

eseguito: executed, carried out
esemp. *see* esemplare
esempl. *see* esemplare
esemplare: copy
eserc. *see* esercizio
esercizio: exercise
est. *see* esterno
esterno: external, exterior
estero: foreign, abroad
estratto: extract, reprint;
  extracted
estremamente: extremely
etichetta: label
ex-libris: bookplate

f.c. *see* fuori commercio
f.comm. *see* fuori commercio
f.t. *see* fuori testo
facciata: page, face
facsim. *see* facsimile
facsimilato: done in facsimile
facsimile: facsimile
fasc. *see* fascicolo
fascic. *see* fascicolo
fascicolo(i): fascicule(s), part(s)
fastosamente: ostentatiously,
  magnificently
faticato: worn, worked over
fattura: craftsmanship, work-
  manship
fedele: faithful
fedelissimo: extremely faithful
fenditura: break
fermagli: clasps, ties
ferro(i): tool(s)
fianco: side
fig. *see* figura, figurato
figg. *see* figure
figur. *see* figurato
figura: figure, illustration
figurato: decorated with designs
figure: figures, illustrations
fil. *see* filetto
filettatura: line pattern, border
filetto(i): line(s), fillet(s)
fili: line patterns
filigrana: watermark
filigranato: watermarked

final. *see* finalino
finale: tailpiece
finaletto: tailpiece
finalino: tailpiece
finem. *see* finemente
finemente: beautifully
finto: imitation
fior. *see* fioriture
fiordaliso: fleur-de-lys
fiorellini: small floral designs
fioretti: floral designs
fiorit. *see* fioriture
fiorito: flowered
fioriture: flowered designs
fioroni: large floral designs
firma: signature
firmato: signed
fitt. *see* fittizio
fittizio: artificial, fictitious
fless. *see* flessibile
flessibile: flexible
fodera: lining, *doublure*
foderato: lined
fogli chiusi *see* a fogli chiusi
fogli di guardia: end papers
fogliame: scrollwork, resembling
  foliage
foglietto: small leaf, sheet
foglio: sheet, leaf
foglio volante: broadside
fondo: end, background
forature di tarlo: wormholes
forellini di tarlo: wormholes
fori di chiodo: nail holes
fori di tarlo: wormholes
form. *see* formato
formato: format
forte: strong
fotocalcografia: photoengraving
fotogr. *see* fotografia, fotografico
fotografia: photograph, photography
fotografico: photographic
fotoincisione: photoengraving
fotolito: photolith
fotolitografia: photolithography
fotoriprod. *see* fotoriproduzione
fotoriproduzione: photoreproduction
fototipia: phototype

116

fr. *see* fregi, frontispizio
frammento: fragment
franco: carriage paid, postpaid
franco di porto: carriage paid,
  postpaid
freddo *see* a freddo
fregi: ornaments, decorations
fregiato: decorated
freschezza: freshness
freschissimo: very fresh, clean
fresco: fresh, clean
front. *see* frontispizio
frontisp. *see* frontispizio
frontispizio: frontispiece
fulvo: fawn-colored, tawny
fuori comm. *see* fuori commercio
fuori commercio: not for sale
fuori numerazione: unnumbered
fuori testo: not in the text
fustagno: fustian, a coarse cloth

gazzetta: gazette
genuino: genuine
geogr. *see* geografico
geografico: geographic
giallo: yellow
giallognolo: yellowish
giansenista: Jansenist, a plain
  binding
giornale: daily
glossa: gloss
glossario: glossary
goffrato: goffered
gora(e) d'acqua: water stain(s)
gora(e) d'umido: damp stain(s)
got. *see* gotico
gotico: gothic
gr. *see* grande
graf. *see* grafico
graffi: scratches
graffiato: scratched
graffiatura(e): scratch(es)
graffio: scratch
grafico: graphic illustration,
  chart
grana: grain
grana lunga: straight-grained
grana schiacciata: crushed grain

granato: grained
grande: large
grandezza: size
graziosissimo: very pleasing
grazioso: pleasing, gracious
greve: serious, seriously
grezzo: raw
grigio: gray
grossis. *see* grossissimo
grossissimo: extremely large,
  thick
grosso: thick
grossolanamente: coarsely,
  roughly
guarnizione(i): decoration(s)
guasti: tears, damaged parts
guasto: torn, damaged
guazzo: gouache
gustosissimo: most highly
  pleasing

iconografia: iconography
ignorato: unknown
ignoto: unknown
ill. *see* illustrato, illustrazione
illegibile: illegible
illustr. *see* illustrato, illustrazione
illustratissimo: profusely illustrated
illustrato: illustrated
illustratore: illustrator
illustrazione(i): illustration(s)
immacolato: immaculate
imminente: imminent
immune da: free of
imp. *see* impressioni
impag. *see* impaginazione
impaginazione: layout
impastato: pasted up, mounted
impostazione: setup, arrangement
impr. *see* impressioni
impress. *see* impressioni
impressioni: stamping, tooling
impressioni a freddo: blind tooling
impressioni in oro: gold tooling
impresso: blind-tooled
in alto: at the top

117

in blocco: as a lot
in calce: at the foot of the page
in cartella: in portfolio
in corso di stampa: in press
in disordine: in disorder
in fine: at the end
in fogli: in sheets
in fogli sciolti: in loose sheets
in-Fol. *see* in-Folio
in-Folio: folio format, folio
in n. e col. *see* in nero e colori
in nero e colori: in black and
 colors
in parte: partly
in plano: in sheets
in preparazione: in preparation
in princ. *see* in principio
in principio: at the beginning
in ristampa: being reprinted
in simile pelle: in imitation
 leather
in vendita: for sale
in viaggio: now on the way
inc. *see* incisione, inciso
incartonato: bound in boards
incartonatura: board binding
incatenato: chained
incc. *see* incisioni
inchiostro: ink
incis. *see* incisione, inciso
incisione: engraving
incisioni: engravings
inciso: engraved, cut in
incisore: engraver
incoll. *see* incollato
incollato: pasted in, mounted
incompiuto: incomplete, imperfect
incorn. *see* incorniciato
incorniciato: framed
incunabulo(i): incunabulum(a)
indice: index, table of contents
indivisibili: not sold separately
ined. *see* inedito
inedito: unpublished
inesistente: nonexistent
inf. *see* inferiore
infer. *see* inferiore

inferiore: lower, bottom
ing. *see* ingiallito, ingialliture
ingiall. *see* ingiallito, ingialliture
ingiallimento: yellowing
ingiallito: yellowed, foxed
ingialliture: marks of foxing
iniz. *see* iniziale
iniziale(i): initial(s), initial
 letter(s)
inquadrato: framed, bordered
inquadratura: frame, border
ins. *see* insegna
inscrizione: inscription
insegna: mark
insegna del tipografo: printer's
 mark
insegna tipografica: printer's
 mark
insepar. *see* inseparabili
inseparabili: inseparable, not sold
 separately
inserito: inserted
inservibile: unusable
insieme: together
int. *see* interno, intonso
intagliato: cut, carved, engraved
intaglio: engraving
intarsi: inlay, inlaid work
intatto: intact
integralmente: integrally
integro: integral
interamente: entirely, completely
interc. *see* intercalato
intercalato: intercalated, inserted
interess. *see* interessante
interessante: interesting
interfogliato: interleaved
interiore: inner, interior
interno: internal
intonso: untrimmed, uncut
intorno: around, approximately
introd. *see* introduzione
introduttivo: introductory
introduzione: introduction
introvabile: impossible to find
inversione: inversion
invertito: transposed
invio: forward

irregolarità: irregularity
iscr. *see* iscrizione
iscrizione: inscription
iscurito: darkened, obscured
istoriato: historiated, illuminated

laccato: lacquered
lacci: ties
lacer. *see* lacerazione
lacerato: torn
lacerazione(i): tear(s)
lacuna: lack, gap
largh. *see* larghezza
larghezza: width
larghiss. *see* larghissimo
larghissimo: very wide
largo: wide
lato: side
lavabile: washable
lavato: washed, cleaned
lavoraz. *see* lavorazione
lavorazione: craftsmanship
lavoro: work
leg. *see* legato, legatura
legacci: fastenings, ties
legacci di chiusura: ties
legat. *see* legatura
legato: bound
legatore: binder
legatura: binding
legatura d'amatore: three-
  quarter binding
legatura editoriale: publisher's
  binding
legatura uniforme: uniform
  binding
legg. *see* leggero
leggenda: legend
leggerm. *see* leggermente
leggermente: slightly
leggero: slight
leggiadro: graceful
leggibile: legible
legno: wood
lembo: bit, end
les. *see* lesione
lesionare: injuring, to injure
lesione: injury

lessico: lexicon
lett. *see* lettera
lettera(e): letter(s)
letterale: literal
libello: lampoon, pamphlet
libraio: bookseller
libreria: bookstore
libretto: little book
libro: book
libro di festa: holiday book
libro d'ore: Book of Hours
lieve: light
lievem. *see* lievemente
lievemente: lightly, slightly
lieviss. *see* lievissimamente
lievissimamente: very lightly,
  very slightly
lim. *see* limitato
limitato: limited
linea: line
lino: linen
liscio: smooth, flat
listello(i): fillet(s)
listino: list
lit. *see* litografato, litografia
litografato: lithographed
litografia: lithography
litografico: lithographic
logoro: worn
lunghezza: length
luogo: place
lusso: luxe, de luxe
lussuoso: luxurious, costly

m. *see* marocchino, mezzo
m.p. *see* mezza pelle
macch. *see* macchia
macchia: stain
macchiato: stained, soiled
macchiato d'acqua: stained by
  water
macchiato di grasso: stained by
  grease
macchie d'inchiostro: inkstains
macchie d'olio: oil stains
macchie d'umidità: damp stains
macchie d'uso: stains of use
macchie di terriccio: stains of mold

macchietta: small stain, spot
macchiettato: spotted
macchiolina(e): small stain(s)
magistralmente: masterfully
maiuscola: capital letter
malamente: badly
man. *see* manovrato
manc. *see* mancante
manca: lacks
mancante: lacking
mancanza: lack
manoscritto: manuscript
manovrato: worked by hand,
  handmade
manuale: handbook
mappa: map
mar. *see* marocchino
marca: mark
marchio: mark
marezzato: marbled
marg. *see* marginoso
margin. *see* marginale
marginale: marginal
marginalmente: marginally
margine(i): margin(s)
margine esterno: outer margin
margine interno: inner margin
marginosissimo: with very wide
  margins
marginoso: with wide margins
marm. *see* marmorizzato
marmor. *see* marmorizzato
marmoriz. *see* marmorizzato
marmorizzato: marbled
marocch. *see* marocchino
marocchino: morocco
marrone: chestnut-colored
martellato: hammered
mass. *see* massimo
massimo: largest
mat. *see* matita
matita: pencil
medagl. *see* medaglione
medaglione: medallion
medesimo: same
medio: medium, average
mediocre: mediocre
mensile: monthly

meraviglioso: marvelous, wonderful
merlett. *see* merlettatura
merlettatura: dentelle design
merletto: dentelle
metallico: metallic
mezza bazzana: half sheepskin
mezza pelle: half leather
mezza tela: half cloth
mezzo: half
migliorato: improved
mille: thousand
millimetri: millimeters
miniato: illuminated, engraved
miniatura: miniature
minuscolo: diminutive
minutissimo: extremely minute
mirabilmente: admirably
mis. *see* misura
miscellanea: miscellany
misura: measure
mm. *see* millimetri
modesto: modest
molle: flexible, soft
molte: many
molti: many
moltiss. *see* moltissimo
moltissimo(i): a great deal, a
  great number
molto: much, very
monocromo: single color
monogr. *see* monogramma
monografia: monograph
monogramma: monogram
monotipia: monotype
montato: mounted, pasted up
montone: ram's skin
mosaicato: decorated in mosaic
motivo: motif, design
motto: coat of arms
ms. *see* manoscritto
muffa: mildew
muta *see* copertina muta
mutilato: mutilated
mutilo: mutilated, cut

n. *see* nero, numerato
n.n. *see* non numerato

n.t. *see* nel testo
n.t.e f.t. *see* nel testo e fuori
 testo
nastro: ribbon
nel complesso: on the whole, for
 the most part
nel testo: in the text
nel testo e fuori testo: in the text
 and not in the text
nero: black
nervetti: ribs
nervi: cords, raised bands
nervi piatti: flat bands
netto: net
nitidamente: clearly, elegantly
nitido: clean-cut, clear
nn. *see* non numerato
nocciola: nut-brown
nome: name
non autorizzato: unauthorized
non comune: uncommon, unusual
non numerato: unnumbered
non più pubblicato: no longer
 published
non tagliato: pages uncut,
 unopened
non venale: not for sale
nono: ninth
nota(e): note(s)
notaz. *see* notazione
notazione(i): notation(s)
notev. *see* notevole
notevole: notable
notissimo: known, renowned
novanta: ninety
novantesimo: ninetieth
nove: nine
novità: novelty
num. *see* numerato, numerazione,
 numero, numeroso
numer. *see* numerato, numerazione, numero, numeroso
numerato: numbered
numeraz. *see* numerazione
numerazione: numbering
numerazione continua: continuous
 numbering
numero: number

numerosiss. *see* numerossissimo
numerosissimo: extremely
 numerous
numeroso: numerous
nuovo: new
nuvolato: cloudy

obl. *see* oblungo
oblun. *see* oblungo
oblungo: oblong
occasione: secondhand, bargain
occh. *see* occhiello, occhietto
occhiello: half-title page
occhietto: half-title page
offset: offset
ogni: every
ognuno: each, each one
oliva: olive
olona *see* tela olona
oltre: over, beyond
ombreggiato: shaded, hatched
onciale: uncial
op. *see* opera
opera: work
opusc. *see* opuscolo
opuscolo: booklet, pamphlet
or. *see* originale
ordinato: put in order, arranged
ordine: order
orig. *see* originale
origin. *see* originale
originale: original
originario: original
ormai: now
orn. *see* ornamentale, ornato
ornamentale: ornamental
ornamento: ornament
ornato: decorated
oro: gold, gilt
ott. *see* ottimo
ottanta: eighty
ottantesimo: eightieth
ottavo: eighth
ottimo: excellent, the best
otto: eight

p. *see* pelle, pergamena, pieno
p.p. *see* piena pelle

pag. *see* pagina
pagg. *see* pagine
pagina: page
paginatura: pagination
pagine: pages
paglierino: pale, straw-colored
pallido: pale
paraffato: initialed
paraffinato: waxed
paraffo: paraph
paragrafo: paragraph
parecchie: several
parodia: parody
parte(i): part(s)
particolare: especial
pastello: pastel
patinato: coated, coated paper
patito: damaged
pegamoide: imitation leather,
    leatherette
pelle: leather
pelle di scrofa: pigskin
pelle zigrino: shagreen
penna: pen
per il resto: for the rest
percalle: book cloth
perdita del testo: loss of text
perfettissimo: most perfect
perfetto: perfect
perg. *see* pergamena
pergam. *see* pergamena
pergamena: vellum
pergamenato: made to resemble
    vellum
periodico: periodical
pesante: heavy
pezzo(i): piece(s)
piani: sides
pianta: plan, map
piantina: small plan
piatto(i): side(s)
piatto anteriore: front cover
piatto posteriore: back cover
picc. *see* piccolo
piccolo: small
piè di pagina: foot of the page
pieg. *see* piegatile, piegato
piega: fold

piegatile: folding
piegato: folded
pieghevole: folding
piena pelle: full leather
pieno: full
più: several; plus
più volte: several times
placca: plaque, medallion
placchetta: small medallion
pochi: few
poco conosciuto: little-known
poderoso: strong
policromia: polychrome
policromo: polychrome
polveroso: dusty
popolare: popular
portafogli: portfolio
portatile: portable
porto: carriage, shipping costs
posposto: postponed
post. *see* posteriore
poster. *see* posteriore
posteriore: back
posticc. *see* posticcio
posticcio: artificial, imitation
postillato: with marginal notes
postille: marginal notes
postumo: posthumous
pp. *see* pagine
pre-tiratura: prepublication
prefaz. *see* prefazione
prefazione: preface
preg. *see* pregiato
pregev. *see* pregevole
pregevole: esteemed, of fine
    quality
pregevolissimo: highly esteemed,
    praiseworthy
pregiatissimo: highly esteemed
pregiato: esteemed
prel. *see* preliminare
prelim. *see* preliminare
preliminare: preliminary
premiato: prized, having earned
    an award
prezzo: price
prezzo complessivo: complete
    price

prezzo di listino: list price
prezzo di vendita: list price
primissimo: the very first
primo: first
principio see al principio, in
  principio
privilegio: privilege
privo di: without
propr. see proprietario
propriet. see proprietario
proprietà letteraria: copyright
proprietario: owner
prospetto: prospectus; view
prospetto editoriale: publisher's
  announcement
prossimo: near, imminent
prova: proof
proveniente: coming from
provenienza: provenance, source
pseudonimo: pseudonym
pubbl. see pubblicato, pubblicazione
pubblicato: published
pubblicazione: publication
pulito: clean
punta secca: dry point
puntato: etched; separate
punte: corners
punte di tarli: wormholes
punteggiato: stippled
purgato: purged, censored

q. see qualche
qq. see qualche
quà e là: here and there
quaderno: quire
quadrante: face of front cover
quadrato: square
quadratura: frame
quadrimestrale: quarterly
quadro: picture
qualche: a few
qualità: quality
quaranta: forty
quarantesimo: fortieth
quarto: fourth
quattordicesimo: fourteenth
quattordici: fourteen

quattro: four
quindici: fifteen
quindicinale: fortnightly
quindicesimo: fifteenth
quinto: fifth
quotidiano: daily

racc. see raccolta
racchiuso: enclosed
raccoglitore: compiler
raccolta: compilation, collection
racconto: tale
raddoppiato: duplicated
raff. see raffigurante
raffigurante: showing
rafforzato: reinforced
ragionato: commented
rame: copper, copper engraving
rappezzato: patched
rappezzo: patched place
rapporto: report
rarissimo: very rare
rarità: rarity
raro: rare
raschiature: erasures, scrapings
rattoppato: restored, patched
recente: recent
recto: recto
redatto: edited
redazione: editorship
regalo: gift
regolato: ruled, lined
rendiconti: transactions
reperibile: that can be found,
  available
repertorio: list, index
residuo(i): residue(s), remnant(s)
rest. see restaurato
restaur. see restaurato
restaurato: restored, repaired
restauri: restorations, repairs
retro: back side
ribasso: discount
ricamato: embroidered
ricamo: embroidery
riccam. see riccamente
riccamente: richly
ricchiss. see ricchissimo

ricchissimo: very rich
ricercatissimo: in great demand
ricercato: in demand
richiesto: in demand
riconciato: mended
riconciatura(e): mended spot(s)
ricop. *see* ricoperto
ricoperto: recovered
ricordi: memoirs
ricorretto: corrected again
ridotto: reduced
riduzione: reduction
rielaborato: reworked, rewritten
rif. *see* rifatto
rifacimento: restoration, rework-
  ing
rifatto: reworked, rewritten
rifil. *see* rifilato
rifilato: trimmed
rifior. *see* rifioriture
rifioriture: foxing
rifioriture d'acqua: watermarks
riga: line
rigato: lined
rigida: stiff
riinciso: re-engraved
ril. *see* rilegato, rilegatura
rilasciato: weakened, broken
rileg. *see* rilegato, rilegatura
rilegat. *see* rilegatura
rilegato: bound, rebound
rilegatura: binding
rilegatura d'amatore: three-
  quarter binding
rilegatura romantica: binding in
  the romantic style
rilevato: embellished
rilievi: reliefs
rimarginato: margins renewed
rimesso: recased
rimontato: remounted
rinforz. *see* rinforzato
rinforzato: reinforced
rinnov. *see* rinnovato
rinnovato: renewed
rip. *see* ripiegato
ripar. *see* riparato
riparato: repaired

riparaz. *see* riparazione
riparazione(i): repair(s)
ripet. *see* ripetuto
ripetuto: repeated
ripieg. *see* ripiegato
ripiegabile: folding
ripiegato: folded
ripr. *see* riproduzione
riprod. *see* riproduzione
riproduz. *see* riproduzione
riproduzione(i): reproduction(s)
ripubblicato: republished
riquadratura: frame
riquadro(i): border(s)
risguardi: cover linings, *doublures*
rist. *see* ristampa
ristampa: reprint, reimpression
ristampato: reprinted
ristretto: limited
risvolti: linings
ritagliato: cut out
ritaglio: piece cut out, clipping
ritoccato: retouched, reviewed
ritr. *see* ritratto
ritratto(i): portrait(s)
riun. *see* riunito
riunito: combined
riv. *see* riveduto
rived. *see* riveduto
riveduto: revised
rivestito di: covered by, with
rivista: magazine
rlg. *see* rilegato
robusto: sturdy
romant. *see* romantico
romantico: in the romantic style
romanzo: novel
rossore: reddish hue
rotoc. *see* rotocalco
rotocalco: rotogravure
rotogravure: rotogravure
rotto: broken
rottura: break
rovescio: reverse
rovinato: damaged
rubrica: heading, rubric
rubricato: rubricated
rubricazione: rubrication

ruggine: rust
rugginoso: rust-colored
rust. *see* rustica
rustica: stitched, in paper covers

s. *see* senza
s.a. *see* senz'anno
s.d. *see* senza data
s.e. *see* senza editore
s.i.p. *see* senza il prezzo
s.l. *see* senza luogo
s.l.n.a. *see* senza luogo nè autore
s.l.n.d. *see* senza luogo nè data
s.l.n. stamp. *see* senza luogo nè
  stampatore
s. tip. *see* senza tipografo
saggio: sample, specimen; essay
saltato: skipped
salvo: except
sanguigno: sanguine
sano: sound, in good condition
satinato: calendered
sbagliato: in error
sbaglio: error
sbiadito: discolored, faded
sbucciat. *see* sbucciatura
sbucciatura: peeling
scadente: weakening, poor
scarabocchiato: scribbled on
scarabocchio: scribbling
scarso: narrow
scartellato: loose in its binding
scatola: box
scelta: selection
scelto: selected
schemi: schemes
schiacciato: crushed
schizzo(i): sketch(es)
sciolto: loose, unbound
sciup. *see* sciupato
sciupato: spoiled, worn
scollato: unglued
scolorito: discolored, colorless
scolpito: sculptured, carved
scomp. *see* scomparti
scomparti: sections, panels
scompleto: incomplete
sconosciuto: unknown

sconto: discount
scorretto: faulty
scorticato: scratched
scorticatura: scratch
screpolato: split, cracked
screpolatura: split, crack
scrittura: writing
scrittura a stampatello: scriptlike
  type
scrittura bastarda: bastard type
scrittura gotica: gothic type
scrittura rotonda: round, roman
  type
scrofa: pigskin
scucito: unsewn, loose
scudo: armorial shield
scurito: darkened, obscured
scuro: dark
sdrucito: worn out
sec. *see* secolo, secondo
secolo: century
secondo: second
sedicesimo: sixteenth
sedici: sixteen
seg. *see* seguente
segn. *see* segnatura
segnacolo: bookmark
segnalibro: bookmark
segnalini: index marks
segnatura: signature
segni di tarlo: marks of worms
segno: mark
seguente: following
sei: six
semestrale: half-yearly, semi-
  annual(ly)
semiannuale: semiannual
semintonso: partly trimmed
semplice: simple
sensibile: noticeable
senza: without
senz'anno: without year of publication
senza data: without date
senza editore: without publisher
senza il prezzo: without price
senza luogo: without place of
  publication

senza luogo nè autore: without place or author
senza luogo nè data: without place or date
senza luogo nè stampatore: without place or publisher
senza tipografo: without name of printer
separatamente: separately
serico: silken
serie: series
sessanta: sixty
sessantesimo: sixtieth
sesto: size, format; sixth
seta: silk
settanta: seventy
settantesimo: seventieth
sette: seven
settimanale: weekly
settimo: seventh
sfarzoso: splendid, magnificent
sfasc. *see* sfasciato
sfasciato: loosened, weakened
sfascicolato: fascicles undone
sfogl. *see* sfogliato
sfogliato: pages torn loose
sfondo: background
sfuggito: escaped
sgorbio: scribbling in ink
sgraffiato: scratched
sgualcito: rumpled, wrinkled
sigillo: seal
sigla: initial letter(s)
siglato: with initial letter(s)
silogr. *see* silografia
silograf. *see* silografia
silografia: wood-block print
similpelle: imitation leather
simpatico: appealing, attractive
singolo: single
sinistro: left-hand
sinottico: synoptic
sleg. *see* slegato
slegato: binding broken
smalto: enamel
smarginato: trimmed margin
smarginatura: trimming of margins

smussato: corners broken, dog-eared
smusso: broken-cornered
sobrio: sober, plain
solo pubblicato: the only one published
sommario: table of contents, résumé
sontuoso: sumptuous
soppresso: suppressed
sopra: above
soprac. *see* sopracoperta
sopracoperta: wrapper
soprascritta: superscription
sottolin. *see* sottolineature
sottolineato: underlined
sottolineature: underlining
sottoscrittore: subscriber
sottoscrizione: subscription
sottot. *see* sottotitolo
sottotit. *see* sottotitolo
sottotitolo: subtitle
sovr.cop. *see* sovracoperta
sovrac. *see* sovracoperta
sovracoperta: wrapper
sovrapposto: superimposed
spaccato: split
spartito: separate
spazio: space
spedizione: handling, forwarding
spellat. *see* spellatura
spellatura: scratch
spese di porto: costs of carriage
spesso: often
spessore: thickness
spezzato: broken
spiegabile: folding
spieghevole: folding
spostato: misplaced
spruzzato: sprinkled
stacc. *see* staccato
staccab. *see* staccabile
staccabile: detachable
staccato: detached
stamp. *see* stampato, stampatore
stampa: print
stampatello: scriptlike type
stampato: printed

stampatore: printer
stanco: worn
stato: condition
stato di conservazione: state of
  preservation
stato di nuovo: as new
stemma: coat of arms
stemmato: with arms
stesso: same, itself
stile: style
stile monastico: monastic style
stima: esteem, value
stimatiss. *see* stimatissimo
stimatissimo: highly esteemed
stimato: esteemed
stracciato: torn
straniero: foreign
strano: strange
strapp. *see* strappato
strappato: torn away, torn out
strappo: tear
stretto: narrow
stupendo: very fine, wonderful
sul: on the
sunto: summary
sup. *see* superiore
superbo: superb, sumptuous
superexlibris: book stamp
superiore: upper, top
supplementare: supplementary
supplemento: supplement
svanito: missing
svariato: varied, speckled

t. *see* tela
t.p. *see* tutta pelle
t.t. *see* tutta tela
tab. *see* tabelle
tabelle: tables
tagli: edges, cuts
tagli cesellati: goffered edges
tagliato: cut, opened
taglio: edge, cut
taglio dolce: *taille-douce,* copper
  etching
tagliuzzato: with very small cuts
tarlato: worm-eaten
tarlature: wormholes

tarli: worms, wormholes
tartaruga: tortoise
tasc. *see* tascabile
tascabile: pocket-size
tascabilità: suitability for pocket
tass. *see* tassello
tassello: label
tav. *see* tavola
tavola: table
tavole: tables
tavv. *see* tavole
tela: cloth
tela canapa: hemp cloth
tela grezza: raw cloth
tela olona: sailcloth
tempera: water colors
tenuto in pregio: valued
terzo: third
tesi: thesis
tessuto: woven, a woven material
testata: title, running title
testata di capitolo: chapter headpiece
testatine: headings, running title
testimoni: witnesses, untrimmed
  edges
testo: text
timbrato: stamped
timbretto: small stamp, mark
timbro: stamp, mark
timbro di biblioteca: library
  stamp, mark
tinto: tinted
tip. *see* tipografia, tipografo
tipogr. *see* tipografia, tipografo
tipografia: printing firm
tipografo: printer
tiraggio: printing run, edition
tirat. *see* tiratura
tirato: printed
tiratura: edition, printing
tiratura limitata: limited edition
tit. *see* titolo
titolo: title, title page
tomo: volume
top. *see* topografico
topogr. *see* topografico
topografico: topographic

tr. *see* tradotto, traduzione
tracce: traces, marks
tracce di fermagli: traces of clasps, ties
tracce di penna: traces of pen
tracce di tarlo: traces of worms
tracce di tarme: traces of worms
tracce d'umidità: traces of moisture
tracce d'uso: traces of use
trad. *see* tradotto, traduzione
tradotto: translated
traduz. *see* traduzione
traduzione: translation
trascrizione: transcription
trasposto: transposed
tratatto: treatise
tre: three
tredicesimo: thirteenth
tredici: thirteen
trenta: thirty
trentesimo: thirtieth
tricr. *see* tricromia
tricromia: three-color illustration
trimestrale: quarterly
triplice: triple
tutta pelle: full leather
tutta tela: full cloth
tutto: full, all
tutto il pubblicato: all published

ult. *see* ultimo
ultimissimo: most recent
ultimo: last
umid. *see* umidità
umidità: humidity
undicesimo: eleventh
undici: eleven
unghie: hooks
unico: single, unique, only
uniforme: uniform
unito: combined
unitovi: together with
uno: one
usato: worn
uscito: issued, published

vacchetta: calf
variamente: variously
variante: variant
variegato: variegated
vario: various
veduta(e): view(s)
vedutina: small view
vel. *see* velina
velatura d'acqua: shading by water
velina: vellum paper
velina di protezione: protective cover of vellum paper
velluto: velvet
venale *see* non venale
vendita: sale
venduto: sold
ventesimo: twentieth
venti: twenty
verde: green
vergato: ribbed
versione: version
verso: verso
veste: make-up, presentation
vignetta(e): vignette(s)
vitellino: yellow
vitello: calf
vivo: bright
voci: words, terms
vol. *see* volume
voll. *see* volumi
volume: volume
volumi: volumes
volumetto: little volume

xyl. *see* xylografia
xylogr. *see* xylografico
xylografia: woodcut
xylografico: woodcut

zigrinato: made to resemble shagreen
zigrino: shagreen
zincografia: zinc engraving
zincografico: engraved on zinc

128

POLISH

abonament: subscription
abonent: subscriber
abonować: to subscribe
abrewiacja: abbreviation
abstrakcyjny: abstract
adnotacja: annotation, explanatory
  note
adnotowany: annotated
adres: address
adresat: addressee
agencja prasowa: press agency
akademia: academy
akademia nauk: academy of
  sciences
akademicki: academic
akademicki podręcznik: academic
  textbook
akta: records, archives
akwaforta: etching
akwarela: water color
album(y): album(s)
album pamiątkowy: album to
  commemorate
alfabetyczny: alphabetical
almanach: almanac
analityczny: analytical
ang. *see* angielski
angielski: English
anonimowy: anonymous
antologia: anthology

antydatowany: antedated
antykwa: roman type
antykwariat: antiquarian bookshop
antykwariusz: antiquarian bookseller
antykwarnia: antiquarian bookshop
apokryf: apocrypha
archiwalia: archival material
archiwum(wa): archive(s)
arcydzieło: masterpiece
ark. *see* arkusz
arkusz(e): sheet(s)
arkusz próbny: proof sheet
arkusz zamówień: order form
arkusze próbne: proof sheets
artykuł(y): article(s)
atlas(y): atlas(es)
atlas kieszonkowy: pocket atlas
aukcja: auction
autentyczny: authentic
autobiografia: autobiography
autograf(y): autograph(s)
autor: author
autor broszur: pamphleteer
autorstwo: authorship

b.m. *see* bez miejsca
b.m.r. *see* bez miejsca i roku
b.r. *see* bez roku
b.w. *see* bez wydawcy

129

badania porównawcze: comparative studies
badanie: research, investigation
bajeczny: fabulous
bajka(i): tale(s), fairy tale(s)
barania skóra: sheepskin
bardzo: very
bardzo uszkodzony: badly damaged
barwn. *see* barwny
barwne ilustracje: colorful illustrations
barwny: colorful
beletrystyka: belles-lettres, fiction
bez: without
bez miejsca: without place
bez miejsca i roku: without place or date
bez rabatu: no discount
bez roku: without date
bez wydawcy: without name of publisher
bezimienny: anonymous
bezpłatnie: gratis, free of charge
biały: white
bibliogr. *see* bibliografia
bibliograf: bibliographer
bibliografia: bibliography
biblioteka: library
bibliotekarz: librarian
bieżący: current
biografia: biography
biuletyn(y): bulletin(s)
błąd: error
błąd drukarski: misprint
błędnie datowany: misdated
błędny: erroneous
bogato ilustrowany: profusely illustrated
br. *see* broszura
brakuje: lacking, missing
brązowy: bronze-colored
brokat: brocade
brokatowy: brocade
brosz. *see* broszura
broszura(y): paperbound book(s), pamphlet(s)

broszurowany: unbound
brunatny: brown
brzeg(i): edge(s)
brzeg boczny: fore edge
brzeg dolny: lower edge
brzeg górny: top edge
brzegi złocone: gilt edges
bukram: buckram

c.d. *see* ciąg dalszy
całkowity: whole, complete
całość: all together, complete
cały: full, whole
cecha: characteristic, typical feature
cena: price
cena kompletu: price of complete set
cena kupna: purchase price
cena poszczególnego egzemplarza: price for single copies
cena przybliżona: probable, likely price
cena zniżona: reduced price
cennik: price list
cenny: valuable
cenzura: censorship
charakterystyczny: characteristic
chronologiczny: chronological
ciąg dalszy: sequel, continuation
ciągły: continuous
cielęca skóra: calfskin
ciemny: dark, deep
codzienny: daily
cudzoziemski: foreign
cz. *see* czasopismo, część
czarny: black
czasopismo(a): periodical(s), magazine(s)
czcionka(i): type, letter(s)
czerwony: red
część: part
częściowo: partly
częstotliwość: frequency
czterdzieści: forty
czterdziesty: fortieth
czternaście: fourteen
czternasty: fourteenth

cztery: four
czwarty: fourth
czwórka: quarto
czystopis: clean copy
czysty: clean, neat
czyt. *see* czytelnik
czytelnik: reader
czytelny: legible

dalszy ciąg: sequel, continuation
dar: gift
data: date
data wydania: date of publication
datowany: dated
dedykacja: dedicatory note,
  inscription
defekt: defective copy
deska: board
diagram(y): diagram(s)
diariusz: diary
długość: length
dnie: days
do przejrzenia: on approval, for
  review
dobry: good
dobrze zakonserwowany: well-
  preserved
dod. *see* dodatek
dodatek(tki): supplement(s),
  appendix(es)
dodatek źródłowy: appendix of
  sources
dokładna podobizna: facsimile
dokument(y): document(s)
dokumentarny: documentary
dół strony: foot of a page
dopełnić: to supplement
doskonały: perfect
dosłowne tłumaczenie: literal
  translation
dostawa: delivery
doświadczenie: experiment,
  experience
dramat: drama
drugi: second
druk(i): print(s), printing(s),
  printed matter
druk gruby: boldface type

druk tajny: clandestine publication
drukarnia: printing house
drukarz: printer
drukowany: printed
drzeworyt(y): woodcut(s)
dublura: *doublure*
duży: large
dwa: two
dwadzieścia: twenty
dwanaście: twelve
dwubarwny: bicolored
dwudziesty: twentieth
dwujęzyczny: bilingual
dwukolorowy: bicolored
dwum. *see* dwumiesięcznik
dwumiesięcznik: bimonthly
dwunastka: duodecimo
dwuroczny: biennial
dwustronny: two-sided
dwuszpaltowy: two-column
dwut. *see* dwutygodnik
dwutygodnik: biweekly
dwutygodniowy: fortnightly
dysertacja: dissertation
dz. *see* dział, dziennik
dział(y): section(s)
dzieje: history, story
dzieło(a): work(s)
dzieło anonimowe: anonymous
  work
dzieło podręczne: reference work
dzień: day
dzien. *see* dziennik
dziennik: daily, diary
dziesiąty: tenth
dziesięć: ten
dziewiąty: ninth
dziewięć: nine
dziewięćdziesiąt(y): ninety(ieth)
dziewiętnaście: nineteen
dziewiętnasty: nineteenth

egz. *see* egzemplarz
egzemplarz(e): copy(ies),
  issue(s)
egzemplarz numerowany: numbered copy
egzemplarz okazowy: sample copy

egzemplarz przepisany na czysto:
  clean copy
ekspert: expert
elegancki: elegant
encyklopedia: encyclopedia
epilog: epilogue
europejski: European

facsimile: facsimile
faktura: invoice
fałszerstwo: forgery
fasc. see fascykuł
fascykuł(y): fascicle(s)
felieton(y): leaflet(s)
fig. see figura
figura(y): table(s), figure(s)
foliacja: foliation
foliał(y): large volume(s), folio(s)
foliant(y): large volume(s),
  folio(s)
folio wielkie: elephant folio
format: size
format bardzo duży: very large
  format
format kieszonkowy: pocket-size
fot. see fotografia
fotografia(e): photograph(s)
fotooffs. see fotooffset
fotooffset: photo-offset
fotostat: photostat
fragment(y): fragment(s)
fragmentaryczny: fragmentary
franco: postpaid
futerał: slipcase, box
futeralik: small slipcase

gazeta(y): newspaper(s)
glansowany: glazed
górny: top, upper
grawiura(y): cut(s), engraving(s)
grubość: thickness
gruby: thick
grzbiet: spine, back of book
guz(y): boss(es)

haftka(i): clasp(s)
hasło: catchword, heading

i inne: and others
i inni: and others
i tak dalej: and so on
identyczny: identical
il. see ilustracja, ilustrowany
ilość stron: number of pages
iluminacja: illumination
ilustr. see ilustracja
ilustracja(e): illustration(s)
ilustrowany: illustrated
imitacja: imitation
indeks: index
indeks ogólny: general index
indeks osób: index of names
indeks przedmiotowy: subject
  index
informacja bibliograficzna: bibliographical information
informator: guide
inicjał(y): initial letter(s)
inicjał ozdobny: ornamental
  initial letter(s)
inkunabuł(y): incunabulum(a)
instytut: institute
introligator: bookbinder
itd. see i tak dalej

jak następuje: as follows
jak nowy: as new
jak powyżej: as above
jasny: light, clear
jeden: one
jedenaście: eleven
jedenasty: eleventh
jednostronny: one-sided
jedyny: only, unique
jesień: Autumn
jeszcze nie wydany: not yet published
język(i): language(s)

k. see karton
k.tyt. see karta tytułowa
kaligrafia: calligraphy
kanwa: canvas
kapitałka: headband
karta(y): leaf(ves), sheet(s)

karta nieliczbowana: unnumbered leaf

karta nienumerowana: unnumbered leaf

karta ochronna: end paper

karta przedtytułowa: half-title page

karta pusta: blank page

karta tytułowa: title page

kartka(i): leaf(ves), sheet(s)

karton: pasteboard

kartusz: cartouche

kaseta: case

katalog(i): catalog(s)

katalog aukcyjny: auction catalog

katalog licytacyjny: auction catalog

każdy: each

kierunek: direction

kilka: several, few

klamra(y): clasp(s)

klasyfikowany: classified

klucz: key

kodeks: codex

kolacjonowany: collation

kolegium redakcyjne: editorial board

kolejny tom: successive volume

kolofon: colophon

kolor(y): color(s)

kolorowany: colored

kolorowy: in color, colored

kolumna(y): column(s)

komedia: comedy

komentarz: commentary

komitet: committee

komitet redakcyjny: editorial committee

kompilacja: compilation

kompilator: compiler

komplet: complete set, complete

koniec: end

konserwacja: state of repair

konsp. *see* konspekt

konspekt: compendium, synopsis

kontynuacja: continuation

kopia: copy

kordyban: cordovan

korekta: proofreading

koźla skóra: buckskin

krajowy: domestic

kratkowany: chequered

krawędź(ie): edge(s)

kronika(i): annals, chronicle(s)

kropkowana linia: dotted line

krótki: short

krótki zbiór: brief collection, compendium

krótkie streszczenie: short summary

krytyczny: critical

krytyka(i): critique(s), review(s)

książeczka: small book, booklet

książka(i): book(s)

książka dla dzieci: children's book

książka nieobcięta: uncut book

książka nieoprawna: unbound book

książka nierozcięta: unopened book

książka niezbroszurowana: book in sheets

książka obcięta: trimmed copy

książka obłożona: book in wrappers

książka podręczna: reference book

książka używana: secondhand book

książka z notatkami: notebook

księga: book, volume

księga adresowa: directory

księga pamiątkowa: commemorative volume

księgarnia: bookshop

księgarz: bookseller

kurs: a course of lectures

kursywa: cursive, italic

kw. *see* kwadratowy, kwartał

kwadratowy: square, rectangular

kwarta: quarto

kwartał: quarter

kwartalnik: quarterly

łącznie: inclusive

łączny: inclusive
lato: Summer
lekko: slightly
lekko uszkodzony: slightly damaged
libra: quire
lichy: poor, shabby
licytacja: auction
liczba stron: number of pages
liczn. *see* liczny
liczny: numerous
linia(e): line(s)
linia ozdobna: fillet
liryka(i): lyric(s)
list(y): letter(s)
literacki: literary
literatura: literature
litografia: lithography
litografowany: lithographed
luksusowy: de luxe
luź.k. *see* luźne kartki
luźne kartki: unstitched sheets, loose leaves

m.in. *see* między innymi
magazyn(y): magazine(s)
mało znany: little-known
malowniczy: picturesque
mały: little, small
manuskrypt(y): manuscript(s)
mapa(y): map(s)
margines(y): margin(s)
margines boczny: outside margin
margines dolny: lower margin, bottom margin
margines górny: head, top margin
margines grzbietowy: inner margin
marmurkowy: marbled
marokin: morocco
maszynopis: typescript copy
materiał archiwalny: archival materials
materiały: sources, materials
miedzioryt(y): copper engraving(s), etching(s)
między innymi: among others
miejsce wydania: place of publication

mies. *see* miesięcznie, miesięcznik
miesięcznie: monthly
miesięcznik: monthly
miniatura: miniature
miniaturowy: miniature
minimalny: minimal
ministerstwo: ministry
mól książkowy: bookworm
monografia(e): monograph(s)
mozaika: mosaic

na: on, upon
na odwrocie: verso, on the back
na prawach rękopisu: manuscript rights
na przykład: for example
na żądanie: upon request
na zamówienie: on request
na zapotrzebowanie: on request
nabyć: to acquire, to purchase
nadbitka: separate, offprint
nadpis: superscription
nadzwyczajny: extraordinary
nagłówek(i): heading(s), headpiece(s)
najniższa cena: lowest price
nakł. *see* nakład
nakład: edition, impression
nakład i druk: published and printed by
nakład ograniczony: limited edition
nakładem własnym: published by author
naklejka(i): label(s)
napis: inscription
naprawione kartki: patched leaves
naprawiony: mended
naprzeciwko tekstu: opposite, facing the text
narodowy: national
narożnik(i): corner(s)
następny: next
następujący: following, consecutive
nauka: science
nazw. *see* nazwisko
nazwa: name

nazwisko: surname
nazwisko przybrane: pen name
netto: net
nie na sprzedaż: not for sale
nie ukazał się: did not appear
nie w tekście: not in the text
niebieski: blue
nieczysty: unexpurgated
niedatowany: undated
niedrogi: inexpensive
niekompletny: incomplete
nieliczbowany: unpaged
nienaruszony: intact, untouched
nienumerowany: unnumbered
nieobcięty: untrimmed
nieokr. *see* nieokreślony
nieokreślony: indefinite
nieoprawny: unbound
nieopublikowany: unpublished
nieponumerowany: unnumbered
nieporozcinany: pages uncut
niesłychanie: extremely
nietknięty: untouched
niewiele: not many, few
niezmiernie: extremely
nieznany: unknown
niezupełny: incomplete,
   imperfect
niżej: below, lower
nkł. *see* nakład
nlb. *see* nieliczbowany
nota bibliograficzna: bibliographical note
nowe wydanie: new edition
nowela(e): story(ies), novel(s)
nowelka(i): short story(ies),
   novella(s)
nowo-odkryty: newly discovered
nowożytny: modern
nr. *see* numer
numer: number, issue
numerowanie: numbering
numerowanie stronic: pagination
nuta(y): music score(s)

ob. *see* obacz
obacz: see
obcięty: trimmed

obejmować: to contain
objaśniający: explanatory
objaśnienie: explanation,
   explanatory notes
obramowanie: frame, border
obramowany: framed
obraz(y): picture(s)
obrazek: small picture
obrazki: small pictures
obszarpany: shabby
obw. *see* obwoluta
obwódka: border
obwoluta: wrapper, book jacket
oceniony: valued
odbitka z czasopisma: reprint
   from a periodical
oddzielny: separate
odnośnie: concerning
odnośnik(i): footnote(s)
odnowiony: restored, renewed
odwr. *see* na odwrocie
oficjalny: official
oficyna: workshop
ogł. *see* ogłoszony
ogłosić: to publish
ogłoszenie: advertisement,
   announcement
ogłoszony: published, announced
ograniczony: limited
okł. *see* okładka
okładka(i): cover(s), wrapper(s)
okładka ślepa: blank cover
okładka wydawnicza: original
   cover
okładzina przednia: front cover
okładzina tylna: back cover
około: about, approximately
oktawo: octavo
opatrzył: supplied, provided
opis: description
opisany: described
opow. *see* opowiadanie
opowiadanie: story, short novel
opowieść(i): story(ies)
opr. *see* oprawa
opr. luks. *see* oprawa luksusowa
opr. skórk. *see* oprawa skórkowa
oprac. *see* opracowane

135

opracowane: prepared, produced
opracowanie(a): work(s)
oprawa: binding
oprawa luksusowa: de luxe
 binding
oprawa miękka: flexible binding
oprawa nakładowa: publisher's
 binding
oprawa ozdobna: decorative
 binding
oprawa pełna: full binding
oprawa pergaminowa: vellum
 binding
oprawa płócienna: cloth binding
oprawa półskórkowa: half-
 leather binding
oprawa skórkowa: leather binding
oprawa skórzana: leather binding
oprawa trzy czwarte: three-
 quarter binding
oprawa w płotno: in cloth binding
oprawa współczesna: contemporary binding
oprawione razem: bound together
oprawiony: bound
opuszczenie(a): omission(s)
opuszczony: omitted
oryg. *see* oryginał
oryginał: original
oryginalny: original
osiem: eight
osiemdziesiąt(y): eighty(ieth)
osiemnaście: eighteen
osiemnasty: eighteenth
ośle uszy: dog-eared
ósmy: eighth
osobliwość(i): rarity(ies)
osobny: separate
ostateczne wydanie: definitive
 edition
ostatni tom: last volume
ozdoba: ornament, decoration
ozdobny: decorated

p. *see* płótno
p.t. *see* pod tytułem
p.z. *see* praca zbiorowa
paginacja: pagination

paginacja ciągła: continuous
 paging
pamiątkowy: commemorative,
 memorial
państwo: state
papier: paper
papier bezdrzewny: wood-free
 paper
papier chiński: China paper
papier glansowany: glazed paper
papier kredowany: coated paper
papier szmaciany: rag paper
papier welinowy: vellum
papier żeberkowany: laid paper
paragraf(y): paragraph(s)
paszkwil(e): lampoon(s), libel(s)
pełne wydanie: complete edition
perg. *see* pergamin
pergamin: parchment
periodyczny: periodical
periodyk: journal, periodical
 publication
piąty: fifth
pięć: five
pięćdziesiąt(y): fifty(ieth)
piękny: beautiful
pierwodruk: *editio princeps*
pierwsze wydanie: first edition
piętnaście: fifteen
piętnasty: fifteenth
pilny: urgent
pisarz: writer
pisemko(a): pamphlet(s)
pismo tygodniowe: weekly
 publication
pł. *see* płótno
plagiat: plagiarism
plama(y): spot(s)
plamy wodne: water spots
plan: plan, layout
plansza(e): plate(s)
pleśń: mildew
płót. *see* płótno
płótno: cloth binding, cloth
płótno do oprawy: book cloth
po słowie: postscript
poczet: list
poczta lotnicza: airmail

poczytny: widely read
pod tyt. *see* pod tytułem
pod tytułem: under the title, entitled
podarty: torn
podkreślony ołówkiem: with pencil underlining
podłużny: oblong
podobizna: likeness, photo
podobizna autografu: facsimile autograph
podpis: signature
podpisany: signed
podr. *see* podręcznik
podrapany: scratched
podręcznik(i): manual(s), textbook(s)
podręcznik(i) uniwersytecki(e): university textbook(s)
podrobiony: falsified, forged
podstawowy: basic
podszyć: lined
podtyt. *see* podtytuł
podtytuł: subtitle
podwójna kopia: duplicate copy
podwójny egzemplarz: duplicate copy
poemat(y): poem(s)
poezja: poetry
pokrowiec: case, container
polityczny: political
półoprawa: half binding
półpergamin: half-vellum binding
półpłótno: half-cloth binding
półr. *see* półrocznik, półroczny
półrocznik: semiannual
półroczny: semiannual
półskórek: half-leather binding
ponowne wydanie: reprint, second edition
poplamiony: spotted, stained
poprawa(y): correction(s)
poprawione i uzupełnione: corrected and supplemented, amended
poprawiony: corrected, revised
poprawka(i): correction(s)
popularny: popular
poradnik: guidebook

porównawczy: comparative
portr. *see* portret
portret(y): portrait(s)
postrzępiony: ragged
poświęcony: dedicated
poszczeg. *see* poszczególny
poszczególny: separate, individual
poszerzony: enlarged
poszukiwany: sought
potwierdzenie: confirmation, approval
powiększony: enlarged, increased
powiel. *see* powielony
powielony: duplicated, reproduced
powieść(i): novel(s)
powieść detektywistyczna: detective story
powyżej: above
powyżej wzmiankowany: above-mentioned, above-cited
poz. *see* pozycja
poza tekstem: not in the text
później: later
pozostały: remaining
pozycja(e): entry(ies), position(s)
płpł. *see* półpłótno
praca(e): work(s)
praca zbiorowa: collective work
prawo przedruku: copyright
prenumerata: subscription
prenumerata kwartalna: quarterly subscription
prenumerata roczna: annual subscription
prenumerować: to subscribe
próbna kopia: specimen copy
próbny egzemplarz: specimen copy
prospekt: prospectus
prospekt wydawnictwa: publication prospectus
proweniencja: provenance
prywatnie drukowany: privately printed
przed: before
przedmiot: subject
przedmowa: preface, introduction
przedpłata: payment in advance
przedr. *see* przedruk

przedruk(i): reprint(s)
przedrukowany: reprinted
przedwojenny: prewar
przedwstępny: preliminary
przegląd(y): review(s)
przejrzane: revised
przekł. *see* przekład
przekład: translation
przerobiony: revised
przerwany: discontinued
przestarzały: obsolete, outdated
przewodnik(i): guide(s),
  directory(ies)
przyczynek: contribution
przygotować: to prepare
przyklejony: glued, pasted on
przypis(y): annotation(s),
  remark(s)
przypisek(ki): footnote(s)
pseudonim: pseudonym
publikacja(e): publication(s)
pytanie: question

r. *see* rok
rabat: discount
raport(y): report(s)
raz na trzy lata: triennial
recenzja(e): review(s)
recto: recto
ręcznie malowany: hand-painted
red. *see* redagowany, redakcja
redagowany: edited
redakcja: editorship, editorial
  office
redaktor: editor
redaktor naczelny: editor in chief
redaktorski: editorial
redaktorstwo: editorship
referat(y): lecture(s)
regularny: regular
rejestr(y): index(es), register(s)
rękopis(y): manuscript(s)
relacja: report, version
reportaż: press report
reprodukcja: reproduction
restauracja: restore, renew
retrospekcyjny: retrospective
rewizja: revision

rocznik: yearbook, annual
  register
roczniki: annals
roczny: yearly
rodz. *see* rodzaj
rodzaj: type
rok: year
rok bieżący: current year
rok wydania: year of publication
ros. *see* rosyjski
rosyjski: Russian
również: also
równoległy tekst: parallel text
rozdział(y): chapter(s), section(s)
rozkaz: order
rozprawa(y): treatise(s)
rozprawa naukowa: dissertation,
  scholarly work
rozprawy: proceedings
rozsprzedany: sold out
rozszerzony: enlarged
rubryka: rubric
rubrykowany: rubricated
ryc. *see* rycina
rycina(y): engraving(s), illus-
  tration(s)
rys. *see* rysunek
rysunek: drawing, sketch
rysunki: drawings, sketches
rytowany: engraved
rzadki: rare
rzadkość: rarity

s. *see* seria, strona, stronica
safian: crushed morocco
ścięgno: bands
sekcja: section
ser. *see* seria
seria: series
setny: hundredth
siedem: seven
siedemdziesiąt(y): seventy(ieth)
siedemnaście: seventeen
siedemnasty: seventeenth
siódmy: seventh
sklep antykwaryczny: antiquarian
  bookshop
skóra: leather

skóra cielęca: calfskin
skóra marokańska: morocco
skóra szagrynowa: shagreen
skorowidz: index, table
skrócenie: abbreviation,
   abridgment
skrócone: abridged
skrót(y): abbreviation(s),
   abridgment(s)
słowniczek: small dictionary
słownik: dictionary
słownik kieszonkowy: pocket
   dictionary
specialny: special
śpiewnik: songbook
spis: list, catalog; index
spis przedmiotowy: subject list
spis rycin: list of illustrations
spis rzeczy: table of contents
spłowiały: faded
spółdzielnia wydawnicza: co-
   operative publishing house
sprawozdania: proceedings
sprawozdanie: report, account
średniowieczny: medieval
staloryt: steel engraving
staranny: elaborate
starodruk: early printed book
statystyczny: statistical
stempel: stamp
sto: hundred
str. see strona
streszcz. see streszczenie
streszczenie: summary
strona(y): page(s)
strona tytułowa: title page
stronica(e): page(s)
strzępiony: deckled
stulecie: century
sucha igła: dry point
światłodruk: photoprint
sygnet drukarski: printer's mark
szagryn: shagreen
szeroki margines: wide margin(s)
sześć: six
sześćdziesiąt(y): sixty(ieth)
szesnaście: sixteen
szesnasty: sixteenth

szkic(e): sketch(es)
szósty: sixth
szp. see szpalta
szpalta(y): column(s)
sztych: engraving
sztycharz: engraver

t. see tom
tab. see tabela
tabela(e): table(s), index(es)
tabl. see tablica
tablica(e): table(s), plate(s)
tablica barwna: table in colors
tani: cheap
targi księgarskie: book fairs
techniczny: technical
teczka(i): small portfolio(s)
teka(i): portfolio(s)
tekst: text
tekstura: black letter
temat(y): theme(s)
teza(y): thesis(es)
tłok: stamp, tool
tłum. see tłumaczenie
tłumacz: translator
tłumaczenie(a): translation(s)
tłumaczenie autoryzowane: authorized translation
tłumaczenie dosłowne: literal
   translation
tłumaczył: translated
tłusty druk: boldface type
tom(y): volume(s)
tom dodatkowy: additional volume
tomik(i): small volume(s)
towarzystwo naukowe: learned
   society
traktat(y): treatise(s)
transliteracja: transliteration
tranzakcje: transactions
treść: contents
trochę uszkodzony: slightly
   damaged
trudny: difficult
trylogia: trilogy
trzeci: third
trzy: three
trzydzieści: thirty

trzydziesty: thirtieth
trzynaście: thirteen
trzynasty: thirteenth
tyg. *see* tygodnik
tygodnik: weekly
tygodniowy: weekly
tylko: only
tylko dla prenumeratorów: for
    subscribers only
tymczasowy: preliminary,
    temporary
typ: type
tysiąc: thousand
tyt. *see* tytuł
tytuł: title
tytuł grzbietowy: title on spine
tytuł nadrzędny: collective title
tytuł okładkowy: cover title
tytuł oryginału: original title
tytuł wstępny: half title

ukazało się drukiem: just
    published
ukaże się niebawem: to be pub-
    lished soon
układ alfabetyczny: alphabetical
    order
ulepszony: improved
ulotka: broadside
umiejętność: knowledge
unikat: unique copy
uniwersytet: university
uprawniony: authorized
urzędowy: official
uszkodzony: damaged, defective
utwór(y): work(s)
uwagi marginesowe: marginal
    notes
uzupełnienie: supplement
uzupełnione: supplemented
używany: used, secondhand

w: in, into
w. *see* wiek
w dobrym stanie: in good condi-
    tion
w doskonałym stanie: in excellent
    condition

w druku: in press
w niektórych miejscach: in some
    places
w prenumeracie: by subscription
w przygotowaniu: in preparation
w rękopisie: in manuscript
w rkpsie. *see* w rękopisie
w sprzedaży: in the book trade
w tekście: in the text
wada: defect
Warszawa: Warsaw
wartość: value
wartościowy: valuable
warunki prenumeraty: conditions
    of subscription
wąski: narrow
ważny: important
według: according to
welin: vellum
wersja: version
wewnątrz: inside
wewnętrzny: inner
wg. *see* według
więcej nie wyszło: no more
    published
wiek: century, age
większość: most, majority
wielobarwny: many-colored
wielu: many
wierzch: top
wierzchni: upper
wilgoć: moisture
winieta(y): vignette(s)
winieta końcowa: tailpiece
winieta tytułowa: headpiece
wiosna: Spring
wkl. *see* wklejka
wkładka(i): insert(s)
wklejka(i): insert(s)
włącznie: inclusive, including
wspaniały: splendid, magnificent
współczesny: contemporary
współudział: participation
wspomnienia: memoirs
wstęp: preface, introduction
wszelkie prawa zastrzeżone: all
    rights reserved
wszystkie prawa zastrzeżone: all

rights reserved
Wwa. *see* Warszawa
wybór: selection
wybór pism: selected works
wybrane prace: selected works
wycisk: tooling, embossing
wycisk ślepy: blind tooling
wycisk złocony: gold tooling
wyczerpany: out-of-print
wyd. *see* wydanie, wydawnictwo
wydać dzieło: to publish
wydanie: edition, printing,
publication
wydanie bezprawne: pirated
edition
wydanie bibliofilskie: bibliophile
edition
wydanie jubileuszowe: jubilee
edition
wydanie kieszonkowe: pocket
edition
wydanie masowe: popular edition
wydanie nowe: new edition
wydanie ocenzurowane: expurgated edition
wydanie ostateczne: definitive
edition
wydanie poprawione: revised
edition
wydanie popularne: popular
edition
wydanie wyczerpane: out-of-print
wydawca: editor, publisher of a
book
wydawnictwo(a): publishing
house(s); publication(s)
wydawnictwo ciągłe: serial
publication
wydawnictwo periodyczne: periodical
wydawnictwo zawieszone: sus-
pended publication
wydawnictwo zeszytowe: book
published in parts
wydawnictwo(a) zwarte: mono-
graph(s)
wydłużony: elongated
wyjątkowy: exceptional

wykaz: list
wykaz alfabetyczny: alphabetical
list
wykład: lecture, reading
wykłady akademickie: series of
academic lectures
wyklejka: end papers
wykr. *see* wykres
wykres(y): diagram(s), graph(s)
wykreślony: crossed out
wyłączny: exclusive
wyłączone ze sprzedaży: not for
sale
wymiana: exchange
wymiar: size
wypukły: embossed
wysortowany: assorted
wysprzedany: sold out
wysprzedaż: sale
wystawa: display, exhibit
wyszukany: extremely elaborate
wzmocniony: reinforced
wznowione: renewed

z: with
z. *see* zbiór, zeszyt
za granicą: abroad
za lata: covering the period
za wyjątkiem: except for
zagadnienia: problems
zagraniczny: foreign
zajmujący: interesting
zakład: establishment, institution
zakończenie: conclusion
zakonserwowany: preserved
zakurzony: dusty
zał. *see* załącznik
załącznik: enclosure, annex
zaliczka: prepayment, advance
payment
zaopatrzył: supplied by
zapiski: short notes
zapowiedzi wydawnicze: publisher's announcements
zarys(y): outline(s), sketch(es)
zarys monograficzny: monographic
study
zasadniczy: fundamental

141

zasięg: scope
zatwierdzono do druku: approved for printing
zawartość: contents
zawiera: contains
zbieracz: collector
zbiór(y): collection(s)
zbroszurowany: stitched in paper covers
zdobnictwo: ornamentation
zepsuty: spoiled, damaged
zestawienie: compilation
zestawił: compiled
zeszyt(y): fascicle(s), part(s), issue(s)
zielony: green
zima: Winter
złamany: broken
złocenie: gilt, gilding
złoto: gold

złożony: folded
zmazany: effaced, rubbed off
zmieniony: changed, altered
znacznie rozszerzony: considerably enlarged
znak(i): mark(s)
znak drukarski: printer's mark
znak(i) wodny(e): watermark(s)
znak wyd. *see* znak wydawnictwa
znak wydawnictwa: publisher's mark (trade-mark)
znany: known
znawca: expert
zniszczony: damaged, destroyed
żółte plamy: yellow stains
źródło: source
zsumowanie: summary
zt. *see* zeszyt
zwięzły: concise
zwykły: ordinary, usual

142

PORTUGUESE

a cabeça: at the head
a côres: in colors
a duas colunas: in two-column
  format
à ferros secos: blind tooling
à frente: opposite, facing
a maneira de: in the manner of
à mão: by hand
a melhor: the best
a negro: in black
a ofertas: subject to offers
à parte: apart
à pena: by pen
a sêco: blind tooling
à tinta: in ink
à venda: for sale
aberta a buril: worked by tool
aberto: open; engraved
acabado: finished, completed
acêrca de: concerning
acima: above
aço: steel
acompanha: accompanies
acontecimento(s): event(s)
acrescentado: enlarged
actualizado: brought up to date,
  modernized
adapt. *see* adaptação
adaptação: adaptation
adornado: adorned

adôrno: ornament
afora: excluding, except
agua-forte(s): etching(s)
agua-tinta(s): aquatint(s)
aguarela(s): water color(s)
aguarelado: colored with water
  colors
ainda: still, yet
alegórico: allegorical
além de: in addition to, beyond
alg. *see* algumas
algodão: cotton
algumas: some
aliás: otherwise
alto: high, height
amador *see* encadernação amador
amarelejado: yellowed
amarelo: yellow
ambas as pastas: both covers
ambos os lados: both sides
amp. *see* ampliação
ampliação: enlargement
ampliado: enlarged
anais: annals, chronicles
anal: annual
anexo(s): annex(es), supplement(s)
ângulo(s): corner(s)
annotado: annotated
ano: year
anônimo: anonymous

143

anotação(ões): annotation(s)
anotado: annotated
ante-rosto: frontispiece; half-
title page
anterior: front, former
antigo: old, antique
antiguidades: antiquities
antologia: anthology
anual: annual, yearly
anuário: yearbook
aparado: trimmed
aparar *see* por aparar
aparatoso: magnificent, ornate
aparte: not in the text
apenas: scarcely, only
apêndice(s): appendix(es)
apenso: added, appended
aperfeiçoado: perfected
apostilha(s): marginal note(s)
apreciado: valued
aprêço *see* de aprêço
apresentação: presentation,
appearance
armoreado: decorated with
coats of arms
arrancado: torn out
artigo(s): article(s)
artístico: artistic
aspecto: aspect, condition
ass. *see* assinado
assaz: very
asseado: clean
assetinado: with satin finish
assin. *see* assinatura
assinado: signed
assinante(s): subscriber(s)
assinat. *see* assinatura
assinatura: signature; subscription
assunto: subject
atinge: touches, affects
atingido: lightly damaged
atribuido: attributed
atribuindo: attributing
atual. *see* atualizado
atualizado: brought up to date
aum. *see* aumentado
aumentado: enlarged, increased

aumento: increase
autenticar: to authenticate
autêntico: authentic
autografado: autographed
autógrafo: autograph; autographic
autor: author
autoria: authorship
avaria: damage
avariado: damaged
avulso: separate, loose
azul: blue

b. *see* bom, brochura
baixo: bottom, lower
baixo-relêvo: bas-relief
bast. *see* bastante
bastante: rather, sufficiently
belamente: beautifully
beleza: beauty
belíssimo: most beautiful
belo: beautiful
bem acabado: well-finished
bem tratado: well-kept
bibl. *see* biblioteca
bibliografia: bibliography
bibliográfico: bibliographic
biblioteca: library
bibliotecário: librarian
biografado: biographee
biografia: biography
biográfico: biographical
boa: good
boletim: bulletin
bôlsa: pocket
bom: good
bonito: pretty
borda(s): border(s)
borrado: erased
br. *see* brochado, brochura
branco: blank, white
brasão(ões): coat(s) of arms
broch. *see* brochado, brochura
brochado: stitched in paper covers
brochura: pamphlet, pamphlet-
style binding
brunido: burnished
buril: graver
buscado: sought, wanted

cabeça: head
cabeçal: vignette at top of page
cabeçalho: title page; heading
cabeção(ões): headpiece(s),
    vignette(s)
cabeceira(s): headband(s)
cada: each
caderninho(s): small copybook(s)
caderno(s): quire(s), signature(s);
    notebook(s)
caixa: case, box
caixa de proteção: protective box
caixa protectora: protective box
caligrafia: handwriting
cansado: worn-out
canto(s): corner(s)
capa(s): cover(s)
capa de resguardo: protective
    cover
capital(ães): capital letter(s)
capitular(es): initial letter(s) of
    chapter(s)
capítulo(s): chapter(s)
caracteres góticos: gothic letters
característico: typical
carecendo: lacking
carecente: lacking
caricatura: caricature
caricaturista: caricaturist
carimbo: rubber stamp, seal
carn. see carneira
carneira: sheepskin
cart. see cartonado
cartolina: light cardboard
cartonado: bound in boards
cartonador: bookbinder
cartonagem: cardboard box,
    carton; binding
cartonagem do editor: publish-
    er's binding
casa editôra: publishing house
castanho: chestnut-colored
cat. see catálogo
catálogo: catalog
catorze: fourteen
célebre: famous
cem: hundred
censura: censorship

centena(s): hundred(s)
centésimo: hundredth
centímetros: centimeters
centro: center
cerca de: near, about
cercadura(s): panel(s)
chapa: plate
chapa de aço: steel engraved plate
chapa de cobre: copper engraved
    plate
chapa de madeira: wood block
chapa de metal: metal engraved
    plate
charneira: joint
cheia: excess, abundance
cinco: five
cinzento: gray
circundado: encircled
citado: cited
claro: clear
clássico: classic
cm. see centímetros
co-autor: joint author
cobre: copper
códice: codex
coetâneo: contemporary
coevo: contemporary
coiro: leather
col. see coleção
colaboração: collaboration
colação: collation
colado: glued
coleção(ões): series, set(s)
coleção de livros: set of books
colecionador: collector
coletânea: collection
coligido: compiled, collected
colocado: placed
colofão: colophon
colorado: reddish color
colorido: color, coloring
cols. see colunas
coluna(s): column(s)
com cantos: with corners
com falta de: lacking
começando: beginning
comentário(s): commentary(ies)
como novo: as new

145

comp. *see* compilado
compilação: compilation
compilado: compiled
compilador: compiler
completo: complete
completo de margens: with full
  margins, untrimmed
composto: composed, made
compre(h)endido: included
comum: common
concluido: concluded
concordância: concordance
condicionado: prepared for
confeccionado: executed,
  compiled
conhecido: known
conhecimento: knowledge
conjunto com: together with
conserva: retains
conservação: conservation
conservado: retained
conservando: conserving,
  preserving
constituido: constituted
contemporâneo: contemporary
conteúdo: contents
continuação: continuation
contra: against
contrafação: forgery, imitation
cópia: copy, imitation
cópia figurada: facsimile copy
copiosamente: copiously
côr(es): color(s)
coroado: awarded a prize;
  completed
correcção(ões): correction(s)
correcto: correct
correição(ões): correction(s)
correto: correct
corrigido: corrected
cortado: cut, trimmed
corte: cut, incision
cortes: edges
cosedura: stitching
cotado: quoted, priced
couché: coated, glazed
couro: leather
couro de bezerra: calfskin

creme: cream-colored
crítico: critical, in bad state
crônica: chronicle
crônicas: annals
cuidado: careful, considered
cuidadosamente: carefully
curioso: curious, rare

da frente: front, of the front
dactilografado: typewritten
danificado: damaged
data: date
de aprêço: valuable
de consulta: for research
de grande estimação: highly
  esteemed
decimo: tenth
decimo nono: nineteenth
decimo oitavo: eighteenth
decimo quarto: fourteenth
decimo quinto: fifteenth
decimo setimo: seventeenth
decimo sexto: sixteenth
decimo terceiro: thirteenth
decorado: decorated
decorativo: decorative
ded. *see* dedicatória
dedicatória: dedication note
def. *see* defeito
defectivo: defective
defeito(s): defect(s)
defeituoso: defective
defendido: protected; prohibited
definitivo: definitive
delgado: thin
demais: besides
demasia: excess, too much
demasiadamente: excessively
dentro: within
des. *see* desdobrável, desenho
descolorido: faded
desconhecido: unknown
desconjuntado: unstitched,
  loosened
descontinuado: discontinued
descosido: unstitched
descrição: description
descripção: description

descritivo: descriptive
desdobr. *see* desdobrável
desdobrar: to unfold
desdobrável: unfolding
desencad. *see* desencadernado
desencadernado: unstitched,
  covers gone
desenhado: designed
desenho(s): sketch(es), design(s)
destruido: destroyed
deteriorado: deteriorated
detrás: in back, behind
deveras: truly
dez: ten
dezena(s): ten(s)
dezenove: nineteen
dezesseis: sixteen
dezessete: seventeen
dezoito: eighteen
difícilmente: with difficulty
dimensões: dimensions
direção: direction, supervision
direito: right-hand
direitos autorais: author's
  copyright
dirigido: directed
disperso: scattered
dissertação(ões): dissertation(s)
distribuido: distributed
dobrado: folded
dobrável: folding, folded
dobre: double
documentado: documented
documento(s): document(s)
dois: two
douração: gilding, gold decoration
dourado: gilt, decorated with gold
dourado por fôlhas: gilt edges
dourados: gold designs
doze: twelve
duas: two
duodecimo: twelfth
dupla página: double page
duvidoso: doubtful, dubious

e. *see* encadernação, encadernado
ed. *see* edição

edição(ões): edition(s)
edição esgotada: out of print
edição limitada: limited edition
edição primitiva: first edition
edição príncepe: first edition
edição romântica: edition in
  romantic format
edição vulgar: ordinary edition
editado: edited
editor: publisher
editôra: publishing house
elegante: elegant
elevado: high
em breve: soon
em contrapartida: in offset
em data próxima: at an early date
em demasia: excessive
em diante: forward, following
em enteira: full binding
em extra-texto: not in the text
em grande papel: on large paper
em página enteira: in full page
em papel: in sheets
em separado: not in the text
em tôda a volta: on all sides, all
  around
emblema: emblem
embora: though, even
embutido: inlaid, inlay; mosaic
emenda(s): emendation(s)
emendado: emended
em(m)oldurado: framed, bordered
empastado: bound in boards
empregado: used
enc. *see* encadernação,
  encadernado
enc. da época. *see* encadernação
  da época
encad. *see* encadernação,
  encadernado
encadernação(ões): binding
encadernação amador: three-
  quarter binding
encadernação característica: usual
  binding, characteristic binding
encadernação da época: contemporary binding
encadernação de amador: three-

147

quarter binding
encadernação de editor: publisher's binding
encadernação do tempo: contemporary binding
encadernação vulgar: common binding
encadernado: bound
encadernador: binder
encerra: includes
encimado: above, surmounted by
encorpado: thick, heavy; solid
enegrecido: darkened
enfeite(s): ornament(s)
enquadrado: framed
enriquecido: enriched, adorned
enrugado: wrinkled
ensaio: essay
entre o texto: within the text
enumerado: enumerated, enumerative
envernizado: glossy, coated
enxovalhado: dirty, soiled
epígrafe: inscription
epílogo: epilogue, postface
época: time period, epoch
errado: erroneous
êrro(s): mistake(s)
erudição: erudition
esbôço: draft, rough outline
esclarecimento(s): explanation(s), explanatory note(s)
escolhido: selected
escrito(s): writing(s)
escritor(es): writer(s)
escuro: dark
esfolado: scratched, abraded
esfoladura(s): abraded spot(s)
esfumado: tinted, shaded
esgotado: exhausted, out-of-print
esmaltado: embellished; enameled
esmeradamente: perfectly
esmerado: perfect
espalhado: scattered
especial: special
especialidade: specialty
espécimen: sample

espelhado: polished, smooth
espessura: thickness
esplendido: splendid
esquadria: right angle
est. *see* estampa
estado: condition
estado de novo: as new
estalado: split
estampa: print, engraving
estilo: style
estimação: esteem, value
estimado: valuable
estôjo: box, case
estragado: deteriorated, damaged
estrangeiro: foreign
estreito: narrow
estropiado: mutilated
estudo(s): study(ies)
etiquêta: label
ex. *see* exemplar
ex-libris: *ex libris*
exausto: exhausted
excluido: excluded
excluindo: excluding
execução: execution
executado: executed
exemplar(es): copy(ies)
existente: existing
expl. *see* exemplar
expungido: expunged, deleted
expurgado: expurgated
extra-texto *see* em extra-texto
extraido: extracted
extremo: extreme

f. *see* fôlha
fac-símile(s): facsimile(s)
facs. *see* fac-símiles
facsimilado: reproduced in facsimile
factício: factitious, imitation
falha: break, split; defect
falsamente: falsely
falso: fake
falta: defect; lacks
fasc. *see* fascículo
fascículo: fascicule, part
fecho(s): clasp(s)

ferro(s): tooled design(s)
ferros do romantismo: tooling in the romantic style
ferros secos *see* à ferros secos
ff. *see* fôlhas
figura(s): chart(s): figure(s)
figurinha(s): small chart(s), figure(s)
filête(s): fillet(s)
filigrana: watermark
fim: end
final(aes): tailpiece(s)
fino: fine, thin
fl. *see* fôlha
flht. *see* folheto
florão(ões): floral design(s)
fol. *see* fôlha
fôlha(s): leaf(ves), sheet(s)
fôlha dupla: double page
folheto(s): pamphlet(s)
fólio: folio
fonte(s): source(s)
fora de dúvida: without doubt
fora de texto: not in the text
fora do comércio: not for sale
fora do mercado: not for general sale, privately printed
forma: form
formato: format
formosíssimo: very beautiful
formoso: beautiful
foto(s): photograph(s)
fotocópia: photocopy
fotogravura(s): photoengraving(s)
fotóstato: photostat
fotozincogravura: photozincography
fragmento(s): fragment(s)
frente a: facing
freqüente: frequent
frescura: freshness
friso: frieze
front. *see* frontispício
frontispício: frontispiece
fundido: molded
fundo: background
furo(s): hole(s)
furo de traça: wormhole

g. *see* grande
galante: gallant
gasto: worn-out
geografico: geographic
glosa(s): gloss(es), note(s)
glossário: glossary
gôsto: taste
gr. *see* grande
gráf. *see* gráfico
gráfico: graphic
grande: large
granido: stippled
gratuito: free
grav. *see* gravura
gravado: engraved
gravador: engraver
gravura(s): engraving(s)
gravura(s) a água forte: etching(s)
gravura(s) em madeira: woodcut(s)
gravurinha(s): small engraving(s)
grosseiramente: grossly, coarsely
grosso: thick, voluminous
grossura: thickness
guarda(s): end paper(s)
guarda(s) de seda: silk lining(s)

heliográfico: engraved
heliogravura(s): engraving(s)
heliótipo: heliotype, photoengraving

igual: equal, similar
il. *see* ilustrado, ilustrador
iluminado: illuminated
iluminura(s): illumination, illuminated page(s)
ilustr. *see* ilustração, ilustrado
ilustração(ões): illustration(s)
ilustrado: illustrated
ilustrador: illustrator
imaculado: immaculate
imitação: imitation, copy
imitando: imitating
imp. *see* impresso
impecável: impeccable
imprensa: press, printing plant
impressão(ões): printing(s)
impresso: printed; pamphlet

impressor: printer
impressos: printed matter
incluído: included
incontestável: incontestable
incunábulo(s): incunabulum(a)
ind. *see* indicação
indicação: indication
índice(s): index(es)
indispensável: indispensable
inédito: unpublished
In-F. *see* infólio
inferior: lower
infólio: in folio format, folio
informação: information
inicial(aes): initial letter(s)
inscrição: inscription
inscripção: inscription
inserto: inserted
int. de pele *see* inteira de pele
intacto: intact, undamaged
intacto de margens: with full
  margins
integral: complete
inteira de pele: full leather
inteira de pele de carneira: full
  sheepskin
inteira de pelica inglesa: full kid
  leather
inteira de pergaminho: full vellum
inteira de vitela: full calf
inteiramente: entirely
inteiro: full, whole
intercalado: intercalated
interessante: interesting,
  attractive
interessantíssimo: most interesting, attractive
interior: inner, interior
interiormente: internally
interpretação: interpretation
intitulado: entitled
intrínseco: intrinsic
inum. *see* inumerado
inumerado(s): unnumbered
inúmero: innumerable

já: now, already
jóia: jewel
150

jornal: newspaper
juntamente: together
junto: together

l. *see* lugar
lacre: sealing wax
lado: side
lado a lado: parallel
lápis: pencil
largamente: largely, generously
largura: width
lavado: washed
ldo. *see* limitado
letra(s): letter(s), type
letra(s) capitular(es): chapter-
  heading letter(s)
letra gótica: gothic type
letra(s) inicial(aes): initial
  letter(s)
letra(s) maiúscula(s): capital
  letter(s)
letra(s) minúscula(s): lower-case
  letter(s)
leve: slight, light
levemente: slightly
léxico: lexicon, dictionary
libelo infamatório: lampoon
licença(s): authorization(s),
  license(s)
ligeiramente: slightly
ligeiro: light, slight
liminar: preliminary
limitado: limited
limpado: cleaned
limpo: neat, clear
lindo: attractive
linho: linen
liso: smooth
lista: list
lito(s): lithograph(s)
litografado: lithographed
litografia(s): lithograph(s),
  lithography
litográfico: lithographic
liv. *see* livraria
livraria: bookshop
livreiro: bookseller
livrete: small book
livrinho: small book

livro: book
local: place
local de impressão: place of
  printing
lombada: back of a book, spine
lona: canvas
lote: lot
lug. *see* lugar
lugar: place
lugar de impressão: place of
  printing
luxuosamente: luxuriously
luxuoso: de luxe, luxurious

má: bad
maculado: spotted
madeira: wood
magnifíco: magnificent
maior formato: large format
maioria: majority
mais: plus, more
mais encorpado: thicker
maiúsculo(s): capital letter(s)
mal: badly
maleável: flexible
mancha: spot, stain
mancha(s) de agua: water stain(s)
mancha(s) de umidade: moisture
  stain(s)
manchado: spotted, stained
manchado de umidade: damp-
  stained
manuscrito: manuscript
mapa: map
mar. *see* marroquim
marca(s): mark(s)
marfim: ivory
margem(ens): margin(s),
  border(s)
marmoreado: marbled
marroquim: morocco
mau: bad
máx. *see* máxima
máxima: very large
medalhão: medallion
medíocre: mediocre
meio: half
meio de chagrin: half-morocco
  binding

melh. *see* melhorado
melhor: better
melhorado: improved
melhoramento(s): improvement(s)
mensal: monthly
mercado: market, trade
merecimento: merit, worth
mesmo: same
mil: thousand
milhar(es): thousand(s)
miniatura: miniature
minuciosamente: minutely
miscelânea: miscellany
moderno: modern
modificação: modification
moldura: frame, molding
monografia: monograph
monográfico: monographic
monograma: monogram
monumental: monumental
mosaico: mosaic
ms. *see* manuscrito
mto. *see* muito
muitíssimo: very much
muito(s): much; numerous
muito procura: eagerly sought
multicolor: varicolored
mus. *see* música
música: music
mutilado: mutilated

não cortado: uncut, unopened
não vulgar: not common
negro: black
nem: nor
nenhum: any, none
nervos: (raised) bands
nítidamente: neatly, clearly
nítido: neat, clear
no mercado: in the trade, available
no prelo: in press
no texto: in the text
nome: name
nonagesimo: ninetieth
nono: ninth
notas: notes
notas marginães: marginal notes
notável: notable
notícias: news, announcement

nove: nine
novo: new
numeração: numbering
numerado(s): numbered
número(s): number(s)
numerosíssimos: in great
  numbers
numeroso(s): numerous
numes. see numerados
nums. see numerados
nunca: never

oblongo: oblong
obra(s): work(s)
obra espúria: spurious work
observações: observations
octagesimo: eightieth
of. see oficina
ofertas see a ofertas
ofic. see oficina
oficina: shop, print shop
oitavo: eighth
oito: eight
onomastico: onomastic
onze: eleven
op. see opúsculo
ops. see opúsculos
óptimo: the best, the finest
opúsculo(s): small work(s)
org. see organizado
organizado: organized
original(aes): original(s)
orla: border, edge
orlado: bordered
ornado: decorated, adorned
ornamentação: decoration
ornamentado: decorated
ornato: decorated, adorned
ostentando: showing
ótimo: the best, the finest
ouro: gold

p. see página
padrão(ões): pattern(s)
pág. see página
página(s): page(s)
página de rôsto: title page
paginação: pagination
paginação seguida: continuous
152

paging
págs. see páginas
pano: cloth
papel: paper
papel assetinado: glazed paper
papel avergoado: laid paper
papel comum: common paper
papel couché: coated paper, art
  paper
papel de algodão: rag paper
papel de linho: linen paper
papel de pergaminho: parchment
  paper
papel extra: extra-quality paper
papel Japão: Japan paper
papel pergaminho: parchment
  paper
papel velino: vellum paper,
  parchment
para cima de: more than
paragrafo: paragraph
parte(s): part(s)
pé: foot, bottom
peça(s): piece(s), part(s)
pedaço(s): piece(s)
pele: skin, leather
pen(n)a: pen
penúltimo: next to last
peq. see pequeno
pequeno: small
perc. see percalina
percal: percale
percalina: percaline
perda de têxto: loss of text
perfeito: perfect
perg. see pergaminho
pergaminho: parchment
pergaminho vegetal: parchment
  paper
pergaminho velino: vellum
periódico: periodical
perito: expert
pesado: heavy
picado: wormholed, perforated
pico(s) de traça: wormhole(s)
pintado: colored
pleno: full
pobre: poor
polêmica: polemic

policromia: polychrome
polvoroso: dusty
por abrir: pages uncut
por aparar: pages uncut
por fôlhas: in sheets
porém: still, yet, however
pormenorizadamente: in detail
porta-fólio: portfolio
porte pago: postpaid
posterior: later, subsequent
póstumo: posthumous
pouco: little
pouco comum: uncommon
pouco frequente: rare
pouco vulgar: uncommon
pouquíssimo: very few
prancha(s): plate(s)
prec. see preciso
preciosidade: preciousness
precioso: precious, costly
preciso: necessary; exact, distinct
preço: price
pref. see prefação
prefação: preface
prefaciado: prefaced
prefaciador: writer of preface
prefácio: preface, foreword
preferível: preferable
prega: fold
prejudicado: damaged, injured
prejuízo: damage, injury
prel. see preliminar
preliminar(es): preliminary
  page(s)
prelo: printing press
prels. see preliminares
premiado: prize-winning
prêto: black
prezado: prized, esteemed
primeiro: first
primitivo: original
primoroso: first-class, excellent
princípio: beginning, front
processo: process
procura: sought, in demand
procurado: sought, searched for
profusamente: profusely
prólogo: prologue

próprio: own; fitting, exact
prova: proof
pseud. see pseudônimo
pseudônimo: pseudonym,
  pseudonymous
publicação(ões): publication(s)
publicado: published

quadro: picture
qualidade: quality
quanto possível: as much as
  possible
quarentesimo: fortieth
quarto: fourth; quarto
quatro: four
quinquagesimo: fiftieth
quinto: fifth
quinze: fifteen

rareando: becoming rare
raridade: rarity
raríssimo: very rare
raro: rare
rascadura: scratch, abrasion
rascunho: draft, outline
rasgado: torn, ripped
rasgão(ões): tear(s)
raspado: scratched, erased
rasurado: scraped
realização: presentation, format
recolhido: collected
recopilação: compilation
recortado: cut out
redação: editing
redator: editor
reduzido: reduced
reedição: re-editing
reeditado: re-edited
ref. see refundido
reforçado: reinforced
refundido: recast
registo: index
registro: index
relação(ões): story(ies), report(s);
  list(s)
relevado: embossed
rematado: finished off
remate: finishing, final touch
repleto: replete

reprodução(ões): reproduction(s)
reproduzindo: reproducing
resguardo: protective cover
restante: remainder
restauração: repair
restaurado: restored
restauro: restoration
restituido: restored
restrito: limited
resumo: abstract
ret. *see* retrato
retocado: improved; retouched
retrato: portrait
rev. *see* revisão, revista
revestido: provided with
revisado: revised
revisão(ões): revision(s)
revista: review, journal
revisto: reviewed, revised
ricamente: richly
roçado: rubbed, worn away
rompimento: break
rôsto: title page, frontispiece
rôto: torn
rotogravura: rotogravure
rótulo: label, inscription
roxo: purple
rúbrica: rubric, flourish
rubricado: rubricated

s. *see* sem
s.d. *see* sem data
s.d. de impressão *see* sem data
  de impressão
s.ed. *see* sem editôra
s.l.n.d. *see* sem lugar nem data
s.lugar *see* sem lugar
saído: appeared
salpicado: sprinkled
sanguíneo: blood-colored
sátira: satire, lampoon
se(c)ção: section
sêco *see* a sêco
seguidamente: in succession
seguido de: followed by
seguinte(s): following
segundo: according to; second
seis: six
sele(c)ção: selection

sêlo: seal, stamp
sem: without
sem data: without date
sem data de impressão: without
  date of publication
sem data nem local: without date
  or place
sem editôra: without publisher
sem ferir o texto: without damaging the text
sem lugar: without place
sem lugar nem data: without place
  or date
sem mancha: spotless
sem numeração: unnumbered
sem o nome do autor: without the
  author's name
sem ofenso do texto: without
  touching the text
sem prejuízo do texto: without
  touching the text
sem valor: without value
semelhante: resembling, similar
sep. *see* separata
separata: separate, reprint
septuagesimo: seventieth
ser. *see* série
série: series
sete: seven
sétimo: seventh
sexagesimo: sixtieth
sexto: sixth
simili-gravura: halftone engraving
simplificado: simplified
só: sole, only
sob: under
soberbo: superb
sobre: on, upon
sóbrio: modest, discreet
sofrido: suffered
solicitado: requested
sôlto: loose
sômente: only
sortido(s): assorted
sumário: summary
super-libros: ownership stamp
superior: upper; better
suplementar(es): supplementary
suplemento: supplement

suposto: imaginary, supposed
supresso: suppressed

t. *see* tomo
tabela: table, index
tábua(s): table(s)
talhe doce: *taille-douce*
talvez: perhaps
tamanho: size
tarja: black border design;
   ornamental painted border
tarjado: bordered in black;
   with ornamental border
tecido: cloth
tela: cloth
tela alemã: German cloth
terceiro: third
texto: text
tip. *see* tipografia
tipo: type, type face
tipo graúdo: huge type
tipocromia: color printing
tipografia: typography
tipográfico: typographic
tiragem: edition, printing
tiragem especial: special
   printing
tiragem limitada: limited edition
tiragem reducida: limited edition
tiragem restrita: limited edition
tiragem vulgar: ordinary edition
título: title, title page
tôda a volta: all edges
todas as margens: full margins
todos os lugares: everywhere
tomo: tome
tôpo: top
trabalhado: tooled, worked
trabalho: work
traça(s): worm(s)
traçado: wormholed
trad. *see* tradução, tradutor
tradução: translation
tradutor: translator
traduzido: translated
transposto: transposed
tratado: treated
três: three
treze: thirteen

tricromia: three-color printing
trigesimo: thirtieth
trocado: exchanged, out of place;
   replaced by
truncado: truncated
tudo: everything, all
tudo quanto se publicou: all published until now

último: last
um: one
uma: one
umidade: humidity, moisture
undecimo: eleventh
únicamente: solely
único: unique, sole
usado: worn, secondhand
útil: useful
utilidade: utility
utilizado: utilized

v. *see* volume
valiosíssimo: extremely valuable
valioso: worthy, important
valor: value
valorisado: enhanced in value
variadíssimo: extremely varied
variante: variant
várias: various, several
vastíssimo: very vast
verdadeiro: true
verde: green
verde-escuro: dark green
verificado: verified
vermelho: red
versão: version, translation
verso: verso
vestígio(s): trace(s)
vigésimo: twentieth
vinheta: vignette
vinte: twenty
vista: view, panorama
vitela: calf
vocábulo(s): word(s)
vol. *see* volume
volume: volume
vulgar: common, ordinary

xilogravura(s): woodcut(s)

RUSSIAN ALPHABET

А	а		Р	р
Б	б		С	с
В	в		Т	т
Г	г		У	у
Д	д		Ф	ф
Е	е		Х	х
Ё	ё		Ц	ц
Ж	ж		Ч	ч
З	з		Ш	ш
И	и		Щ	щ
Й	й		Ъ	ъ
К	к		Ы	ы
Л	л		Ь	ь
М	м		Э	э
Н	н		Ю	ю
О	о		Я	я
П	п			

RUSSIAN

А.Н. *see* Академия наук

абзац(ы): paragraph(s), indent(s), break(s)

абон. *see* абонент

абонем. *see* абонемент

абонемент: subscription; loan (libraries)

абонент(ы): subscriber(s)

авиапочта: airmail

авт. *see* автор

авт. не указан *see* автор не указан

автобиог. *see* автобиографический

автобиографический: autobiographical

автограф(ы): autograph(s)

автор(а): author(s)

автор не указан: no author, author not indicated

автореферат: author's abstract

авториз. *see* авторизованный

авторизованный: authorized

авторитетный: authoritative

авторский указатель: author index

авторское право: copyright

автотипия: autotype, halftone engraving

адрес: address

Ак. Н. *see* Академия наук

Ак. Нк. *see* Академия наук

Акад., акад. *see* академия

Акад. наук *see* Академия наук

академический: academic

академия(и): academy(ies)

Академия наук: academy of sciences

акварель: water color

акватинта: aquatint

алфавитный каталог: alphabetic catalog

алфавитный список: alphabetic list, register

алфавитный указатель: alphabetic index

альб. *see* альбом

альбом(ы): album(s)

альбом иллюстраций: album of illustrations

альбомный формат: oblong format

амер. *see* американский

американский: American

аналитич. *see* аналитический

аналитический: analytical

анастатический: anastatic

анг. *see* английский

английский: English

анналы: annals, chronicles

аннотация(и): annotation(s), note(s), commentary(ies)

анонимные произведения: anonymous works

анонимный: anonymous

антикварный: secondhand, used
антикварный магазин: antiquarian
 bookstore
антикварный рынок: antiquarian market
антология(и): anthology (ies)
аппретированный холст: buckram
арабеска: arabesque
архив(ы): archive (s)
атлас(ы): atlas(es)
аукцион(ы): auction(s), sale (s)
аутентичный: authentic

б. *see* без, большой, брошюра,
 буква
б–ва *see* буква
б.г. *see* без года
б.г.п. *see* без года печатания, без
 года публикации
Б. загл. листа *see* без заглавного
 листа
б–ка *see* библиотека
б.л. *see* большие листы
Б.м. и г.п. *see* без места и года
 публикации
Б.о.м. и г.п. *see* без обозначения
 места и года публикации
Б.у.м. и г.п. *see* без указания места
 и года публикации
б.ф. *see* большой формат
б–фия *see* библиография
б.ц. *see* без цены
б–чка *see* библиотечка
баранья кожа: sheepskin
бархатный: velvet
без: without
без года: no date
без года печатания: without date of
 printing
без года публикации: no publishing
 date
без заглавного листа: without title
 page
без задатка: without deposit, no advance payment
без места: no place
без места и года публикации: no
 place or date of publication

без обозначения места и года публикации: without indication of place
 or date of publication
без пер. *see* без переплёта
без переплёта: unbound
без пересылки: shipping charge not
 included, without shipping charge
без тит.л. и обл. *see* без титульного
 листа и обложки
без титульного листа и обложки: without title page and cover
без указания места и года публикации:
 no place or date of publication
без цены: no price, price not indicated
беллетристика: fiction
бескрасочное тиснение: blind tooling
беспл. *see* бесплатно
бесплатная доставка: free delivery
бесплатно: free of charge, gratis
бесценный: priceless
библ. *see* библиографический, библиотечный
библ. очерк *see* библиографический
 очерк
библ. указатель *see* библиографический указатель
библ. штемп. на загл. *see* библиотечный
 штемпель на заглавии
библиогр. *see* библиограф, библиографический
библиограф(ы): bibliographer(s)
библиограф. *see* библиографический
библиографическая(ие) редкость(и):
 bibliographical rarity (ies)
библиографический: bibliographical
библиографический(ие) очерк(и): bibliographic survey (s)
библиографический(ие) указатель(и):
 bibliographical index(es)
библиография(и): bibliography (ies)
библиотека(и): library (ies)
библиотекарь(и): librarian(s)
библиотечка(и): small library (ies);
 small series
библиотечная марка: *ex libris*, bookplate
библиотечная скидка: library discount
библиотечный: of or pertaining to the
 library

библиотечный знак: *ex libris,* bookplate

библиотечный штемпель на заглавии: library stamp on the title page

библиофил(ы): bibliophile(s), booklover(s); amateur collector (s)

бинт(ы): raised band(s)

биогр. *see* биографический

биографический: biographical

биография(и): biography(ies)

блекнувший: faded

блокнот(ы): notebook (s)

богато иллюс. *see* богато иллюстрированный

богато иллюстрированный: well-illustrated, many illustrations

более не выходило: no more published

более не издано: no more published, issued

большие листы: large leaves, pages, sheets

большой: big, large

большой формат: large size

бордюр(ы): border (s), ornamental border (s), edge(s)

брайлевская печать: Braille

бронзированный: bronzed

брошюра(ы): brochure(s), pamphlet(s), opuscule (s)

брошюрованный: sewed, stitched

буква(ы): letter (s)

буквально: literally

бум. л. *see* бумажный лист

бумага: paper

бумажная обложка: paper cover

бумажный(ые) лист(ы): sheet(s), signature(s)

бумажный переплёт: paperbound

бюлл. *see* бюллетень

бюллетень(и): bulletin (s)

в: in, into

в. *see* век

в вып. дан. *see* в выпускных данных

в выпускных данных: included in imprint

в красках: in color

в начале: at the beginning

в некоторых местах: in some places

в о.б.л. *see* в очень больших листах

в обложке: paperbound

в одн. пер. *see* в одном переплёте

в одн. т. *see* в одном томе

в одном переплёте: bound together

в одном томе: in one volume

в отличной сохранности: excellently preserved

в отличном состоянии: in excellent condition

в оч. б.л. *see* в очень больших листах

в очень больших листах: in very large leaves

в папке: in pasteboard case

в пер. *see* в переплёте

в перепл. *see* в переплёте

в переплёте: bound

в печати: in press, at the printer's

в полном виде: complete set, edition

в полях: on margins

в портфолио: in portfolio

в продаже: in the book trade, book market

в пятнах: stained

в столбцах: in columns

в т.ч. *see* в том числе

в том числе: including, inclusively

в хорошем состоянии: in good condition

вв. *see* века

введение: introduction, preface, foreword

вводная статья: introductory article

век(а): century(ies)

велен. *see* веленевый

веленевый: vellum

великолепно сохранено: in excellent condition

вероятная цена: approximate price

верхний: upper, top

весна: Spring

вестник: review

весьма: extremely

виньетка: vignette

вкл. *see* вкладка, включая, включительно

вкладка: supplementary sheet, insertion

вкладной(ые) лист(ы): loose supplementary leaf(ves), sheet(s)

включ. *see* включая, включительно

включая: including, inclusively

включенный(ые) лист(ы): intercalated leaf(ves)

включительно: inclusively

включительный: inclusive

влож. *see* вложение

вложение: enclosure

внешний: outside; foreign

внешняя книжная торговля: foreign book trade

внутр. *see* внутренний

внутренний: inner, inside

водян. знак *see* водяной знак

водяное пятно: moisture stain, water stain

водяной(ые) знак(и): watermark(s)

восемнадцатый: eighteenth

восемнадцать: eighteen

восемь: eight

восемьдесят: eighty

восемьдесятый: eightieth

восьмой: eighth

временный: temporary

все права сохранены: all rights reserved

всерос. *see* всероссийский

всероссийский: all-Russian

всес. *see* всесоюзный

всесоюзный: all-union

всё изд. *see* всё издание

всё издание: whole edition, complete set

всё что вышло до с. п. *see* всё что вышло до сих пор

всё что вышло до сих пор: all published so far

всё что издано: all published

вступ. *see* вступительный

вступительная статья: introductory article

вступительный: preliminary, introductory

вступление: foreword, introduction

второй: second

вывод: conclusion

выйдет из печати: will be published, to be published

вып. *see* выпуск

вып. дан. *see* выпускные данные

выпуск: issue, number, part; edition; fascicle

выпуск серии: series

выпускные данные: imprint

выпустить в свет книгу: publish a book

вырванный: torn out

вырез. *see* вырезка

вырезанный: engraved, carved, cut out

вырезка(и): cut(s), engraving(s); clipping(s)

выставка: exhibition, show

выход в свет: appearance, publication

выходит ежемесячно: published monthly

выходной лист: title page

выходные данные: imprint

выходные сведения: imprint

вычеркивание: expurgation

вычеркивать: score out, cancel

вышитый: embroidered

вышло из печати: just published

г. *see* год

газ. *see* газета

газета(ы): newspaper(s)

гг. *see* годы

гелиогравюра(ы): heliogravure(s)

герб(ы): coat(s) of arms

гербовый: heraldic

гибкий: flexible

гл. *see* глава, главный

глав. *see* главный

глава(ы): chapter(s)

главная редакция: main editorship

главный: main, chief, principal

главный редактор: editor in chief

гладкий: smooth; crushed (leather)

глазированный: glazed, coated, calendered

год(ы): year(s)

год издания: imprint date, year of publication

годовой: annual, yearly

Гос. издат–во *see* Государственное издательство

Госиздат. *see* Государственное издательство

Государственное издательство: State publishing house

готический шрифт: gothic type

готовить к печати: prepare for publication, make ready for the press

гр. *see* графа

грав. *see* гравёр, гравированный, гравюра

гравёр: engraver

гравир. *see* гравированный

гравирование: engraving, etching

гравированный: engraved

гравюра(ы): engraving(s), cut(s), print(s), plate(s)

гравюра на дереве: wood engraving, woodcut

гравюра на меди: copper engraving

гравюра на стали: steel engraving

гравюра сухой иглой: dry-point etching

гравюры исполнены пунктиром: stippled engravings

гражданский шрифт: ordinary (as contrasted with Church Slavic) type

гранка: proof, galley

графа(ы): column(s)

графика: drawing

гротесковый шрифт: block-letter type

грубо раскраш. *see* грубо раскрашенный

грубо раскрашенный: crudely colored, painted

грубый: crude

грязный: soiled, dirty

д. *see* доллар

давно: long since

дарственная надпись: presentation inscription

дарственный экземпляр: presentation copy

дата издания: date of publication

датир. *see* датированный

датированный: dated

датированный неверно: misdated

два: two

двадцатый: twentieth

двадцать: twenty

двенадцатый: twelfth

двенадцать: twelve

двойной: double

двухлетний: biennial

двухмесячный: bimonthly

двуязычный: bilingual

девиз: motto, device

девяносто: ninety

девяностый: ninetieth

девятнадцатый: nineteenth

девятнадцать: nineteen

девятый: ninth

девять: nine

действительный выход: actual date of publication

деревянная печатная форма: block

деревянный переплет: wood covers

десятый: tenth

десять: ten

деф. *see* дефектный

дефектный: defective, imperfect

дешевое издание: inexpensive, cheap edition

дешевый: cheap, inexpensive

диагр. *see* диаграмма

диаграмма(ы): diagram(s), drawing(s), charts(s)

дисконт: discount

дисконтировать: discount

дисс. *see* диссертация

диссертация(и): dissertation(s), thesis(es)

дл. *see* длина

длина: length

до с.п. *see* до сих пор

до сих пор: till now

добавл. *see* добавление

добавление: appendix, supplement

дозволено цензурой: passed by the censor

докл. *see* доклад

доклад(ы): report(s)

документ(ы): document(s)

дол. *see* доллар

доллар(ы): dollar(s)

доп. *see* дополнение, дополнительный

допеч. *see* допечатка

допечатка(и): additional, supplementary print(s)

допол. *see* дополнение, дополнительный

дополнение: addition, supplement, addenda

дополненное издание: enlarged edition

дополнительный: supplementary, extra

допущ. к печати *see* допущенный к печати

допущенный к печати: approved for printing

дошущено к изданию: privilege

дорогой: costly

доска(и): board(s), cover(s)(of a book); wooden board(s)

дослов. *see* дословный

дословный: literal, textual

дословный перевод: literal translation

доставка: delivery

достойный особого внимания: worthy of special attention

др. *see* другие

драма: drama

другие: others

дубликат(ы): duplicate(s), duplicate copy(ies)

дырка(и) проделанная личинкой: wormhole(s)

европ. *see* европейский

европейский: European

единообразный: uniform

единств. *see* единственно, единственный

единственно: only, solely

единственный: only, sole, unique

ежегод. *see* ежегодник, ежегодный

ежегодник: annual, yearbook; almanac

ежегодный: yearly

ежедневн. *see* ежедневный

ежедневная газета: daily paper

ежедневный: daily

ежеквартальник: quarterly

ежемесячн. *see* ежемесячный

ежемесячный: monthly

еженедельн. *see* еженедельник, еженедельный

еженедельник: weekly

еженедельный: weekly

еще не вышло: not yet published, not yet printed

ж. *see* журнал

желанный: desired, sought

желаемый: in demand

желтый: yellow

живописный: picturesque, pictorial

жирный шрифт: boldface

жур. *see* журнал

журн. *see* журнал

журнал(ы): journal(s), magazine(s); review(s)

за исключ. *see* за исключением

за исключением: except for

за наличное: for cash

заг. лист *see* заглавный лист

загл. *see* заглавие, заглавный

заглавие: title

заглавного листа нет: no title page

заглавный лист: title page, title leaf

загнутый угол страницы: dog-eared

заголовок(ки): rubric(s), heading(s), caption title(s)

заграничная книжная торговля: foreign book trade

заграничный: foreign

загрязненный: soiled, dirty

задняя часть обложки: back cover

заказ(ы): order(s)

заказное письмо: registered letter

заказы направлять: order from

заключение: conclusion

законченный: completed, finished

зам. редактора *see* заместитель редактора

заменительный экземпляр: substitute copy

заменять: replace

заместитель редактора: assistant editor

заметка(и): marginal note(s), paragraph(s); notice(s)

заметки на полях: marginal notes

замечательной происхождении: provenance

записная книжка: notebook
заплаченный вперёд: prepaid
заплесневелый: moldy
запрещенное издание: forbidden edition
запрос: inquiry, request
заруб. печать *see* зарубежная печать
зарубежная печать: foreign press
зарубежное издание: foreign edition, foreign publication
зарубежный: foreign
заставка(и): headpiece(s)
застежка(и): clasp(s)
застежки утрачены: clasps lost
зел. *see* зелёный
зелёный: green
зима: Winter
знак(и): mark(s), sign(s), trace(s)
знак пользования: trace, mark of use
знак сноски: reference mark
знак тома: volume number
золот. *see* золото, золотой
золото: gold
золотое тиснение: gold tooling
золотой: gilt, gilded
золотые обрезы: gilded edges

и. *see* иллюстрация
и др. *see* и другие
и другие: and others
и мн. др. *see* и многие другие
и многие другие: and many others
и проч. *see* и прочее
и прочее: and so on, etc.
и т.д. *see* и так далее
и т.п. *see* и тому подобные
и так далее: etc., and so on
и тому подобные: likewise, and so on
идеальный: ideal, perfect
идентичный: identical
избр. *see* избранный
избран. *see* избранный
избранные произведения: selected works
избранные сочинения: selected works
избранные труды: selected works
избранный: selected
изв. *see* известия, извлечение
известия: news, information

извлечение: extract
изд. *see* издание, издатель
изд—во *see* издательство
издат. *see* издатель
издавать: publish
издается: in course of publication; published by
издание: edition, publication
издание некоммерческой типографии: privately printed edition
издание неофиц. *see* издание неофициальное
издание неофициальное: unofficial edition
издание прекратилось: publication discontinued, ceased
издание с лимитированным тиражом: limited edition
издат. *see* издатель, издательство
издатель(и): publisher(s)
издательский лист: publisher's signature
издательское объявление: prepublication announcement
издательство: publishing house; published by
издать: publish
изм. *see* изменение, измененный
изменение: correction, revision
измененный: corrected, revised
изношенный: worn-out
изображ. *see* изображение
изображение: picture, portrait
изрезанный: with cuts
изящная литература: fiction; belles-lettres
изящный: refined, de luxe
илл. в красках *see* иллюстрации в красках
иллюс. *see* иллюстрация, иллюстрированный
иллюстрат. *see* иллюстратор
иллюстратор(ы): illustrator(s)
иллюстрации в красках: color illustrations
иллюстрация(и): illustration(s), plate(s)
иллюстрированный: illustrated
им. *see* имени

163

имеется в наличии: available
имени: by name, named
имени (e.g., Библиотека имени Ленина):
   named for (e.g., The Lenin Library)
именной указатель: author index
имеются в продаже (книги): (books)
   available for sale
ин—т *see* институт
индийская бумага: India paper
инициал(ы): initial(s)
инкрустированный: mosaic, inlaid
инкунабуль(и): incunabulum(a)
иностр. *see* иностранный
иностранный: foreign
инст. *see* институт
институт: institute
интерпретация: interpretation
искаженный: mutilated
исключительной красоты: of exceptional beauty
исключительный: exceptional
искусственный: artificial, imitation
испачканный: soiled, stained, dirty
использованная литература: literature consulted, sources
испорченный: spoiled
испр. *see* исправленный
исправление(я): correction(s)
исправленный: corrected, revised
иссл. *see* исследование
исследование: paper, research, investigation
исторический: historical
источенный личинками: wormholed
истрёпанная книга: frayed, torn book
истрёпанный: worn-out
исчерпано: out-of-print
итог: sum, total, result

к: to, for
к. *see* копейка
к.—л. *see* какой-либо
к.—н. *see* какой-нибудь
к (пятидесяти) летию: on the (50th)
   anniversary; *Festschrift* on the
   (50th) anniversary
к—т *see* комитет
какой—либо: some, any
какой—нибудь: some, any

каллиграф. *see* каллиграфический
каллиграфический: calligraphic
кант(ы): edge(s)
капитальный труд: major work
каптал(ы): headband(s), turn-in
карандашные пометки: annotations in
   pencil
карикатура(ы): caricature(s), car-
   toon(s)
карманное издание: pocket edition
карманный: pocket
карманный размер: pocket-size
карманный словарь: pocket dictionary
карманный формат: pocket-size
карт. *see* карта, картина
карта(ы): map(s), chart(s)
картина(ы): picture(s), illustration(s)
картогр. *see* картограмма
картограмма(ы): cartogram(s)
картографический: cartographical
картон: binding board, pasteboard
картонаж: pasteboard case, portfolio
картушь: cartouche
кат. *see* каталог
каталог(и): catalog(s)
квадратный формат: square format
квартал: quarter
квартальный: quarterly
кварто: quarto
кириллица: Cyrillic alphabet
китайская бумага: China paper
клеенка: buckram
клеенчатый переплёт: buckram binding
клей: glue
клише: block
кн. *see* книга
кн—во *see* книгоиздательство
книга(и): book(s)
книгоиздатель: book publisher
книгоиздательство: publishing house
книгообмен: book exchange
книгопродавец(ы): bookseller(s)
книготорговец(ы): bookseller(s)
книготорговля: book trade
книготоргующая организация: bookselling organization
книгохранилище: book repository

книжка(и): booklet (s), notebook (s), book (s) of little value

книжная закладка: ribbon, bookmarker

книжная лавка: bookstore

книжная торговля: book trade

книжный базар: book fair

книжный знак: bookplate

книжный магазин: bookstore, bookshop

книжный переплёт: bookbinding, book cover

книжный червь: bookworm

кож. пер. *see* кожаный переплёт

кожа: leather

кожа покрыта тисненными квадратиками: diced leather

кожаный переплёт: leather binding

козлиная кожа: morocco

кол. *see* коллекция

коленкор: calico, buckram

коленкор. пер. *see* коленкоровый переплёт

коленкоровый переплёт: buckram binding

колич. *see* количество

количество: quantity, amount, number

коллация: collation

коллектив авторов: joint authors

коллектив редакторов: editorial staff

коллективный: collective

коллектор: book-supply agency

коллекция(и): collection (s)

колонка(и): column (s)

колофон: colophon

ком. *see* комиссия, комитет

ком-т *see* комитет

комиссия(и): commission (s), committee (s)

комитет(ы): committee (s)

коммент. *see* комментарий

комментарий: commentary

компенд. *see* компендиум

компендиум: compendium, digest

компилятивный труд: compilation

компилятор(ы): compiler (s)

компиляция: compilation, compiling

комплект(ы): set (s), complete set (s)

конец: end

конкордация: concordance

конспект(ы): compendium (ia), synopsis(es)

конфискованный: seized, forbidden

концовка(и): tailpiece (s)

коп. *see* копейка

копейка(и): kopeck (s)

копия(и): copy (ies), duplicate (s), transcription (s)

корешковое заглавие: spine title

корешок: spine of a book

краешек: narrow edge

край(я): edge (s)

крайне: extremely

крайняя цена: lowest price

крапчатый обрез: sprinkled edge

краска(и): color (s)

красочный: colorful

крат. *see* краткий

краткий: short

краткое заглавие: short title

краткое изложение: summary

критицизм: criticism

критические замечания: critical notes

крупный: large, big

крышка переплёта: case, book jacket

ксилографическая книга: block book

ксилография: xylography

курсив: italics

курсивный шрифт: italic type

Л. *see* Ленинград

л. *see* лист

латин. *see* латинский

латинский: Latin

латинский алфавит: roman alphabet

лауреат: laureate

лекция(и): lecture (s)

Ленинград: Leningrad

лента(ы): ribbon (s), bookmarker (s)

—лет: years

—летие (пятидесяти-): the (50th) anniversary; *Festschrift* on the (50th) anniversary

лето: Summer
летопись(и): chronicle (s)
летучее издание: fugitive publication
линия(и): line(s)
линованный: lined, ruled
лирика: lyric poetry
лист(ы): leaf(ves), sheet(s), signature(s)
листки вступительной части: preliminary pages
листовка(и): small pamphlet(s)
листы подклеенные: patched leaves
лит. *see* литература, литературный
лит-ра *see* литература
литература: literature
литературный: literary
литогр. *see* литография
литограф. *see* литографированный, литографический, литография
литографированный: lithographed
литографический: lithographic
литография: lithography
лл. *see* листы
Лнг. *see* Ленинград
Лнгд. *see* Ленинград
Лнгр. *see* Ленинград
ложн. *see* ложный
ложный: false, fictitious
лозунг: catchword
льняной: (of) linen
любопытное издание: curio

М. *see* Москва
м. *see* масштаб
м.с. *see* малая серия
м.ф. *see* малый формат
м. форм. *see* малый формат
малая серия: small series
мало: little, few
малоизвестный: little-known
малотиражный: small, limited edition
малоупотребительный: rarely used
малоценный: of little value
малочисленный: not numerous
малый: small, little
малый формат: small size
манускрипт(ы): manuscript(s)

маргиналии: marginal notes, marginalia
марокен: morocco
масса: many, numerous
массовое издание: popular edition
масштаб: scale
медальон(ы): medallion(s)
межбиблиотечный абонемент: interlibrary loan
междустрочный: interlinear
мелкая печать: small print, small type
меловая бумага: art paper, enamel paper
мемориальный экземпляр: copy with mark of important collection
мемуары: memoirs
месяц(ы): month(s)
месячный: monthly
металическое украшение: boss
метод. *see* методический
методический: methodical, systematic
мешо-тинто: mezzotint
микрофильм(ы): microfilm (s)
миллиметр(ы): millimeter(s)
миниатюра(ы): miniature(s)
миниатюрный: tiny, miniature
минимальный: minimum
мм. *see* миллиметр
мн. *see* многие, множество
многие: many
много: much
многовековый: century(ies) old
многокрасочный: multicolored, polychromatic
многотиражный: large edition
многотомное издание: edition of many volumes
многочисленный: numerous
множество: many, the majority
множит. аппар. *see* множительным аппаратом
множительным аппаратом: mimeographed
модель(и): pattern(s)
мозаичный: mosaic

монография(и): monograph (s)
монотип: monotype
монументальный: monumental
Моск. *see* Москва
Москва: Moscow
мрам. *see* мраморный
мраморн. обл. *see* мраморная обло-
    жка
мраморная обложка: marbled cover
мраморный: marbled
мраморный обрез: marbled edge
муаровый: moire, watered silk
музейная редкость: museum piece
мягк. обл. *see* мягкая обложка
мягкая обложка: soft cover
мягкий: soft

н. *see* номер, народный, научный
н.э. *see* нашой эры
на: on
на обороте: verso, on the back
на обороте заглавного листа: on
    verso of the title page
на отзыве: on approval
на правах рукописи: all rights re-
    served
на просмотр: on approval
на складе: in stock
надпись(и): superscription (s), inscrip-
    tion(s), epigraph(s)
назв. *see* название
название: title
название главы: chapter heading
накл. *see* наклеенный, наклейка
наклеен *see* наклеенный
наклеенный: pasted on, mounted
наклейка(и): label (s), patch(es)
накрашенный: painted
наличные деньги: cash
наличный расчет: cash purchase
наново: anew, again
напеч. *see* напечатано
напечатано: printed
написано: written
написано от руки: handwritten
нар. *see* народный
народный: national
науч. *see* научный

научн. *see* научный
научный: scientific, scholarly
находится в печати: at the printer's,
    being printed
находится в производстве: in process
    of printing, being printed
находится в самом ограниченном
    числе: available in a very limited
    number
нац. *see* национальный
национальный: national
нач. *see* начальный
началось печататься: printing started
начальный: first, original
начитанный: scholarly
нашой эры: A.D.
не для общей продажи: not for gener-
    al sale
не для продажи: not for sale
недельно: weekly, every week
неделя(и): week(s)
недостает: lacking, missing
недостаточный: insufficient, scanty
незаконная перепечатка: pirated re-
    print
незаконное издание: pirated edition
незаконченный: incomplete
незначительный: insignificant, slight
неизвестный: unknown
неизданный: unpublished
некролог(и): obituary(ies)
нем. *see* немецкий
нем. обл. *see* немая обложка
немая обложка: blank cover
немецкий: German
немногочисленный: not numerous
немножко: slightly, little
немножко поврежден: slightly dam-
    aged
ненаходимый: impossible to find
ненумер. *see* ненумерованный
ненумерованный: not paginated, un-
    numbered
необрезанный: untrimmed
неоконч. *see* неоконченный
неоконченный: unfinished, not com-
    pleted
неопубликованный: unpublished; un-
    publicized

неофициальный: unofficial

непериодический: irregular serial publication

неподписанный: unsigned

неполный: incomplete

непоступивший в продажу: not for sale

неразрезанный: uncut, unopened

нерегулярный: irregular

несколько: several, few

нетто: net

неудовлетворительный: unsatisfactory

нечетная страница: right-hand page, recto

нигде: nowhere

ниже: lower, below

нижнее поле: bottom margin, foot of page

но. *see* номер

новое издание: new edition

новый: new

номер(а): number(s), issue(s)

номинальная цена: list price

нотификация: notification

нр. *see* номер

нумер. *see* нумерование, нумерованный

нумерация: numbering, pagination

нумерование: numbering, pagination

нумерованное издание: numbered edition, limited edition

нумерованный: numbered, paginated

о: about, of

о. *see* очень

о—во *see* общество

об—во *see* общество

оба: both

обгорелый: burned

обесцвеченный: faded

обёртка(и): portfolio(s), case(s) for a pamphlet set

обзор: survey, review

обл. *see* обложка

обложка(и): dust cover(s), book jacket(s)

обмен: exchange

обозначение: designation

обозр. *see* обозрение

обозрение(я): review(s)

оборван. *see* оборванный

оборванный: ragged, torn

оборот заглавия: verso of title

оборотная сторона: verso

оборотное заглавие: title on verso

оборотный: verso, back

обр. *see* обрез, обрезанный

обраб. *see* обработанный

обработанный: edited

образец(зцы): pattern(s)

обрамленный: framed

обратная почта: return post

обрез(ы): edge(s)

обрез книги с рисунком: painted edge

обрезанный: trimmed

обрезанный край: trimmed edge, cut edge

общ. *see* обший

общ. тит. л. *see* общий титульный лист

общ—во *see* общество

общая нумерация: consecutive numbering

общее заглавие: collective title

общество: society, association, company

общий: common, general

общий титульный лист: common title page, general title page

объедин. изд. *see* объединенное издание

объединенное издание: collection

объём: size

объявл. *see* объявление

объявление(я): announcement(s), advertisement(s), notice(s)

объясн. *see* объяснение, объяснительный

объяснение(я): explanation(s)

объяснительный: explanatory

обыкновенный: ordinary

обязательный: compulsory

обязательный экземпляр: legal deposit copy

огл. *see* оглавление
оглавление: table of contents
огласка: publicity
огранич. колич. экз. *see* ограниченное
  количество экземпляров
ограниченное количество экземпляров:
  limited number of copies
ограниченный: limited
один: one
одиннадцатый: eleventh
одиннадцать: eleven
одобр. *see* одобренный
одобренный: approved
означение: meaning, significance
окаймленный: bordered, edged
окаймлены золотым бордюром: gilded
  borders, edges
окрашенный обрез: combed, colored
  edge
окружен бордюром: bordered, edged
октаво: octavo
оленья кожа: buckskin
опечатка(и): misprint(s), printing er-
  ror(s), corrigendum(a)
оптовая книжная торговля: wholesale
  book trade
оптовый: wholesale
опублик. *see* опубликовано
опубликованные труды: published
  works
опубликованный в печати: printed,
  published in press
опубликовано: announced, advertised;
  published
опущ. *see* опущенный
опущенный: omitted
ориг. *see* оригинальный
оригинал(ы): original(s)
оригинальный: original
орнамент(ы): ornament(s)
орнаментированный(ые) инициал(ы):
  ornamental initial(s)
осень: Fall
особый: special
от руки: by hand
отв. ред. *see* ответственный редактор
ответственный редактор: editor in
  chief, editor in charge

отд. *see* отдел, отделение, отдельный
отд. отт. ж. *see* отдельный оттиск
  журнала
отд—ние *see* отделение
отдел: division, section
отделение(я): part(s), section(s)
отдельный оттиск журнала: separate
  reprint from a magazine
отзыв: comment, review; reference
отличный: excellent, perfect
отметка(и): annotation(s), note(s),
  mark(s)
отпеч. множит. аппар. *see* отпечатано
  множительным аппаратом
отпечатано множительным аппаратом:
  mimeographed
отпечатанный: printed
отпечатать весь тираж книги: print
  the whole edition of the book
отпечаток: imprint, impress
отсутствует: missing, lacking, ab-
  sent
отт. *see* оттиск
оттиск(и): reprint(s)
отчет(ы): report(s), account(s)
отчетливый шрифт: distinct print,
  clear type
отчетный доклад: report
офиц. *see* официальный
официальный: official
офорт(ы): etching(s)
оценка: appraisal
оч. *see* очень, очерк
оч.б.л. *see* очень большие листы
очень: very
очень большие листы: very large
  sheets, leaves
очень редкий: very rare
очерк(и): sketch(es), essay(s)

П. *see* Петербург, Петроград
п. *see* портрет
п.л. *see* печатный лист
п.с.с. *see* полное собрание сочинений
п.с.соч. *see* полное собрание сочинений
паг. *see* пагинация
пагинация: pagination

памфлет(ы): pamphlet(s), brochure(s); lampoon(s)

папка(и): portfolio(s), pasteboard case(s)

параграф(ы): paragraph(s)

паралл. *see* параллельно

параллельно: in parrallel, simultaneously

параллельный текст: parrallel text

парчевый: brocaded

пер. *see* перевод, переплёт

первой свежести: in very good condition

первый: first

перг. *see* пергамент

пергам. *see* пергамент

пергамент: parchment

перев. *see* перевод

перевод(ы): translation(s), translated by

переводчик(и): translator(s)

перед заглавием: at the head of title

переделка(и): adaptation(s)

передний: first, front

передний обрез: fore edge

передняя доска: front cover

передняя часть обложки: front cover

перезаказывать: reorder

переизд. *see* переизданный

переизданный: republished, reprinted

переклеенный: reglued

перенумерованный от руки: renumbered by hand

перепл. *see* переплёт

перепечатание: reprint, another printing, unchanged edition

перепечатанный: reprinted

перепечатка(и): reprint(s), another printing

перепечатка воспрещается: copyright reserved

переписка: transcription

переплетенный: bound

переплёт(ы): binding(s)

переплёт из телячей кожи: calf binding

переплётная крышка: case

переплётная ткань: book cloth

переплётчик: bookbinder

перер. *see* переработанный

перераб. *see* переработанный

переработанный: reworked, revised, re-edited

пересм. *see* пересмотренный

пересмотренный: revised, checked

переставленный: transposed

переставший выходить: ceased publication

пересылка: cost of shipping

пересылка включена: postpaid, post free

период. *see* периодический

периодический: periodic, serial

периодическое издание: serial, periodical publication

песенник(и): songbook(s)

Пет. *see* Петербург, Петроград

Петербург: St. Petersburg

Петроград: St. Petersburg

печ. *see* печатный

печ. л. *see* печатный лист

печатается: in process of printing, being printed

печатание: printing

печатная(ые) буква(ы): block letter(s)

печатный: printed

печатный лист: signature (of a book); printer's sheet, quire

печать: stamp, seal, press

печать для слепых: Braille

писатель(и): author(s), writer(s)

письмо(а): letter(s)

план(ы): plan(s); map(s)

платить по частям: to be paid by installments

плесень: mildew

плохо связанный: loose in binding

по ошибке напечатано: printer's error

по подписке: for subscribers only

по случаю (50-летн.) юбилея: on occasion of the (50th) anniversary

по требованию: on request

повесть(и): story(ies)
поврежден: damaged, mutilated
поврежден в корешке: back, spine damaged
повышенной прочности: reinforced (binding)
под заглавием: under the title, under the heading; headed, entitled
под ред. *see* под редакцией
под редакцией: edited by
подарочное издание: gift edition
подбитый: lined
подделка(и): falsification, forgery(ies)
поддержанный экземпляр: used, secondhand copy
подзаголовок: subtitle, subheading
подклейка(и): pasted patch(es), pasting(s)
подмочен. *see* подмоченный
подмоченный: damaged by moisture
подносный экземпляр: complimentary copy
подп. к печати *see* подписано к печати
подписано к печати: officially approved for publication
подписанный: signed
подписка: subscription
подписка продолжается: subscription time extended, subscription still accepted
подписная цена: subscription price
подписное издание: subscription edition
подписной лист: subscription list
подпись(и): personal signature(s)
подпись автора: autograph
подпись иллюстрации: legend
подстроч. *see* подстрочный
подстрочное примечание: footnote
подстрочный: interlinear
подстрочный перевод: interlinear translation
подчеркнутый: underlined, underscored
пожелтелый: yellowed, browned
поискивается: in demand, wanted, sought after

покрытый бурными пятнами: foxed
покрытый плесенью: mildew-spotted
покрытый пятнами: spotted
пол. *see* половина
поле(я): margin(s)
полигр. *see* полиграфический, полиграфия
полиграфический: typographical
полиграфия: typography
полированный: burnished
полит. *see* политический
политипаж: polytype
политический: political
полное издание: complete edition
полное собрание сочинений: complete works
полностью разошлось: completely sold out
полный: full, complete
полный комплект: full set
половина: half
полоска орнамента: fillet, ornamental line
полосная(ые) иллюстрация(и): full-page illustration(s)
полотн. *see* полотняный
полотняная бумага: linen paper
полотняный: of linen
полугодовый: semiannual
полукож. с угл. пер. *see* полукожаный с углами переплёт

полукожаный с углами переплёт: three-quarter binding
полумесячный: semimonthly
полупереплёт: half binding
полусафьян: half morocco
полутом(ы): half volume(s)
полушагр. *see* полушагреневый
полушагреневый: half shagreen
пометка(и): mark(s)
попорчен сыростью: damaged by moisture
поправка(и): correction(s)
попул. *see* популярный
популярный: popular
портр. *see* портрет
портрет(ы): portrait(s)

посвящен: dedicated
посвящение: dedication
посеребренный: silver (edge)
последний: last
послесловие: epilogue, afterward
посмертное издание: posthumous edition, work
пособие(я): textbook(s)
постоянный: regular
поступило в продажу: on the market, on sale
потертый: shabby
потеря: loss
потрёпанный: tattered
починенный: repaired
появится в печати: to come out, to be published
пояснительный: explanatory
Пргр. *see* Петроград
превосходный: excellent, perfect
предварительный: preliminary
предисл. *see* предисловие
предисловие: preface, introduction
предполагаемая цена: probable price
предстоящий выпуск издания: to be published shortly
предыдущий: previous
прекрасно сбережен: well-preserved
прекрасный: beautiful, fine
прекратилось: discontinued
прекратилось изданием в (1915 г.): last edition in (1915), no more published since (1915)
премированная книга: prize book, book having won an award
преподношение: complimentary copy
приб. *see* прибавление
прибавл. *see* прибавление
прибавление(я): supplement(s), appendix(es)
прибл. *see* приблизительно
приблизительно: approximately
приготовлено к печати: readied for publication, readied for printing
приготовляется к печати: in process of preparation for publication
прил. *see* приложение
прилож. *see* приложение

приложение(я): enclosure(s); appendix(es), supplement(s), annex(es), addendum(a)
прим. *see* примечание
примеч. *see* примечание
примечание(я): footnote(s), annotation(s), marginal note(s)
пробный экземпляр: specimen, sample copy
прод. *see* продолжение
продаваться: to be on (for) sale
продажа: sale
продано: sold
продолг. *see* продолговатый
продолговатый: elongated
продолж. *see* продолжение
продолжающие издаваться: in progress
продолжение: continuation
продолжение следует: to be continued
проза: prose
произведение(я): work(s)
прокладный(ые) лист(ы): interleaf(ves)
прописная(ые) буква(ы): capital letter(s)
пропуск(и): omission(s)
просм. *see* просмотренный
просмотренный: revised
просмотрено цензурой: censored
проспект(ы): prospectus(es)
простой переплёт: ordinary binding
протёрто: perforated by erasure
против текста: opposite, facing the text
пряжка(и): clasp(s)
прямой корешок: flat band
прямой шрифт: roman type
псевд. *see* псевдоним
псевдоним(ы): pseudonym(s), pen name(s)
Птгр. *see* Петроград
Птрг. *see* Петроград
публикация: publication; publishing
пунктир: dotted line
пунктирная манера: dotted print
пунктирный: stippled
путеводитель(и): guidebook(s)
пыльный: dusty

пятнадцатый: fifteenth
пятнадцать: fifteen
пятно(а): stain(s), spot(s)
пятый: fifth
пять: five
пятьдесят: fifty
пятьдесятый: fiftieth

р. *see* рубль
разд. *see* раздел
раздел(ы): division(s), section(s)
раздельный: detached, separated
размер: size
разнообразные литературные произве-
    дения: miscellaneous pieces, works
разноцветный: many-colored
разорванный: torn
разошлись: sold out
разошлись полностью: completely
    sold out
разработка: elaboration, treatment
разрезанный: cut, opened
разрозненный: detached, separated
разукрашенный: painted, colored
разъяснение: explanation, interpreta-
    tion
разъяснительный: explanatory
рамка(и): border(s), frame(s)
ранее *see* раньше
раньше: earlier, previously
раскр. от руки *see* раскрашенный от
    руки
раскраска(и): coloring(s), illumina-
    tion(s)
раскрашенная рукопись: illuminated
    manuscript
раскрашенный: colored, illuminated
раскрашенный от руки: hand-colored
расписка в получении: receipt
распоряжение(я): order(s), direc-
    tion(s)
распродажа: sale, clearance sale
распродано: sold out, out of print
рассказ(ы): story(ies)
рассмотренный: revised
расставленный: spaced
растительный орнамент: floral de-
    sign, ornament

расчет(ы): account(s)
расширенный: enlarged
регулярный: regular
ред. *see* редактор
редактирование: editing, editorship
редактор(ы): editor(s)
редакц. *see* редакционный
редакционная коллегия: editorial
    board
редакционный: editorial
редкий: rare
редко попадается: hard to find
редкость: rarity
редчайшее издание: rarest edition
рез. на дереве *see* резанный на дере-
    ве
резан. *see* резанный
резан. на меди *see* резанный на меди
резанный: carved, engraved
резанный на дереве: woodcut
резанный на меди: copper-engraved
резюме: summary, résumé
репр. *see* репродукция
репродукция(и): reproduction(s), fac-
    simile(s)
реставр. *see* реставрированный
реставрированный: restored, mended
ретроспективный: retrospective
ретуш. *see* ретушированный
ретушированный: retouched
реферат(ы): abstract(s)
реферативный журнал: abstracting
    journal

рецензия(и): review(s)
рис. *see* рисунок
рисунок(нки): drawing(s), illustra-
    tion(s), design(s)
розничная продажа книг: retail book-
    selling, book trade
розничная цена: retail price
роман(ы): novel(s)
романские цифры: Roman numerals
роскошн. *see* роскошный
роскошный: de luxe, magnificent
росс. *see* российский
российский: Russian
руб. *see* рубль
рубль, рубля, рублей: ruble(s)

рубрика(и): rubric(s)
рубчик(и) переплета: joint(s) (of the binding)
руководство: manual, handbook, treatise
рукопись(и): manuscript(s)
русск. *see* русский
русский: Russian
ручной выделки: made by hand

с: with
с. *see* сантиметр, серия, страница
с автографом: autographed
с инициалами: rubricated, with initials
с оттенком: tinted
с пересылкой: postpaid, shipping charge included
с подписью: signed
с примечанием: with annotation
с проложенными чистыми листками: interleaved
с тиснением: tooled
с.ф. *see* средний формат
с.фр. *see* средний формат
самая редкая книга: most rare book
самый выдающийся: most distinguished
самый популярный: most popular
самый точный: most accurate
сантиметр(ы): centimeter(s)
сафьяновый: morocco
сб. *see* сборник
сбереженный хорошо: in good condition
сборник: collection
сборный лист: preliminary pages
сверенный: verified, collated
свиная кожа: pigskin
сгиб(ы): fold(s)
седьмой: seventh
семидесятый: seventieth
семнадцатый: seventeenth
семнадцать: seventeen
семь: seven
семьдесят: seventy
сер. *see* серия
серия: series
сигнатура(ы): signature(s)

сильно поврежденный: badly damaged
систем. указ. *see* систематический указатель
систематический указатель: classified index
сказка(и): tale(s), story(ies)
скидка: discount
скл. *see* складный
складный: folded, folding
слабые водяные пятна: slight moisture spots
славянский шрифт: Slavic type, Slavic print
слегка подмочен: slightly damaged by moisture
след. *see* следующий
след. обр. *see* следующим образом
следующий: following, next
следующим образом: as follows
слепой шрифт: blind type
словарь(и): lexicon(s), dictionary(ies)
слоновая бумага: very large folio
см. *see* сантиметр, смотри
см. также *see* смотри также
смотри: see
смотри также: see also
снабженный примечаниями: annotated
снабжено: provided, furnished
сниженная цена: reduced price
снимк. *see* снимок
снимок(мки): photograph(s)
сноска(и): footnote(s), note(s)
сноски на полях: marginal notes
соавтор(ы): coauthor(s), joint author(s)
собиратель(и): collector(s)
собр. *see* собрание
собр. сочинений *see* собрание сочинений
собрание(я): collection(s)
собрание сочинений: collected works
сов. *see* совет, советский
совет: Soviet, council
советский: Soviet
совр. *see* современный
соврем. *see* современный
современный: contemporary

содерж. *see* содержание
содержание: table of contents
сокр. *see* сокращение, сокращенный
сокращ. *see* сокращение, сокращенный
сокращение(я): abbreviation(s),
  abridgment(s)
сокращенное заглавие: catchword title
сокращенный: abbreviated, abridged
сообщение(я): proceeding(s), re-
  port(s)
сорок: forty
сороковый: fortieth
сост. *see* составитель
составитель(и): compiler(s)
составление(я): compilation(s), com-
  position(s)
составной переплет: half-cloth binding
состояние: condition
сотрудник(и): contributor(s), collab-
  orator(s)
сотый: one hundredth
сохран. *see* сохранённый
сохранённый: preserved
сохранность великолепная: very good
  condition
сохранность превосходная: excellent
  condition
сохранность средняя: medium condition
сочинение(я): work(s)
СПБ. *see* Ст. Петербург
Спб. *see* Ст. Петербург
спец. *see* специальный
специальный: special, specific
спиральный орнамент: lettered scroll
список(ски): list(s)
список дезидератов: want list
список опечаток: errata list
сплетанный орнамент: interlacing
сплошная нумерация: consecutive
  numbering
справочная книга: reference book
справочник(и): reference book(s)
ср. *see* сравни
сравни: compare
средн. форм. *see* средний формат
средневековый: medieval

средний формат: medium size
ст. *see* статья
Ст. Петербург: St. Petersburg
старинная рукопись: codex
старинный: ancient
стат. *see* статистический, статья
статистический: statistical
статья(и): article(s), paper(s)
стереотип. *see* стереотипный
стереотип: stereotype
стереотипный: stereotype
стержень(жни): guard(s)
стертый: effaced, faded
стлб. *see* столбец
сто: one hundred
стоимость: value, cost
стоимость пересылки: mailing charges, shipping charges
столб. *see* столбец
столбец(бцы): column(s)
столетие(я): century(ies)
сторона(ы): side(s)
стр. *see* страница
страница(ы): page(s)
строчная(ые) буква(ы): small let-
  ter(s)
суперобложка(и): book jacket(s),
  dust cover(s), wrapper(s)
сфальцованная иллюстрация: folding
  plate
сфальцованный: folded
схема(ы): diagram(s), chart(s)
схематич. *see* схематический
схематический: schematic, outlined
счет(ы): account(s)
сшитый: sewed, stitched

т. *see* том
т—во *see* товарищество
т.е. *see* то есть
т.к. *see* так как
т.н. *see* так называемый
таб. *see* таблица
табл. *see* таблица
таблица(ы): table(s), plate(s),
  chart(s)
таблица в красках: color plate
так как: as, since

175

так называемый: so-called
тезис: thesis
текст(ы): text(s)
телячья кожа: calf leather
тем. пл. *see* тематический план
тематический план: thematic plan,
   topical plan
темнозел. *see* темнозелёный
темнозелёный: dark green
темносин. *see* темносиний
темносиний: dark blue
тесьма(ы): tie(s)
тетрадь(и): section(s), fascicle(s)
тех. *see* технический
техн. *see* технический
технический: technical
тип. *see* типографический, типография
типо—лит. *see* типолитографический,
   типолитография
типогр. зн. *see* типографический знак
типограф. *see* типографический,
   типография
типограф. знак *see* типографический
   знак
типографический: typographic
типографический знак: printer's mark
типография: printing house
типографская марка: printer's device,
   mark
типографская ошибка: printer's error
типолитогр. *see* типолитографический, типолитография
типолитографический: typolitho-
   graphic
типолитография: typolithography
тираж: edition, printing, run
тисн. *see* тиснение, тисненый
тиснение: stamping, tooling
тисненый: tooled, stamped, embossed
тит. *see* титул
тит.л. *see* титульный лист
титул(ы): title(s)
титульный лист: title page
тифдрук: mezzotint
то есть: that is, i.e.
товарищество(а): company(ies), so-
   ciety(ies)

того времени: contemporary
толкование: interpretation, commentary
только: only
только для подписчиков: for subscribers only
том(ы): volume(s)
том разрозненного комплекта: odd
   volume
торшонированный обрез: goffered
   edge
точный: exact
трактат(ы): treatise(s)
транскрипция: transcription
транслитер. *see* транслитерация,
   транслитерованный
транслитерация: transliteration
транслитерованный: transliterated
третий: third
трёхлетний: triennial
трёхмесячный: quarterly
три: three
тридцатый: thirtieth
тридцать: thirty
тринадцатый: thirteenth
тринадцать: thirteen
трудно находимый: hard to find
труды: transactions, scientific works
труды научного общества: transactions of a scientific society
тт. *see* томы
тщательно: thoroughly
тысяча: thousand

убористая печать: close print, close
   type
увеличенный: enlarged, increased
угл. *see* угол
угол(глы): corner(s), angle(s)
удлинен. *see* удлиненный
удлиненный: oblong, elongated
удовлетворительный: satisfactory
узкий: narrow
ук. *see* указатель
указ. *see* указание, указатель
указание: indication, direction, instruction
указанный: indicated

указатель(и): index(es)

укомплектов. *see* укомплектованный

укомплектованный: full, completed set

украш. *see* украшение, украшенный

украшение(я): decoration(s), ornament(s), illumination(s)

украшенный: ornamented, decorated, illuminated

укрепленный: reinforced

улучш. *see* улучшенный

улучшен. *see* улучшенный

улучшенный: improved, revised, amended

уменьшенный: reduced

умнож. *see* умноженный

умноженный: enlarged

ун–т *see* университет

унив. *see* университет

университет(ы): university(ies)

уникум: unique

унциальная(ые) буква(ы): uncial letter(s)

упаковка: packing, wrapping

уполномоч. *see* уполномоченный

уполномоченный: authorized

упущение(я): omission(s)

урез. *see* урезанный

урезанный: cut off

условно: on condition

усовершенствованный: perfected, improved

уст. *see* устарелый

устар. *see* устарелый

устарелый: obsolete, archaic

утв. *see* утверждение, утвержденный

утверждение: confirmation, affirmation, approval

утвержденный: confirmed, affirmed, approved

утеря: loss

утрачен. *see* утраченный

утраченный: lost, missing

уцелевший: intact, untouched

учеб. *see* учебник

учебник(и): textbook(s), manual(s)

ученый: learned, scientific

факс. *see* факсимиле

факсимиле: facsimile

факультативный: optional

фальсификация(и): forgery(ies), falsification(s)

фальсифицированный: forged

фальц(ы): fold(s)

фантастический: fantastic

фантастичный: fabulous

фиг. *see* фигура

фигура(ы): figure(s), diagram(s)

фиктивный год издания: fictitious date of publication

фолио: folio

форзац: flyleaf; lining paper

форм. *see* формат

формат: size, format

фот. *see* фотография

фотогелиотипический: photoheliotyped

фотограв. *see* фотогравюра

фотогравюра(ы): photogravure(s), photoengraving(s)

фотография(и): photograph(s)

фотолит. *see* фотолитографический

фотолитогр. *see* фотолитографический

фотолитографический: photolithographic

фотомех. *see* фотомеханический

фотомеханический: photomechanical

фотостат. *see* фотостатический

фотостатический: photostatic

фототип. *see* фототипический

фототипич. *see* фототипический

фототипический: phototype

фр. *see* французский

фрагментарный: fragmentary

фрактура: black-letter type

франкированный: prepaid

франц. *see* французский

французский: French

фрахт: freight

фронт. *see* фронтиспис

фронтиспис: frontispiece

фундаментальный: fundamental

фундаментальный труд: basic work

футляр(ы): container(s), portfolio(s)

ходкая книга: best seller

холст: canvas, cloth

177

холщ. пер. *see* холщевый переплёт
холщевый переплёт: canvas binding
хор. *see* хороший, хорошо
хорош. *see* хороший
хороший: good
хорошо: well
хрестоматия: reader
хромолит. *see* хромолитографированный, хромолитография
хромолитографированный: chromolithographed
хромолитография: chromolithograph, chromolithography
хромотипография: chromotypograph, chromotypography
хроника(и): chronicle(s), annals
хронолог. *see* хронологический
хронологический: chronological
худое состояние: poor condition
худож. *see* художественный
художественная литература: fiction, belles-lettres
художественное произведение: work of art
художественный: artistic

ц. *see* цена
цвет: color
цветн. *see* цветной
цветная гравюра: colored print, colored engraving
цветная обложка: colored cover
цветная продукция: color printing, printed in colors
цветная фотография: color photograph
цветной: colored, in colors
целый: full, whole
цена: price
цена без пересылки: mailing charges not included
цена без упаковки: packing charges not included
цена включая пересылку: price including mailing charges
цена за том по подписке: subscription price per volume
цена каждой части отдельно: price for each separate part

цена комплекта в обёртке: price for set in portfolio
цена нетто: net price
цена повысилась: price increased
цена с пересылкой: price postpaid
цензура: censorship
ценность: value
ценный: valuable
сентиметр(ы): centimeter(s)
центр. *see* центральный
центральный: central
церк.–слав. *see* церковнославянский
церковнославянский: Church Slavonic type, print
цинкограф. *see* цинкографический
цинкографический: zincographic
цитата(ы): quotation(s)
цифра(ы): figure(s), cipher(s)

ч. *see* часть, число
часто: frequently, often
частый: frequent
часть(и): part(s)
частью: partly
черный: black
черт. *see* чертёж
черта(ы): scoring, line(s)
чертёж(и): drawing(s), sketch(es), chart(s)
четвёртый: fourth
четная(ые) страница(ы): left-hand page(s), verso(s)
четыре: four
четырнадцатый: fourteenth
четырнадцать: fourteen
чиароскуро: chiaroscuro
число: date, number
чистая обложка: blank wrapper, plain cover
чистописание: calligraphy
чистый: clean, blank, plain
читатель(и): reader(s)
член(ы): member(s)
чрезвычайный: extraordinary, extreme
чудесный: wonderful
чч. *see* части

шаблон(ы): stencil(s), pattern(s)
шагр. *see* шагреневый

шагреневый: shagreen
шагрень: shagreen
шарж(и): cartoon(s), caricature(s)
шедевр(ы): masterpiece(s)
шелковый: silk
шестидесятый: sixtieth
шестнадцатый: sixteenth
шестнадцать: sixteen
шестой: sixth
шесть: six
шестьдесят: sixty
широкий: broad, wide
широта: width
шифр: pressmark
шмуцтит. *see* шмуцтитул
шмуцтитул: half title, bastard title
шнур(ы): raised band(s)
шрифт: print, type
штамп(ы): stamp(s), seal(s)
штандарт: standard
штемп. *see* штемпель
штемпель(я): stamp(s)
штриховка: hatching
штриховой рисунок: line drawing

эквивалент. *see* эквивалентный
эквивалентный: equivalent
экз. *see* экземпляр
экземпляр(ы): copy(ies), issue(s)
экслибрис: *ex libris*, bookplate
экспериментальный: experimental
экспертный: expert
экспортная торговля: export trade
экстракт(ы): extract(s)

экстраординарный: extraordinary, unusual
элегант. *see* элегантный
элегантный: elegant
эмблема(ы): emblem(s), device(s)
энцикл. *see* энциклопедия
энциклопедический словарь: encyclopedic dictionary
энциклопедия: encyclopedia
эпиграф(ы): epigraph(s)
эпика: epic(s)
эпилог(и): epilogue(s), postface(s)
эпический: epic
эпоха(и): epoch(s)
эра(ы): era(s)
эскиз(ы): sketch(es), outline(s)
эстамп(ы): print(s), plate(s)
этюд(ы): study(ies), sketch(es)

юбил. *see* юбилей
юбилей: anniversary, jubilee
юбилейное издание: jubilee publication, *Festschrift*
юмористич. *see* юмористический
юмористический: humorous, comic
юридич. *see* юридический
юридический: legal, juridical
юфть: Russian leather

явный: evident, obvious
яз. *see* язык
язык(и): language(s)
японская бумага: Japan paper
ясный: clear, lucid

SPANISH

a. *see* año
a colores: in colors
a doble folio: double folio
a doble página: two-page
a doble plana: two full pages
a doble texto: parallel text
a dos columnas: in two columns
a dos tintas: in two colors
a frío: blind-tooled
a grandes márgenes: with wide
  margins
a la bandeja: like a tray
a la rom. *see* a la romántica
a la romántica: in the style of
  the romantic period
a la venta: on sale
a mano: by hand
a página entera: full page
a pesar de: in spite of
a plana: full page
a plena página: full page
a seco: blind-tooled
a toda plana: full page
a todo color: in full color
a todo lujo: de luxe
a varias tintas: in various colors
abigarrado: variegated
abreviación: abridgment
abreviatura: abbreviation
acaba de: just, has just

acabado de publicar: just published
acanelado: cinnamon-colored
acero: steel
aclaratorio: clarifying
aconsejado: advised
acta: proceedings
actualmente: currently
acuarela(s): water color(s)
acuarelado: water-colored
acuatinta: aquatint
adentro: inside, within
adicional: additional
adiciones: addenda
adolecido: defective, damaged
adornado: decorated
adorno(s): ornament(s)
afectando: affecting
aficionado: amateur
afuera: outside
agot. *see* agotado
agotadísimo: scarce
agotado: out-of-print
agregado(s): addition(s), added
aguafuerte(s): etching(s)
agujereado: wormholed
agujero(s): wormhole(s)
ahuesado: tinted, off-white,
  bone-color
al acero: in steel
al aguafuerte: etched

al cromo: in colors
al día: up to date
al fin: at the end
al final: at the end
al mercado: to market, for sale
al parecer: apparently
al respaldo: on the back
alargado: long, elongated
álbum: album
alisado: smooth
almanaque: almanac
alterado: altered
amarilleado: yellowed
amarillento: yellowed
amarillo: yellow
amenidad: amenity
ampliado: enlarged
amplio: ample
amplitud: amplitude, fullness
anales: annals
análisis: abstract
anaranjado: orange-colored
anastatico: anastatic
ancho: wide
anchura: width
anchuroso: very wide
anejo(s): annex(es), supplement(s)
ángulo: corner, angle
año: year
anónimo: anonymous
anotación(es): note(s), annota-
   tion(s)
anotado: annotated
ant. *see* antiguo
antaño: in olden times
antep. *see* anteportada
anteportada: half-title page
anteportadilla: small half title
anticuado: out of date
antiguo: old
antología: anthology
anual: annual
anual. *see* anualmente
anualmente: annually
anuario: yearbook, annual
anverso: recto, front side
apais. *see* apaisado
apaisado: oblong

aparatoso: sumptuous
aparecido: appeared
aparición: appearance, publication
aparte: separately
aparte texto: separate from the
   text
apenas: scarcely
apéndice: appendix
aplic. *see* aplicaciones
aplicaciones: appliqués
apolillado: perforated by worms,
   worm-eaten
aprec. *see* apreciado
apreciable: valuable
apreciado: esteemed, valued
aproximadamente: approximately
aproximado: approximate
apuntes: notes
arabesco(s): arabesque(s)
archivo: archives
armas: arms
arpillera: coarse cloth
arrancado: torn out
arreglo(s): repair(s)
arrugado: wrinkled
artístico: artistic
atacado: attached; damaged
aterciopelado: made to resemble
   velvet
atlas: atlas
atrasado: out of date, delayed
aum. *see* aumentado
aumentado: enlarged
autobiografía: autobiography
autocromía: color print
autografiado: autographed
autógrafo: autograph
autor: author
autorizado: authorized
autorretrato: self-portrait
avellana: nut-colored
aviso: notice
azul: blue
azulado: bluish
azurado: bluish, azure blue

badana: sheepskin
bajo-relieve: bas-relief

bajorrelieve: bas-relief
banda(s): border(s), strip(s)
barbas: witnesses, uncut edges
barroco: baroque
bastante: rather, somewhat
bastardilla: bastard type
becerrillo: calf
bellamente: beautifully
bermellón: vermilion
bibliófilo: bibliophile
bibliografía: bibliography
bibliográfico: bibliographical
biblioteca: library, series,
  collection
bibliotecario: librarian
bicromía: two-color print
bimen. see bimensual
bimensual: semimonthly
bimestral: bimonthly
biografía: biography
biográfico: biographic
bistre: bister
bitono: two-tone
bl. see blanco
blanco: white, blank
blasón: armorial bearing
boj(es): woodcut(s)
boletín: bulletin
bolsillo: pocket
bonito: pretty
bordado: embroidered
borde(s): border(s), edge(s)
borrado: erased
botón(es): boss(es)
bradel: bradel, a cased binding
breve: short
brin: sailcloth, canvas
brocado: brocaded
broche(s) de metal: metal
  clasp(s)
broche(s) metálico(s): metal
  clasp(s)
bronce: bronze
bronceado: bronzed, bronze-
  colored
bruñido: crushed, burnished
btca. see biblioteca
bucarán: buckram

buen: good
bullones: bosses
buscado: in great demand, sought

c. see centímetros, con, corte
cabecera(s): headpiece(s)
cabeza: top
cabezada(s): headband(s)
cada: each
caja (de carton): box (pasteboard)
caja-estuche: slipcase
calcografía: chalcography
calderón(es): paragraph sign(s)
calidad: quality
calígrafo: scribe
cambio: change
camisa: wrapper
cancionero: songbook
cant. see canto
canto(s): edge(s)
cantonera(s): cornerpiece(s)
cap. see capítulo
capa-estuche: slipcase
capitulares: chapter headings
capítulo(s): chapter(s)
caps. see capítulos
caracteres: letters, type
caracteres arábigos: Arabic
  letters, type
caracteres griegos: Greek
  letters, type
caracteres romanos: roman
  letters, type
carátula: title page
carcomido: worm-eaten
carecer see por carecer de
carente: lacking
caricatura: caricature
carpeta: slipcase, portfolio
cart. see cartón
cartilla: primer, hornbook
cartografía: cartography
cartón: cardboard
cartón flexible: flexible cardboard
cartoné: boards, bound in boards
cartulina: bristol board, thin
  cardboard

cartulina gamuzada: yellowed board

cartulina satinada: coated board

castizo: pure

catorce: fourteen

celebérrimo: most celebrated, famous

célebre: celebrated

celofán: cellophane

cenefa: border

censura: censorship

censurado: censored

centenar(es): hundred(s)

centésimo: hundredth

centímetros: centimeters

centro: center

cerdo: pigskin

chagrín: shagreen

chamuscado: scorched, singed

cien: one hundred

ciento: one hundred

cierres: clasps

cierres metálicos: metal clasps

cincelado: engraved, chiseled

cinco: five

cincuenta: fifty

cinta(s): tie(s)

círculos: circular designs, circles

citado: cited

citrón: lemon-colored

claroscuro: chiaroscuro

clave: key

clavo(s): nail(s), peg(s)

cm. *see* centímetros

coautor: coauthor

cobre: copper

códice: codex

codiciable: highly desirable

codiciado: desired, coveted

coetáneo: contemporary

col. *see* colaboración, colección, colorado

colaboración: collaboration

colación: collation

colección: collection, series

coleccionado: collected

colectivo: collective

colocación: placement

colofón: colophon

colorado: colored

coloreado: colored

colorido: colored, coloring

columna: column

com. *see* comentario

comentario: commentary

como nuevo: as new

comp. *see* compartimientos, compilador

compart. *see* compartimientos

compartimientos: line design used in decorating bindings in square or oblong panels

compendiado: organized into a compendium

compilación: compilation

compilado: compiled

compilador: compiler

complemento: complement

completado: completed

completo: complete

compuesto: composed

con: with

con sus márgenes: with original margins

concordancia: concordance

conjunto: together, the group

conservación: conservation

conservado: well-preserved

contemporáneo: contemporary, contemporaneous

contenido: contents

contexto: context

continuación: continuation

contracanto(s): lacework tooling inside edges of covers

contrahecho: counterfeited

contraportada: page opposite the title page

contratapa(s): lining(s), *doublure(s)*

coop. *see* cooperativo

cooperativo: co-operative

copia: copy

corcho: cork

cordobán: cordovan

corr. *see* corregido

corrección: correction
corregido: corrected
corriente: common, current
cort. *see* corte(s)
cortado: opened, trimmed
corte(s): edge(s)
corte delantera: fore edge
corte(s) dorado(s): gilt edge(s)
corte(s) labrado(s): chiseled
  edge(s)
corto: short
cosido: sewing, stitching
costeado: paid for
cotidiano: daily
cotización: price, evaluation
crestomatía: anthology
cribado: dotted
cromo(s): color(s), colored
  illustration(s)
cromo. *see* cromolitografía
cromolitografía: chromo-
  lithography
cromotipia: chromotypography
crónica(s): chronicle(s)
croquis: sketch
cuadernillo: a small notebook,
  a measure of paper
cuaderno(s): notebook(s),
  pamphlet(s); quire(s)
cuadrado: square
cuadrados: pattern of squares
cuadragésimo: fortieth
cuadro(s): picture(s); border(s)
cuajado: highly decorated
cuarenta: forty
cuarterones: quarters
cuarto: fourth
cuatricromías: four-color prints
cuatro: four
cubierta(s): cover(s)
cubierta en blanco: blank wrapper
cubierta protectora: protective
  cover
cubiertas dobladas: folded
  wrapper
cubretapa: wrapper
cuenta: account
cuento: tale

cuero: leather
cuero de avestruz: ostrich leather
cuero de cerdo: pigskin
cuero de Rusia: Russian leather
cuidado: care; carefully done
curioso: curious
curvado: curved

d.c. *see* doble columna
dañado: damaged
dañando: damaging
daño(s): damage(s)
data: date
de época: contemporary
de la época: contemporary
de lujo: de luxe
de mucho aprecio: highly valued
de proxima publicación: to be
  published soon
de suma rareza: of the utmost
  rarity
débil: weak
debilitado: weakened
décimo: tenth
decimo cuarto: fourteenth
decimo nono: nineteenth
decimo octavo: eighteenth
decimo quinto: fifteenth
decimo séptimo: seventeenth
decimo sexto: sixteenth
decimotercio: thirteenth
decoración(es): decoration(s)
decorado(s): decoration(s),
  decorated
ded. *see* dedicatoria
dedicatoria: dedication
dedicatorio: dedicatory
defecto: defect
defectuoso: defective
definitivo: definitive
delantero: top margin
delgado: thin
dentellado: ornamented with
  dentelle patterns
dentelle: dentelle
dentro del texto: within the text
depurado: cleaned up
derecho: right

desbarbado: trimmed, smoothed
descolorido: discolored, faced
desconocido: unknown
descosido: unsewn, stitching broken
descripción: description
descuidado: careless
desencolado: unglued
desencuadernado: binding loose or gone
desgarro: tear
desgastado: worn away
desgraciadamente: unfortunately
deslustrado: without luster
desmerecer: to decrease in value
desperfecto: imperfection
desplegable: unfolding
desprendido: loosened, separated
destacado: detached
destinado: destined
deteriorado: damaged, deteriorated
diagr. see diagrama
diagrama: diagram
diario: daily publication, daily
dib. see dibujo
dibujado: drawn, sketched
dibujo(s): drawing(s), sketch(es)
dibujo(s) al lapiz: pencil sketch(es)
diecinueve: nineteen
dieciocho: eighteen
dieciseis: sixteen
diecisiete: seventeen
diez: ten
difícil: difficult
diminutivo: diminutive
dirección: address
dirigido: directed
discontinuado: no longer published
diseño: design
disertación: dissertation
disminuido: reduced, diminished
disponible: available
doblado: folded
doble: double
doble columna: double column

doble hilo: double thread, line
doce: twelve
docum. see documento
documento(s): document(s)
donativo: gift
dor. see dorado
dorado(s): gilt, gold decoration(s)
dos: two
duodécimo: twelfth

ed. see edición, editor
edic. see edición
edición(es): edition(s)
edición de bolsillo: pocket edition
edición definitiva: definitive edition
edición limitada: limited edition
edición principe: editio princeps
edición privada: private edition
edit. see editorial
editor: publisher
editora: of the publisher
editorial: of the publisher
ej. see ejemplar
ejecutado: executed
ejecutoria: execution
ejem. see ejemplar
ejemp. see ejemplar
ejemplar: copy
ejemplar en rama: copy in sheets
elenco: list
empastado: bound in boards
empastadura: board binding
en boga: popular, the vogue
en breve: shortly
en buen estado: in good condition
en colores: in colors
en conjunto: all together
en curso de publicación: in course of publication
en el mercado: in the market, for sale
en el texto: in the text
en gran papel: on large paper
en mal estado: in poor condition
en oro: in gold
en perfecto estado: in perfect condition

en pliegos: in folded sheets
en prensa: in press
en preparación: in preparation
en rama: in sheets
en reimpresión: being reprinted
en relieve: in relief
en seco: dry point
enc. *see* encuadernación,
  encuadernado
encabezamiento: heading,
  subject heading
encadenado: chained
encaj. *see* encaje
encaje: inlay
encarnado: flesh-colored
encartonado: bound in boards
encolado: pasted up, mounted
encontrar: to find
encuad. *see* encuadernación,
  encuadernado
encuader. *see* encuadernación,
  encuadernado
encuadernación: binding
encuadernación arpillera: heavy
  cloth binding
encuadernación coetánea: contemporary binding
encuadernación de edición:
  edition binding
encuadernación en cartón: cased
  boards
encuadernación nominal: usual
  binding
encuadernación romántica:
  bound in romantic style
encuadernado: bound
encuadernador: binder
encuadernar: to bind
encuadrado: framed, bordered
encuadre: line pattern forming
  a frame
enmarcado: marked
enmendado: emended
enmienda(s): emendation(s)
ennegrecido: darkened, blackened
enriquecido: enriched, embellished
ensayo: essay; trial

ensuciado: dirtied
entelado: cloth-covered, cloth-
  backed
enteramente: entirely
entero: entire
entredós: strip
entrega(s): part(s), installment(s)
entrel. *see* entrelazados
entrelazados: interlaced fillets
entrelazamientos: interlacings
epígrafe: epigraph, inscription
epilogo: epilogue
epístola: epistle
época: epoch, of the time
equivoca *see* se equivoca
errata: misprint, errata
erróneo: erroneous
escaso: rare
escogido: selected
escolios: critical notes
escribano: scribe
escudo(s): shield(s)
escudo(s) de armas: coat(s) of
  arms
escudo(s) heraldico(s): heraldic
  shield(s)
esmeradamente: carefully
esmerado: careful
especial: special
espécimen: specimen, sample
espléndido: splendid
esquema(s): plan(s), outline(s)
esquina(s): corner(s)
est. *see* estampado
estado: condition, state
estado de conservación: condition,
  state of preservation
estamp. *see* estampado
estampa: print, engraving
estampación: tooling
estampación(es): tooled design(s)
estampado: tooled
estampadura: tooling
estilo: style
estilo romántico: romantic style
estima: esteem, value
estimado: esteemed, valued
estrecho: narrow

186

estrecho-apaisado: narrow and elongated
estropeado: mutilated, torn
estuche: slipcase
estupendo: stupendous
ex-libris: ownership plate or mark
excelente: excellent
excelentemente: excellently
exornado: embellished
explicativo: explanatory
expurgado: expurgated
extracto: extract
extranjero: foreign
extremado: extreme

f. *see* fecha
fabricado: manufactured, made
facsím. *see* facsímile
facsímil: facsimile
facsimilar: facsimile
facsímile: facsimile
facticio: artificial, factitious
factura: invoice, bill
falta: lacking
fantasía: fancy
fascículo: fascicle, part
fatigado: worn
fecha: date
fechado: dated
fielmente: faithfully
figura: illustration
fil. *see* filete
filete(s): fillet(s)
filete de lineas: design of lines
fileteado: adorned with fillets
filiforme: filiform, threadlike
filigrana: filigree, watermark
fils. *see* filetes
fin: end
finales: end
fino: fine, thin
finura: fineness, perfection
firma: signature
firmado: signed
flexible: flexible
flor de lis: fleur-de-lys
floral: floral

floreado: flowered
florones: large floral designs used in tooled bindings
fol. *see* foliación, folio
foliación: foliation
foliado: foliated
foliar: foliate, foliating
folio: a folio, folio-size
folio mayor: large folio
folio menor: small folio
follajes: scroll design
folleto: pamphlet
fondo: background
forrado: lined
forro: jacket, lining
forro(s): cover(s)
foto(s): photograph(s)
fotocopia: photocopy
fotograbado(s): photoengraving(s)
fotograbs. *see* fotograbados
fotografía(s): photograph(s)
fotográfico: photographic
fotolitográfico: photolithographic
fototipia: phototype
fototípico: phototype
fototipográfico: phototypographic
fragmento: fragment
franco: postpaid
frecuente: frequent
frescura: freshness
frío *see* a frío
front. *see* frontispicio
frontis: frontispiece
frontis. *see* frontispicio
frontis-retrato: portrait frontispiece
frontispicio: frontispiece
frotado: rubbed
fuera de comercio: not for sale
fuera de texto: not in the text
fuera texto: not in the text
fuerte: serious, strong

gaceta: gazette
gamuzado: yellowed
garrapatos: scribblings
gastado: worn, soiled, spoiled
glosa: gloss

glosario: glossary
gofrado: goffered
gofreado: goffered
gótico: in gothic type
gr. *see* grano
grab. *see* grabado
grabadito(s): small engraving(s)
grabado(s): illustration(s),
  engraving(s)
grabado al aguafuerte: etched
grabado al boj: woodcut
grabado en acero: steel engraving
grabador(es): engraver(s)
gráf. *see* gráfico
gráfico(s): illustration(s)
gran: large
granate: dark red
grande: large
grano: grain
grano bruñido: crushed, polished
  surface
grano grueso: heavy, thick grain
grano largo: straight-grained
grasa: grease
grbs. *see* grabados
greca(s): ornamental design(s)
grisado: gray
grueso: thick, heavy; thickness
guarda(s): end paper(s)
guardapolvo: dust cover, wrapper
guía: guide
gusto: taste

h. *see* hoja
h. en b. *see* hoja en blanco
hábil: able
hábilmente: ably
hacia: about
hecho: made
heliograbado: helioengraving
heliotipia: heliotype
hermoso: beautiful
hierro(s): tooled design(s)
hierro(s) en seco: blind-tooled
  design(s)
hilo(s): thread(s), line(s)
historiado: historiated
hoj. *see* hoja

hoja(s): leaf(ves)
hoja(s) añadida(s): added leaf(ves),
  cancel(s)
hoja(s) doble(s): double leaf(ves)
hoja(s) en blanco: blank leaf(ves)
hoja volante: broadside
hol. *see* holandesa
holand. *see* holandesa
holandesa: half-leather binding
holandesa chagrín: half-shagreen
  binding
hueco(s): mezzotint(s)
huecograbado(s): mezzotint(s)
huella(s): trace(s)
hule: oilcloth
humedad: dampness
humedades: spots caused by
  dampness

ilegible: illegible
iluminado: illuminated
ilus. *see* ilustración
ilust. *see* ilustración, ilustrado
ilustración(es): illustration(s)
ilustrado: illustrated
ilustrador: illustrator
imitación: imitation
imitado: imitated, artificial
imp. *see* imprenta
impecable: impeccable
imprenta: imprint, press
imprescindible: indispensable
impresión: printing, edition
impresionante: impressive
impreso(s): printed matter,
  printed piece(s)
impresor: printer
inasequible: out of reach,
  unattainable
incisión: cut, scratch
incl. *see* inclusive, incluyendo
inclusive: inclusive
incluso: including
incluyendo: including
incompleto: incomplete
incrustación: embossing
incrustado: embossed
incunable: incunabulum

índ. *see* índice
índice(s): index(es)
indispensable: indispensable
inédito: unpublished
inferior: lower
infinidad: a great number
informe: report
inicial(es): initial letter(s)
inmaculado: immaculate
inmediato: imminent
inmejorable: perfect, could not
  be better
inminente: imminent
inscripción: inscription
inserto: inserted, laid in
insigne: famous
int. *see* interior
íntegramente: completely, wholly
íntegro: complete, whole
intercal. *see* intercalado
intercalado: intercalated
interesa a: affects
interesando: affecting, touching
interfoliado: interleaved
interior: inside, inner
interlineado: interlinear
intitulado: entitled
intonso: uncut
intrasparente: opaque
introducción: introduction
inverso: inverse; obverse
izquierdo: left

jasp. *see* jaspeado
jaspead. *see* jaspeado
jaspeado: marbled
juego de filetes: pattern of lines
juntos: together

keratol: keratol, a book cloth

l. *see* letra, lugar
labrado: polished, worked
ladillos: marginal numbering
lám. *see* lámina
lámina(s): plate(s)
láms. *see* láminas
larg. *see* largo
largo: large, long, wide

lastimado: damaged
lateral: lateral
laureado: prize-winning
lavado: washed
lazos: ties, laces
legajo: packet
legible: legible
lejos de: far from
let. *see* letra
letra: letter, type face
letra bastarda: bastard type
letra(s) capital(es): capital
  letter(s)
letra(s) capitular(es): chapter
  letter(s)
letra cursiva: italics, cursive
  type
letra gótica: gothic type
letra(s) initial(es): initial
  letter(s)
letra redonda: round-letter type
letra romana: roman-letter type
levantado: raised
leve: light, slight
levemente: lightly
lexico: lexicon
librería: bookstore, bookshop
librería de viejo: secondhand
  bookstore
librero: bookseller, bookstore
librito: little book
libro: book
ligeramente: lightly
ligerísimo: very light
ligero: light, slight
limitado: limited
limón: lemon-colored
limpio: clean
limpísimo: very clean
lindo: pretty
lit. *see* litografías
literal: literal
literalmente: literally
litografiado: lithographed
litografías: lithographic prints
lom. *see* lomera
lomera: back strip
lomo: back
lomo liso: smooth back

189

lomo roto: back broken
lugar: place
lujo: de luxe, highest quality
lujosamente: sumptuously
lujosísima: most elaborate
lujoso: elaborate, luxurious

m. see marroquí, medio
m.s. see manuscrito
madera: wood
maderas: woodcuts
magníficamente: magnificently
magnífico: magnificent
mal: bad
maltratado: badly treated
mancha(s): spot(s), stain(s)
manchado: spotted, stained
manchas de agua: water stains
manchas de humedad: damp
  stains
manchas del tiempo: stains of
  time
manuable: portable
manuscrito: manuscript
mapa: map
mapa(s) estado(s): map(s) with
  table(s)
mapa-ruta: route map
mapamundi: world map
marca: device, mark
marca del impresor: printer's
  mark
marcado: marked
marfil: ivory
margen: margin
marginal: marginal
marmoleado: marbled
marr. see marroquí
marrón: chestnut color
marroquí: morocco
marroquín: morocco
más: more, plus
mayor: large
mayoría: majority
mayúscula(s): capital letter(s)
medallón: medallion
media basana: half sheepskin
media piel: half leather

media tela: half cloth
media tinta: mezzotint
mediados: about half
medio: half, center
medio pergamino: half vellum
mediocre: mediocre
mejorado: improved
memorias: memoirs
menor: small
mensual: monthly
meritísimo: very praiseworthy
metálico: metallic
microscópico: microscopic,
  very small
miniado: illuminated
miniatura(s): miniature(s)
miniaturado: painted in miniature
minuciosamente: minutely
minucioso: minute
miscelánea: miscellany
mismo: same
mitad: half
moaré: moire, watered
moderno: modern
modificado: changed
monografía: monograph
monograma: monogram
montado: mounted
morado: violet
mordedura: bite
mordido: gnawed
mosaico(s): mosaic design(s)
mota(s): defect(s)
moteado: with small defects
motivo(s): motif(s)
movible: movable
ms. see manuscrito
muestra(s): sample(s), example(s)
multicolor: many-colored
multitud: a great number
mutilación: mutilation
mutilado: mutilated
muy: very

nácar: mother-of-pearl
nacarado: decorated with mother-
  of-pearl
nada frecuente: not often found

naranja: orange-colored
nervios: raised bands
neto: net
nítido: clean, clear
no es frecuente: infrequent,
  seldom found
no venal: not for sale
nombre: name
nominado: named
nominal: nominal
nonagésimo: ninetieth
nota(s): note(s)
notabilísimo: outstanding
noticia: piece of information
novela: novel
noveno: ninth
noventa: ninety
nro. *see* número
nueve: nine
nuevo: new
num. *see* numerado, numerar,
  número
numeración: numbering
numeración consecutiva: continuous numbering
numerado: numbered
numerar: numbering
número(s): number(s)
nunca: never
nutrido: abundant, full, dense

oblongo: oblong
obra: work
obrita: small work
ochenta: eighty
ocho: eight
octagésimo: eightieth
octavo: eighth
offset: offset
once: eleven
opúsculo: short or small work
ordenado: arranged, put in order
original: original
orla(s): border(s)
orla(s) ornamental(es): ornamental border(s), scroll(s)
orlado: ornamented with a
  decorative border

ornado: ornamented
ornam. *see* ornamento
ornamentación: ornamentation
ornamentado: decorated
ornamento(s): decoration(s)
oscurecido: darkened, obscured
oscuro: dark

p. *see* página
p.e. *see* pasta española
pág. *see* página
página(s): page(s)
paginación: pagination
págs. *see* páginas
palidecido: faded
panfleto: pamphlet
papel: paper
papel acanillado: laid paper
papel ahuesado: tinted paper
papel alfa: esparto paper
papel avitelado: vellum paper
papel biblia: Bible paper
papel corriente: ordinary paper
papel de arroz: rice paper
papel de corcho: cork paper
papel de estraza: brown, coarse
  paper
papel de forro: end papers
papel de hilo: rag paper
papel fantasía: fancy paper
papel fuerte: heavy paper
papel holanda: Dutch paper
papel hueso: off-white, bone-
  colored paper
papel Japon: Japan paper
papel jaspeado: marbled paper
papel medio-satinado: dull-coated
  paper
papel offset: offset paper
papel picado: stippled paper
papel registro: register paper
papel satinado: glazed paper,
  calendered paper
papel satiné: glazed paper
papel verjurado: laid paper
papel vitela: vellum paper
párrafo: paragraph
parte: part

pasta: leather-covered board binding
pasta española: leather-covered board binding
pastoril: pastoral
paulatinamente: little by little, slowly
pauta: line, lines
pautado: lined
pecarí: peccary
pedido: order
pegado: glued, pasted
penúltimo: next to last
peq. *see* pequeño
pequeñísimo: very small
pequeño: small
percal: calico
percalina: book cloth, buckram
pérdida de texto: loss of text
perfecto: perfect
perforación: perforation
perg. *see* pergamino
pergam. *see* pergamino
pergamino: parchment
pericia: craftsmanship
periódico: periodical
perjudicado: damaged
pgs. *see* páginas
picado: wormholed
picado de polilla: perforated by worms
picadura: wormholing
picadura de polilla: wormholing
pico(s): corner(s)
pie de imprenta: imprint
pie de página: foot of the page
piel: leather
piel becerrillo: calfskin
piel chagrín: sheepskin
piel corriente: standard leather
piel de cerdo: pigskin
piel de Levante: Levant leather
piel flexible: flexible leather
piel labrada: carved leather
pieza: piece
pintado: painted, colored
placa: plaque
plancha(s): board(s)

plancha(s) de madera: wood board(s)
plano: design, plan
planos: sides (of a book)
plata: silver
plateado: plated
pleg. *see* plegable, plegado
plegable: folding
plegado: folded
pleno: full
pliego(s): sheet(s)
pliegue: fold, crease
pluricolor: multicolor
poco frecuente: infrequent
pocos márgenes: narrow margins
policromo: polychrome
polilla *see* picadura de polilla
polvoriento: dusty
popular: popular
por: by
por ambas caras: on both sides
por carecer de: for lack of
por lo demás: for the remainder
pórfido: porphyry (color)
port. *see* portada
portada: title page
portadillo: half title
portaf. *see* portafolio
portafolio: portfolio
porte pagado: costs of carriage paid
post. *see* posterior
posterior: back; later
postizo: stuck on, artificial
póstumo: posthumous
pp. *see* páginas
precedente: preceding
precedido: preceded
precio: price
precio estimado: estimated price
precio fuerte: firm price
precioso: precious
prefacio: preface, foreword
prel. *see* preliminar
preliminar(es): preliminary(ies)
premiado: prize-winning
prensa: press
prestigiado: highly esteemed

prestigio: prestige, esteem
prestigioso: very highly esteemed
primera tirada: first printing
primero: first
primorosamente: elegantly
primoroso: elegant, handsome
principio: beginning
priv. *see* privilegio
privado: private
privilegio: privilege, permit to
  publish
prof. *see* profusión
profus. *see* profusamente,
  profusión
profusamente: profusely
profusión: profusion
pról. *see* prólogo
prologado: prefaced
prólogo: preface
prolongado: elongated
promedio: average number
propio: suitable
próximo: imminent
prueba: proof
ps. *see* páginas
publicación: publication
publicado: published
puesto en venta: offered for sale
pulcritud: cleanliness, neatness
pulcro: clean, neat
pulido: polished
pulimentado: polished, smooth
punt. *see* punta, puntera
punta(s): corner(s)
punta seca: dry point
puntas rotas: with broken corners
puntera(s): corner(s)
puntillado: stippled

quebradura: break, crack
quemado: burned
quemadura: burn, burning
quince: fifteen
quincenal: fortnightly
quinquagésimo: fiftieth
quinto: fifth

raído: chafed, worn

rama(s): sheet(s)
rareza: rarity
raridad: rarity
rarísimo: very rare
raro: rare
raro en comercio: rarely offered
  for sale
rascado: scraped, scratched
rascadura: scraped spot, scratch
rasgado: rubbed, torn
rasgadura(s): tear(s)
rasguño(s): scratch(es)
raso: satin
rayado: decorated with a line
  pattern
razonado: commented
rca. *see* rústica
real: royal
realizado: completed
rebajo: discount, reduction
recién: recently
recientísimo: very recent
recio: thick
reclamo(s): catchword(s)
recobrado: recovered
recogido: collected again
recop. *see* recopilado
recopilación: compilation
recopilado: compiled
recopilador: compiler
recortado: trimmed; cut out
recorte: cutting, clipping
recto: recto
recuadrado: laid out in square or
  oblong line patterns
recuadro(s): square or oblong
  line pattern(s)
recubierto: covered
redacción: editing; editorial staff
redactado: edited, arranged
redactor: editor
redondeado: rounded
redondo: round
reducido: reduced
reedición: republication
reemplazado: replaced
reforzado: reinforced
refuerzo: reinforcing

refundición: adaptation
refundido: reworked, re-edited
regalo: gift, present
regiamente: royally
regio ejemplar: magnificent copy
registro: register
registro de propiedad: copyright
reglado: ruled, lined
regocijante: pleasing, very
  amusing
rehecho: renovated, restored
reimpresión: reprint
reimpreso: reprinted
rejilla: grid, textured material
relato: story
relieve: relief
remarg. *see* remarginado
remarginado: margins reworked,
  improved
remendado: mended
renglón: line
renombrado: renowned
renovado: renewed
reparación: repair
reparado: repaired
repartido: divided, separated
repertorio: list, index
repetido: repeated
reproducción: reproduction
repujado: embossed
respaldo: back
restante: remainder, remaining
restaurado: restored
resto: remainder
resumén: résumé, synopsis
retocado: retouched
retrato: portrait
reunir: to bring together, collect
reverso: verso
revisado: revised
revisión: review
revista: journal, review
rodado: encircled, surrounded
rodeado: encircled, surrounded
roido: gnawed, eaten
rojizo: reddish
romano: roman
romántico: in the style of the

romantic period
rombal: rhombic
rombo: lozenge- or diamond-
  shaped
rompimiento: break, tear
roto: damaged, broken
rótulo: label
rotura: break
rozado: rubbed, scuffed
rstca. *see* rústica
rtca. *see* rústica
rúbrica: rubric
rubricado: rubricated
rueda: circular design
rueda greca: lace pattern
ruedas de cadenas: chain design
rúst. *see* rústica
rústica: sewed

s. *see* siglo, sin
s.a. *see* sin año
s.f. *see* sin fecha, sin foliar
s.i.t. *see* sin indicaciónes
  tipográficas
s.l. *see* sin lugar
s.l.i.ni a. *see* sin lugar de
  impresión ni año
s.l.n.a. *see* sin lugar ni año
s.l.ni a. *see* sin lugar ni año
s.l.y.a. *see* sin lugar y año
s.n. *see* sin numerar
s.n.d.p. *see* sin nota de precio
s.p.d.i. *see* sin pie de imprenta
s.p.i. *see* sin pie de imprenta
salta: skips, jumps
salvado: preserved
satinado: coated, glazed
se equivoca: errs, is mistaken
sección: section, passage
seco: blind tooling
seda: silk
según: according
segundo: second
seis: six
sellado: bearing a seal
sello(s): seal(s), stamp(s)
sello de biblioteca: library stamp
semanal: weekly

194

semes. *see* semestral
semestral: semiannual(ly)
semintonso: half-cut, trimmed
seña(s): mark(s)
señalando: indicating
señas: address
separadamente: separately
separado: separated
separata: reprint, separate
septimo: seventh
septuagésimo: seventieth
serie: series
sesenta: sixty
sesentésimo: sixtieth
setenta: seventy
setentésimo: seventieth
seud. *see* seudónimo
seudónimo: pseudonym
sexagésimo: sixtieth
sexto: sixth
siete: seven
sig. *see* signatura
sigla: initials, monogram
siglo: century
signatura(s): signature(s)
sigue: there follows
siguiente: following
silografía: wood-block print
símil-cuero: imitation leather
sin: without
sin abreviar: unabridged
sin abrir: unopened
sin afectar el texto: without
  affecting the text
sin año: without year
sin cortar: untrimmed, unopened
sin coser: unsewn
sin cotización: without price
sin dañar: without damaging
sin enc. *see* sin encuadernar
sin encuadernar: without binding
sin expurgar: unexpurgated
sin fecha: without date
sin foliación: without foliation
sin foliar: without foliation
sin i.t. *see* sin indicaciónes
  tipográficas
sin importancia: unimportant

sin indicaciónes tipográficas:
  without name of publisher
sin interesar: without affecting,
  without touching
sin las tapas: without its covers
sin lugar: without place
sin lugar de impresión: without
  place of publication
sin lugar de impresión ni año:
  without place of publication or
  year
sin lugar ni año: without place or
  year
sin lugar y año: without place or
  year
sin nota de precio: without indication of price
sin numerar: without numbering
sin paginación: without pagination
sin pie de imprenta: without
  imprint
sin recortar: untrimmed
sin signar: unsigned
sin signatura: without signature
sin tasación: without price
sinóptico: synoptic
sobado: shopworn, mauled
soberbio: superb, splendid
sobrecubierta: book jacket
sobrescrito: superscription
sobretiro: reprint, separate
sobrio: sober
solapa: book jacket
sólidamente: solidly
sólido: firm, solid
sombreado: shaded by cross-
  hatching
ss. *see* siguiente
subrayado: underlined
subscribir: to subscribe
subscripción: subscription
subscriptor(es): subscriber(s)
subtitulo: subtitle
sucio: dirty
suelto: odd, single
suelto(s): loose, detached
sumamente: extremely
sumario: summary

suntuoso: sumptuous
sup. *see* superior
super-libros: property stamp
superior: top, upper
suplemento: supplement
suplido: supplied, made up
suprimido: suppressed, censored
suscripción *see* subscripción

t. *see* taller, tomo
tabla: table, table of contents;
  board
tachado: spotted
tachadura(s): spot(s), stain(s)
tafilete: morocco
taladrado: with holes
taladro(s): hole(s)
taladro(s) de polilla: wormhole(s)
tall. *see* taller
talla dulce: *taille-douce*
taller: shop
tamaño: size, format
tapa(s): side(s) of a book
tapa(s) de cartón: board(s),
  cased binding
tapa inferior: back cover
tapa(s) suelta(s): loose board(s)
tapa superior: front cover
tapado: covered
tasación: appraisal, price
tejuelo: label
tela: cloth
tela chagrín: morocco cloth,
  cloth grained to imitate shagreen
teñido: tinted
tercero: third
terciopelo: velvet
tesis: thesis
texto: text
tinta: color, tint; ink
tip. *see* tipografía
tipo: type, font
tipo gótico: gothic type
tipografía: printing house
tipográfico: typographical
tirada: edition, printing
tirada aparte: offprint, separate

tirada corta: limited edition
tirada limitada: limited edition
tirada nominal: ordinary edition
tirada numerada: numbered
  edition
tirada reducida: small edition
tirada única: sole printing
tirado: printed
tiraje: printing
tít. *see* título
título: title
título colectivo: collective title
tocado: touched
toda tela: full cloth
todo lo publicado: all published
tomito: small volume
tomo(s): volume(s)
tono: color, hue
trabajado: worked
trabajo: work
trad. *see* traducción, traducido,
  traductor
traducción: translation
traducido: translated
traductor: translator
transcripción: transcription
transpuesto: transposed
tratado: treated; treatise
trece: thirteen
treinta: thirty
tres: three
tres cuartos cuero: three-quarter
  leather binding
tricolor: three-color
tricromía: three-color print
trigésimo: thirtieth
trim. *see* trimestral
trimestral: quarterly
trocito: small piece
trozo(s): bit(s), piece(s)
ts. *see* tomos

último: last, latest
un: one
uncial: uncial
undécimo: eleventh
únicamente: solely
único: sole, unique

196

uniforme: uniform
usado: worn, soiled
uso: wear

v. *see* verso
v. en b. *see* verso en blanco
valenciana: Valencian leather,
  usually colored green
valioso: worthy, valuable
vaqueta: calfskin
variante(s): variant(s)
veinte: twenty
venal: for sale
vendido: sold, sold out
venta: sale
venta al contado: cash sale
verde: green
verde oliva: olive green
versión: version

verso: back side, verso
verso en blanco: verso blank
veteado: grained
viejo: old
vigésimo: twentieth
viñeta(s): vignette(s), border(s)
vista(s): view(s)
vistoso: beautiful, colorful
vit. *see* vitela
vitela: parchment, vellum
volante: fugitive
volumen(es): volume(s)
volumen suelto: single, odd
  volume
voluminoso: voluminous

xilografía: wood-block print,
  wood engraving
xilográfico: xilographic

SWEDISH

å: on, upon
a.a. *see* akademisk avhandling
a.s.u. *see* allt som utkommit
a.u. *see* allt som utkommit
ABC-bok(böcker): hornbook(s),
  primer(s)
aderton: eighteen
adertonde: eighteenth
afsats(er): paragraph(s)
ägarestämpel: owner's stamp
ägo: possession
akad. *see* akademisk
akad.avh. *see* akademisk
  avhandling
akademisk: academic
akademisk(a) avhandling(ar):
  thesis(es), dissertation(s)
akvarell(er): water color(s)
akvatint: aquatint
album: album(s)
äldre: older
aldrig: never
allt som utkommit: all published
almanack(or): almanac(s)
amatörband: three-quarter
  binding
anastatisk: anastatic
andra: second, other
andre: second, other
ang. *see* angående

angående: concerning
anmärkning(ar): comment(s),
  note(s)
ann. *see* annons(er), annotation(er)
annan: other
annars: otherwise, besides
annat: other
annons(er): advertisement(s)
annotation(er): annotation(s),
  note(s)
anonym: anonymous
ansv. *see* ansvarig
ansvarig: authentic, responsible
ant.-bl. *see* anteckningsblad
antages: presumably
antal: number, amount
anteckn. *see* anteckning
anteckning(ar): note(s)
anteckningsblad: note page(s)
anteckningsbok(böcker): note-
  book(s)
antikva: roman type
antikvariatbokhandlare: antiquarian bookseller
antikvarisk: used, secondhand
antologi: anthology
appendix: appendix
appreterad: calendered
år: year(s)
arabesk: arabesque

198

arb. *see* arbete
arbete: work, item
årg. *see* årgång
årgång: year, annual volume
ark: signature(s), sheet(s) of
  paper
arkiv: archives
arrangerad: arranged
års-: annual
årsbok(böcker): yearbook(s)
årtalet: year, date
atlas(er): atlas(es)
åtta: eight
åttio: eighty
åttionde: eightieth
åttonde: eighth
auktion: auction sale
auktoriserad: authorized
autograf(er): autograph(s)
autotypi: halftone
avbildn. *see* avbildning
avbildning(ar): illustration(s)
avd. *see* avdelning
avdelning(ar): part(s), section(s)
även: also
avgiven: delivered
avh. *see* avhandling
avhandling(ar): dissertation(s)
avlång: elongated
avriven: torn off, torn out
avskrapning(ar): scratch(es)
avskrift: copy
avtrubbad: dulled
avtryck: copy(ies), impression(s)
avvikande: differing

båda: both, either
bägge: both, either
bakpärm: back (of) cover
bakre: back, rear
baksida: verso
band: binding; volume(s)
banderoll: legend, lettered scroll
barnbok(böcker): children's
  book(s)
bastard typer: bastard type
bd. *see* band
bearb. *see* bearbetad, bearbetning

bearbetad: revised
bearbetning: adaptation
begränsad: limited
beh. *see* behandla
behandla(r): deal(s) with
bemyndigad: authorized
berättare: narrator
berättelse(r): narrative(s), trans-
  action(s)
bestå(r): consist(s)
bestående: consisting
beställning: order
beträffande: dealing with, concerning
betydelsefull: significant
bev. *see* bevarad
bevarad: preserved
bibl.-uppl. *see* bibliofil-upplaga
bibliofil: bibliophile
bibliofil-upplaga: book collector's
  fine edition, de luxe edition
bibliofilband: book collector's
  fine binding
bibliogr. *see* bibliografisk
bibliografi: bibliography
bibliografisk: bibliographic
bibliotek: library
bibliotekarie: librarian
biblioteksstämpel: library stamp
bidrag: contribution(s)
bifogad: added
bihang: supplement
bilaga: supplement
bilagor: supplements
bilagsband: supplement(s)
bild(er): illustration(s), picture(s)
bind: raised band
bind. *see* bindning
bindning: binding
biogr. *see* biografi, biografisk
biografi: biography
biografisk: biographical
bl. *see* blad
bl.a. *see* bland annat
blå: blue
bläcklinjer: ink lines
bläckteckning(ar): pen and ink
  drawing(s)

blad: leaf(ves), sheet(s)
bladornament: floral scrollwork
bland annat: among others
blank: blank
blek: faded, pale
blindpressning(ar): blind tooling
blindstämpel(stämplar): blind stamp(s)
blockbok(böcker): block book(s)
blomsterperiod: golden age, climactic period
blott: only
blyertsstreckad: pencil-marked
böcker: books
bok: book
bokband: cover, binding
bokbindare: bookbinder
bokh. *see* bokhandel
bokhandel: bookstore
bokhandlare: bookdealer
bokhist. *see* bokhistoria
bokhistoria: history of books
bokrygg: spine
bokstav(stäver): letter(s), character(s)
boktr. *see* boktryckeri
boktryckarmärke: printer's mark
boktryckeri: printing firm
bomärke: flourish, paraph
bordyr: ornamental border
början: beginning
borta: missing
bortraderad: erased
bortskärning: clipping, excision
bortskuren: cut off, trimmed
bortskurits: been cut off
brändes: was (were) burned, destroyed
brandrök: smoke
brandskada: fire damage
brandskadad: damaged by fire
bredd: width
bredrand. *see* bredrandig
bredrandig: with wide margins
brist(er): defect(s)
broderad: embroidered
brokig: varicolored
bronserad: reddish-brown

broschyr: booklet, pamphlet
broschyromsl. *see* broschyromslag
broschyromslag: stitched wrappers
brott: break
brottskada: break
brunfl. *see* brunfläckad
brunfläckad: foxed
bunden: bound
bundna: bound

c:a. *see* cirka
censur: censorship
censurerad: censored, suppressed
chagrin: shagreen
chagrinband: bound in shagreen
cirka: approximately
ciselerad: chiseled
clairobscur: chiaroscuro
clot: cloth

d. *see* del
då: since, when, then
dammig: dusty
därtill: in addition to this
daterad: dated
dåtida: contemporary
ded. *see* dedikation
dedikation: dedication
definitiv: definite, definitive
dek. *see* dekoration, dekorerad
dekor. *see* dekorerad
dekoration: decoration, ornamentation
dekorerad: decorated
del(ar): part(s)
delbeteckning(ar): designation(s) of parts
delvis: partly
denna: this, the latter
denne: this, the latter
denteller: dentelle tooling
dessutom: besides, in addition
devis: device, motto
diagram: diagram
diagramblad: diagram leaf
differerad: differing

differerande: differing
dikt(er): poem(s)
dir. *see* direkt
direkt: direct
disponibel: available
dissertation(er): dissertation(s)
dittils: up to that date, previously
djuptryck: photogravure
dlr. *see* delar
dokument: document
dubbel: couple, double
duplic. *see* duplicerad
duplicerad: mimeographed

edition: edition
efter: after, according to, from
efterfrågad: in demand, sought
  after
efterlämnad: posthumous
efterskrift: postscript
eftersökt: sought after
eftertryck: reprint
egentlig: real, actual
ej heller: neither
ej i bokhandeln: not in the trade,
  privately printed
eleg. *see* elegant
elegant: elegant, elegantly
elfte: eleventh
eljest: otherwise
elva: eleven
elvte: eleventh
emaljband: enamel binding
en: one
end. *see* endels
enda: unique
endast: only
endels: partly
engelsk band: limp binding
enkel: simple
enl. *see* enligt
enligt: according to
ersatt(s) med: replaced by
etikett: label
etsn. *see* etsning
etsning(ar): etching(s)
ett: one
ett par: a few

ettbladstryck: broadside
ex. *see* exemplar
exemplar: copy(ies)
exlibris: *ex libris*
exlibrisstämplar: marks of
  ownership
expl. *see* exemplar

f.ö. *see* för övrigt
faksimil: facsimile(s)
faksimilupplaga: facsimile edition
fals(ar): joint(s)
falsad: folded
falsarium: forgery
falsk: wrong, false
fält: panel(s)
färg(er): color(s)
färglagd: colored
färglitografi: color lithography
färglitografi(er): color litho-
  graph(s)
färgplansch(er): color plate(s)
färgtryck: color printing, color
  prints
färgtrycksplansch(er): color
  plate(s)
färgtrycksplr. *see* färgtryck-
  splanscher
fårskinn: sheepskin
fäste(n): tie(s)
fastlimmad: reglued
fåtal: few
felaktig: erroneous, incomplete
feltryckt: misprinted
fem: five
femte: fifth
femtio: fifty
femtionde: fiftieth
femton: fifteen
femtonde: fifteenth
festskrift: commemorative volume
ficka: pocket
ficklexikon: pocket dictionary
fig. *see* figur
figur: figure, illustration
filet: fillet
fin: fine, delicate

fjärde: fourth
fjorton: fourteen
fjortonde: fourteenth
fl. *see* fläckad, flera
fläck: spot
fläck. *see* fläckad
fläckad: spotted
fläckfri: spotless
flera: several
flerfärgstryck: multicolor printing
flertal: most, majority
flock: group(s), section(s)
flygblad: broadside
foder: lining, *doublure*
fodral: case, slipcase
föga: little
folierad: foliated
foliering: foliation
följd(er): series
folkupplaga: popular edition
för övrigt: otherwise, in addition
förbjuden: forbidden, banned
före: before, in front of
föreg. *see* föregående
föregående: preceding
föregiven: fictitious
förekomma: occur
föreläsning(ar): lecture(s)
föreligga: be (are) present
föreliggande: present
företal: preface
förf. *see* författare
författare: author
författarkollektiv: team of
  authors, joint authors
författarrätt: copyright
förgylld: gilt
förhållandevis: relatively
förhandlingar: proceedings
förklaring(ar): explanation(s),
  notice(s)
förkortad: abbreviated, short
förkortning(ar): abbreviation(s)
förl. *see* förlag
förlag: publishing firm
förläggare: publisher(s)
förlagsstämpel: publisher's

stamp
format: format, size
förminskad: reduced
förnyad: renewed
förord: preface
försäljning: sale
försättsblad: flyleaf
försättspapper: end paper
försedd: furnished
förskuren: trimmed
första(te): first
förstärkt: reinforced
förteckn. *see* förteckning
förteckning: list
förtitel: half title
förtitelblad: half-title page
fortsättning(ar): continuation(s)
förut: previously
fotografi(er): photograph(s)
fotografisk: photographic
fotogravyr(er): photogravure(s)
fotolitografi: photolithograph,
  photolithography
fotostatkopi(or): photostatic
  copy(ies)
fototypi: phototype
fr. *see* främre, från, fräsch
fraktur: black letter
främmande: different
frampärm(ar): front cover(s)
främre: front
främre omslag: front wrapper
främre snitt: fore edge
framsida: recto
från: from
frånsett: apart from, except
franskt band: leather binding,
  calf binding
fräsch: clean
fris(er): heading(s), headpiece(s)
frontispis(er): frontispiece(s)
frsp. *see* frontispis
fuktfl. *see* fuktfläckad
fuktfläck(ar): damp stain(s)
fuktfläckad: damp-stained
fullständig: complete
fyra: four
fyrtio: forty

fyrtionde: fortieth

gammal: old, contemporary
gång(er): time(s)
ganska: quite, altogether
gått upp i limningen: loose in
  binding
gedigen: well-made, strong
gemensam titel: collective title
genom: through
genomgående: all through, con-
  sistently
genomsedd: revised
genomskinlig: transparent
ggr. *see* gånger
glättad: calendered, burnished
glättad marokäng: crushed
  morocco
gldsn. *see* guldsnitt
gotisk: gothic
gott: good
granskad: revised
gråpappersomsl. *see* gråpappersomslag
gråpappersomslag: plain wrap-
  per(s)
grav. *see* graverad
graverad: engraved
gravör: engraver
gravyr(er): print(s), etching(s)
grön: green
groteska typer: block letter(s)
grundritning: outline
gul: yellow
gulbrun: fawn-colored
guld: gold
gulddekor: gold ornamentation
guldorn. *see* guldornerad
guldornerad: decorated in gold
guldpress. *see* guldpressad
guldpressad: gilt-stamped
guldsnitt: gilt edge(s)
gulnad: yellowed

h. *see* häfte
häftad: stitched, sewed
häfte(n): issue(s), part(s)
häfteomsl. *see* häfteomslag

häfteomslag: issue cover(s)
häftning: sewing, stitching
hål: hole(s)
halvår: half-year, semiannual
  volume
halvband: half binding
halvfr. *see* halvfranskt
halvfranskt: half leather, half calf
halvfransktband: half-calf binding
halvfrbd. *see* halvfransktband
halvklotband: half-cloth binding
halvklotbd. *see* halvklotband
halvläderband: half-leather binding
halvmarokängband: half-morocco
  binding
halvmarokgbd. *see* halvmarokängband
halvnummer: half issue(s)
halvpergamentband: half-vellum
  binding
halvpergmtbd. *see* halvpergamentband
handgjord: handmade
handgjordt: handmade
handkolorerad: hand-colored
handlar om: deals with
handpresstryckeri: hand press
handskrift: manuscript, handwriting
handskriven: handwritten
här: here
hårt: hard, close
hel: entire, whole
helförgylld: entirely gilt
heliogravyr: photoengraving
helkbd. *see* helklotband
helklotband: full-cloth binding
helsida: full page
helsidesbild(er): full-page
  picture(s)
helsidesillustration: full-page
  illustration
helsidesplansch(er): full-page
  plate(s)
helskinnband: full-leather binding
hfn. *see* häften
hfr. *see* halvfranskt

hfrbd. *see* halvfransktband
hjortskinn: buckskin, doeskin
hklot. *see* halvklotband
hög: tall
högra: right-hand
högst: extremely
högt: highly, greatly
hopvikt: folded
hörn: corner(s)
hörnbit: cornerpiece
hörnlagad: corner(s) repaired
hörnskada: corner(s) damaged
höst: Autumn, Fall
hundöron: dog-ears
hundra: hundred
hundrade: hundredth
huvudsakligen: mainly
hygglig: nice
hyst: contained

i allt: altogether
i press: in press, being printed
i st.f. *see* i stället för
i stället för: instead of
icke: not
ifall annat icke angives: unless
    otherwise indicated
ill. *see* illustration, illustrerad
illuminering: illumination, color-
    ing
illustr. *see* illustration,
    illustrerad
illustration(er): illustration(s)
illustratör: illustrator
illustrerad: illustrated
in-folio: in folio format
inalles: in all, a total of
inb. *see* inbunden
inbunden: bound
inciselerad: carved in
indragen: withdrawn from
    circulation
initial(er): initial(s)
inkl. *see* inkluderad
inklistr. *see* inklistrad
inklistrad: pasted in, glued in
inkluderad: included
inkunabel(bler): incunabulum(a)

inl. *see* inledning
inlagt: loosely inserted, laid in
inledande: introductory
inledn. *see* inledning
inledning: introduction
innehåll: contents
innehåller: contains
innehållsförteckning: table of
    contents
inramad: framed, bordered
inre: internal, interior, inner
inskjuten: intercalated
inskrift: inscription
inte: not
interfol. *see* interfolierad
interfolierad: interleaved
intryckt: embossed
invikt: folded in

jämför: compare
jämne: smooth
jämte: together with
jansenistband: Jansenist binding
japanpapper: Japanese vellum
jmfr. *see* jämför

kallnål: dry point
källor: sources
kalv: calf
kalvband: calf binding
kalvskinn: calfskin
kapitälband: headband
kapitel: chapter(s)
kapitelöverskrift: chapter heading
karikatyr(er): caricature(s)
kart. *see* kartonnerad
karta: map, chart
kartbild: picture map
kartbl. *see* kartblad
kartblad: map(s)
kartografi: cartography
kartong: pasteboard, cardboard
kartongpärmar: boards
kartonnerad: paper boards
kartskiss(er): sketch map(s)
kartusch(er): cartouche(s)
kåseri(er): talk(s), light essay(s)
kbd. *see* klotband

kedjeband: chained binding
kemigrafi: photoengraving,
  zincography
klb. *see* klotband
klbd. *see* klotband
klipp: excision, cut, hole
klippt: cut, damaged by excision
klotb. *see* klotband
klotband: cloth binding
klotbd. *see* klotband
klotöverdrag: cloth covers
kluven: split
knapp(ar): boss(es)
knappast: hardly ever
knäppe(n): clasp(s)
knytband: tie(s)
knytremmar: leather ties
kodex: codex
kokbok(böcker): cookbook(s)
kollationering: collation
kolofon: colophon
kolor. *see* kolorerad
kolorerad: colored
kolorering: coloring
komedi: comedy
kommentar(er): comment(s),
  commentary(ies)
kommenterad: commented
kompilation: compilation
kompilator: compiler
kompl. *see* komplett
komplett: complete
konkordans: concordance
konstläder: imitation leather,
  leatherette
konsttryckpapper: fine-coated
  paper
konto: account
koppardjuptryck: photogravure
kopparstick: copper engraving
koppartryck: copperplate printing
korrigering: correction
kplt. *see* komplett
kprst. *see* kopparstick
krönika(or): chronicle(s)
kungl. *see* kunglig
kunglig: royal
kungliga: royal

kungörelse(r): decree(s), official
  announcement(s)
kurvor: curved lines
kväde: verse
kvadratisk: square
kvartal: quarter of a year

lacksigill: wax seal
läder: leather
läderband: leather-bound, leather
  binding
läderbd. *see* läderband
lag: reduced, low
lagad: repaired
lagerfläckad: foxed
lagning: repair
lappad: mended
lätt: light, slightly
lexikon: dictionary
likadeles: equally
liksom: as, like
lilior: fleurs-de-lys
limmad: glued
limning: gluing
linje(r): line(s)
linjerad: ruled, lined
lit. *see* liten
liten: small
litogr. *see* litografi
litografi(er): lithograph(s)
litografierad: lithographed
litteraturförteckn. *see*
  litteraturförteckning
litteraturförteckning: list of
  references
ljus: light-colored
ljustrycksplansch(er): heliogravure plate(s)
ljustrycksplchr. *see*
  ljustrycksplanscher
lös: loose
lösnr. *see* lösnummer
lösnummer: separate number,
  issue
loss: loose, unstitched
lossnad: loosened
löst: odd, loosely
lumpapper: rag paper

lunta: old, unwieldy volume
lyx: de luxe
lyxband: de luxe binding

m.fl. *see* med flera
m.m. *see* med mera
m.u. *see* mer utkommit
mager: thin
måhända: possibly
målad: painted
månadsskrift: monthly
månatlig: monthly
många: many
mängd: lot, quantity
manuskript: manuscript
marg. *see* marginal
marginal(er): margin(s)
marginalsiffror: marginal
  numbers
marinblå: navy blue
märke: mark
marknad: market
marmorerad: marbled
marmorering: marbling
marokäng: morocco
maskhål: wormhole(s)
maskstungen: perforated by
  worms
mästare: master(s)
mattad: tarnished, lusterless
med flera: and others, etc.
med mera: etc., etc.
medaljbeskr. *see* medaljbeskrivning
medaljbeskrivning: description of
  medal(s)
medaljong: medallion
medaljplansch(er): plate(s) of
  medals
medelmåttig: mediocre
medeltida: medieval
medfaren: worn, faded
medföljer: accompanies
medl. *see* medlem
medl.-avg. *see* medlemsavgivet
medlem: member
medlemsavgivet: for members
medverkan: collaboration

memoarer: memoirs
mer utkommit: more published,
  incomplete set
metallfästen: metal clasps,
  fastenings
mezzotint: mezzotint
mindre: less, smaller
miniatyr: miniature
miniatyrbok: miniature book
minneskrift: commemorative
  volume
mitt: middle
mjuk: flexible
mjukt band: flexible binding
moaré: moire
moderniserad: modernized,
  brought up to date
mögelfläck(ar): mildew stain(s)
monografi: monograph
mönster: pattern
mörkare: darker
mörkbrun: dark brown
mosaikinläggning(ar): mosaic
  inlay(s)
musik: music
musikbilaga(or): music supple-
  ment(s)
musiknot(er): music note(s)
mycket: very, highly

n.f. *see* ny följd
n.s. *see* ny serie
naggad: notched
något: somewhat
några: a few, a couple of
namn: name
namnregister: index of names
namnt. *see* namnteckning
namnteckning: signature (name)
näst sista: next to the last
nästan: almost
nätt: nice
nedre: lower, bottom
nedsmutsad: soiled
ngt. *see* något
nio: nine
nionde: ninth
nittio: ninety

nittionde: ninetieth
nitton: nineteen
nittonde: nineteenth
notlinje(r): line(s) for musical
   notation
nötning: use, rubbing
nött: worn
noveller: short stories, novellas
nr. *see* nummer
numera: now
nummer: number(s), issue(s)
numr. *see* numrerad
numrerad: numbered
ny: new
ny följd: new series
ny serie: new series
ny tryckning: reprint
ny uppl. *see* ny upplaga
ny upplaga: new edition
ny utg. *see* ny utgåva
ny utgåva: reissue
nyare: more recent
nyckelroman: *roman à clef*
nygjort omslag: new wrapper(s)
nyinbunden: rebound, newly bound
nypris: list price
nyss utkommen: just published
nytr. *see* nytryck, nytryckt
nytryck: reprint(s)
nytryckt: reprinted
nytt: new, something new

o.a. *see* och andra
o.s.v. *see* och så vidare
obekant: not known
obet. *see* obetydlig
obetydl. *see* obetydlig
obetydlig(t): insignificant(ly)
obunden: unbound
ocensurerad: unexpurgated
och andra: and others
och så vidare: and so forth
oclotbd. *see* originalklotband
offentl. *see* offentlig
offentlig: public
officin: print shop, press
offset: offset
oförändr. *see* oförändrad

oförändrad: unchanged
okänd: unknown
oklot. *see* originalklotband
oktavformat: octavo size
oljefläckad: oil-stained
omarb. *see* omarbetad,
   omarbetning
omarbetad: revised
omarbetning(ar): revision(s)
omfatta: comprise
omfattad: comprised
omfattar: comprises
omkring: approximately
omnämnd: mentioned, listed
omsl. *see* omslag
omslag: wrapper(s)
omslagstitel: cover title
omsorgsfull(t): careful(ly)
omställd: transposed
omtryck: reprint(s)
onumr. *see* onumrerad
onumrerad: unnumbered
opag. *see* opaginerad
opaginerad: unnumbered
ordbok(böcker): dictionary(ies)
ordförklaring: glossary
ordinarie: ordinary
ordlista: word list, glossary
ordspråk: proverb(s)
oregelbunden: irregular
orig. *see* original
origband. *see* originalband
orighäfte: *see* originalhäfte
orighalvklotbd. *see* originalhalvklotband
orighelkbd. *see* originalhelklotband
original: original
originalband: original binding
originaletsning(ar): original
   etching(s)
originalhäfte(n): original issue(s)
originalhalvklotband: original
   half-cloth binding
originalhelklotband: original
   full-cloth binding
originalkartonnage: original
   boards

originalklotband: original cloth
  binding
originallinneband: original linen
  binding
originalomslag: original wrap-
  per(s)
originaltryck: original printing
originaltygband: original fabric
  binding
originalupplaga: first edition
originell: curious, amusing
origkart. *see* originalkartonnage
origkbd. *see* originalklotband
origlinneband. *see* originallinneband
origtygband. *see* originaltygband
ornerad: decorated
osk. *see* oskuren
oskuren: uncut
otryckt: unpublished
ouppskuren: unopened
öv. *see* översatt
ovan: above
ovanlig: unusual
ovanst. *see* ovanstående
ovanstående: above-described,
  the above
över: about, concerning; above
överdragspapper: fancy paper
övers. *see* översatt, översätta,
  översättning
översatt: translated
översätta: translate
översättning: translation
översikt: abstract, synopsis
översiktstabell: synoptic table
överskrift: heading, caption
översnitt: upper edge
överstruken: crossed out
överstycke(n): headpiece(s),
  frieze(s)
övre: top
övrig: other, remaining

på: in, upon
paginerad: paginated
påklistrad: pasted on
pamflett(er): pamphlet(s)

pappband: boards
papper: paper
papper- och pappomslag: paper
  and cardboard cover(s)
pappersfläckad: foxed
pappomslag: hard paperboard
  cover(s)
papp-pärmar: (original) cased
  binding
paraferad: initialed
parallel: parallel
pärm(ar): board(s), cover(s)
pärmbordyr: border on sides
pärmexlibris: book stamp(s)
pärmfals(ar): joint(s)
pärmficka: pocket
pärmfileter: fillet designs on
  side(s)
pärmförgyllning: gilding on
  side(s)
pärmöverdrag: covering of sides
pärmstämpel: stamp, design on
  sides
passepartout: passe partout
pastisch: imitation
per kontant: cash
pergament: parchment, vellum
pergamentband: vellum binding
pergamentbd. *see* pergamentband
pergamentrygg(ar): vellum back(s)
pergrygg. *see* pergamentrygg
pergryggar. *see* pergamentryggar
perkal: calico
perkalin: buckram
personregister: index of names
pl. *see* plansch
pl.-bl. *see* planschblad
pl.-blad. *see* planschblad
pl.-s. *see* planschsida
pl.-sid. *see* planschsida
plagiat: plagiarism
planritning(ar): plan(s), design(s)
plansch(er): plate(s)
planschbild(er): picture(s) on
  plates
planschblad: plate(s)
planschpapper: plate paper
planschserie: set of plates

planschsida(or): plate(s)
platta bind: flat bands
plchr. *see* planscher
plr. *see* planscher
plschr. *see* planscher
portf. *see* portfölj
portfölj(er): portfolio(s)
porträtt(er): portrait(s)
porträttplansch(er): portrait
  plate(s)
ppbd. *see* pappband
ppomslag. *see* pappomslag
ppr. *see* papper
pr. *see* pro
präglad: embossed
praktbilder: splendid illustrations
praktverk: de luxe publication
preliminär: preliminary
prenumeration: subscription
pris: price
prisbelönad: prize-winning
prislista: price list
privattryck: privately printed
  publication
pro: for, per, each
prospekt: prospectus, booklet
prov: sample(s)
proveniens: origin, provenance
provisoriskt band: temporary
  binding
prydd: decorated
prydl. *see* prydlig
prydlig: neat
pseudonym(er): pseudonym(s)
publ. *see* publicerad
publicerad: published
publiceras: (to) be published
publiceringsdatum: date of
  publication
publikation: publication
punkterad: dotted, stippled
putsad: trimmed

rabatt: discount
rad: line
raderad: erased
rak: straight
råkanter: untrimmed edges

ram: frame, border
rar: rare
rariss. *see* rarissimum
rarissimum: extremely rare
råsnitt: uncut edges
rättad: corrected
rättelse(r): correction(s)
rättelseblad: errata sheet
rec.-stämpel. *see* recensionsstämpel
recensionsstämpel: review-copy
  stamp
red. *see* redaktion, redaktör,
  redigerad
redaktion: editorship
redaktör: editor
redig. *see* redigerad
redigerad: edited
redogörelse: account, report
reg. *see* register
register: index(es)
registerblad: index page(s)
rem(mar): tie(s)
remsa(or): tie(s), ribbon(s)
ren: clean
renoverad: restored, repaired
rensad: cleansed, expurgated
reproduktion(er): reproduction(s)
rest: balance, remainder
reva(or): tear(s)
revid. *see* reviderad
reviderad: revised
rik: rich
rispa(or): tear(s), scratch(es)
röd: red
rolig: amusing, nice
roman(er): novel(s)
röntgenbilder: x-ray illustrations
rörande: dealing with
rostfläck(ar): rust stain(s)
rött: red
rubricerad: rubricated
rubrik: rubric
rubriktitel: running title
rundad: rounded
rutormönster: checkered design
rygg: spine
ryggdekor: decorated spine

ryggfält: panel(s) on spine
ryggförgyllning: gilding on spine
ryggornerad: decorated on spine
ryggornering: ornaments on spine
ryggskylt(ar): label(s) on spine
ryggtitel: back title, title on spine
rysk: Russian
ryssläder: Russian leather

s. *see* sida
saga: tale
saknas: lacking, missing
sakregister: subject index
sällan: rarely, seldom
sällsynt: rare
samarbete: collaboration
saml. *see* samling
samlad: collected
samling: collection
samlingsband: collective volume
samlingsbd. *see* samlingsband
samlingstitelblad: collective
  title page
samlingsverk: collected work
samma: same
sammanbunden: bound together
sammandrag: abridgment,
  synopsis
sammetliknande: velvet-like
sammetsband: velvet binding
sammetsbd. *see* sammetsband
samt: and also
samtidig: contemporary,
  simultaneous
sångbok(böcker): songbook(s)
sannolikt: probably
särskild: special, separate
särskilt: especial, especially
särtr. *see* särtryck
särtryck: offprint(s), separate(s)
schatterad: hatched, azure-tooled
se: see
sen. *see* senare
senare: later
senast: latest, last
separat: separate, separately
ser. *see* serie
serie: series
sex: six

sextio: sixty
sextionde: sixtieth
sexton: sixteen
sextonde: sixteenth
sid. *see* sida
sida: page
sidnummer: page number
sidor: pages
siffra(or): figure(s), number(s)
sigill: seal
signatur(er): signature(s)
signering: signature
silverbrokadband: bound in silver
  brocade
silverspänne(n): silver clasp(s)
sirad(e): decorated
sista: last
självbiografi: autobiography
sjätte: sixth
sjökort: nautical chart(s)
sju: seven
sjunde: seventh
sjuttio: seventy
sjuttionde: seventieth
sjutton: seventeen
sjuttonde: seventeenth
skad. *see* skadad
skadad: damaged
skådespel: play, drama
skamfilad: chafed, worn
skämt: joke(s), jest(s)
skämtbok(böcker): jokebook(s)
skandalskrift: lampoon
skår(or): (ornamental) cut(s),
  scoring
skåra(or): scratch(es), scoring
skattad: esteemed
skavd: gnawed
skick: state
skiljer sig: differs
skinn: leather
skinnband: leather binding
skinnbd. *see* skinnband
skinnkapitäl: headcap
skinnryggband: bound with leather
  back
skinnryggbd. *see* skinnryggband
skiss(er): sketch(es)
skolbok(böcker): textbook(s)

210

skolier: scholia, critical notes
skönskrift: calligraphy
skrapad: scratched
skrbd. *see* skinnryggband
skrifter: writings
skrivpapper: writing paper
skrynklad: wrinkled, crushed
skuren: trimmed, cut
skyddskartong: slipcase
skyddsomslag: jacket
slät: smooth
slut: end
slutblad: last page
slutord: postface
slutvinjett: tailpiece
små: little
smädeskrift: lampoon
smal: narrow
smärre: minor
småskrift(er): pamphlet(s);
  miscellanea
småtryck: pamphlet(s)
smutstitel: half title
snitt(ar): edge(s)
solblekt: faded
solkad: soiled
som: like, which
sommar: Summer
sönderläst: tattered
sönderriven: torn, lacerated
söndrig: torn
sp. *see* spalt
spalt(er): column(s)
spänne(n): clasp(s)
spår: trace(s)
språk: language(s)
sprängd: sprinkled
spricka(or): break(s), crack(s)
ss. *see* sidor
st. *see* stor
ställvis: in some places
stålstick: steel engraving
stämpel: stamp, tooled design
stämplar: stamps, tooled designs
starkt: much, strongly
stentryck: lithography
stilenlig: in style
stilfull: in good style, tasteful
stiliserad: stylized

stor: large
storlek: dimension, size
större: larger
strimla(or): guard(s)
stycke(n): item(s), matter
styvhäftad: bound in boards
subskriberad upplaga: subscriber's edition
suppl. *see* supplement
supplement: supplement
sv. *see* svensk
svag: slight, weak
svart: black
svärtad: darkened
svartskinnryggsband: half black-
  leather binding
svensk: Swedish
svinläder: pigskin
svit: run; set

t.o.m. *see* till och med
tab. *see* tabell
tabell: table
tabellblad: table(s)
tal: number (e.g., ett 40-tal:
  some forty; 1800-talet: 19th
  century)
talr. *see* talrik
talrik: numerous
teckn. *see* teckning
tecknad: drawn
teckning(ar): drawing(s)
textblad: sheet(s) of text
textfigur(er): figure(s) in the text
textförlust: loss of text
textkom. *see* textkommentar
textkommentar: textual comments
textsid(or): page(s) of text
tid: time
tid. *see* tidigare
tidigare: earlier
tidning(ar): newspaper(s)
tidskrift: journal, periodical
tidstypisk: typical of the age
till och med: up to and including,
  through
tillägg: appendix(es), supple-
  ment(s)
tilläggshäfte: supplementary

211

issue
tillägnad: dedicated
tillägnan: dedication
tillbunden: bound with
tillök. *see* tillökad
tillökad: enlarged
tillökning(ar): addition(s)
tills. *see* tillsammans
tillsammans: in all, together
tillstånd: state
tillverkats: was (were) fabricated
tio: ten
tionde: tenth
tit. *see* titel
titel: title
titelark: title signature
titelblad: title page
titelram: title border
titelsid: title page
titelstämpel: stamp on title page
titelvignett: title vignette
titlar: titles, title pages
tjock: thick
tjugonde: twentieth
tjugu: twenty
tolking(ar): interpretation(s)
tolv: twelve
tolvde: twelfth
tom: empty, blank
tr. *see* tryck, tryckning, tryckt
träblock: wood block
träfritt papper: wood-free paper
trägravyr: wood engraving
transkription: transcription
träpärm(ar): wooden side(s)
trasig: tattered
träsnitt: woodcut
träsnittsplansch: plate with
  woodcut
tre: three
tredje: third
trenne: three, a triad of
treplanskisser: sketches on three
  planes
trettio: thirty
trettionde: thirtieth
tretton: thirteen
trettonde: thirteenth
trevl. *see* trevlig

trevlig: pleasant
troligen: probably
tryck: printing
tryckalster: printed product,
  printing
tryckfel: typographical error,
  misprint
tryckning: printing
tryckort: place of publication
tryckt: printed
tryckt såsom manuskript: privately printed
tryckt som manuskript. *see* tryckt
  såsom manuskript
tryckuppgift: imprint, colophon
tummad: well-worn
tunga: flap
tus. *see* tusen
tusen: thousand
tv. *see* tvär
två: two
tvär: oblong
tvättad: washed
tvenne: two, a couple of
tydlig: obvious, clear
typ: type, genre, class
typisk: typical

u.å. *see* utan år, utan årtal
u.o.o.å. *see* utan ort och år
udda del: odd volume
uncial: uncial
undersökning: investigation
understöd: support, subsidy
understrekad: underlined
undertitel: subtitle
undre: lower, bottom
ungefär: approximately
uniform: uniform
unik: unique
uppdrag: order
uppfodrad: mounted
uppgift(er): information
upphöjda bind: raised bands
uppk. *see* uppköptes
uppköptes: was (were) bought up
uppl. *see* upplaga
upplaga(or): edition(s)
upplysn. *see* upplysning

upplysning(ar): information
uppsats(er): essay(s), article(s)
uppslagslitteratur: reference
  literature
upptagen: listed
upptill: at the top
ur band: out of its binding
urblekt: discolored
urval: selection
utan år: without year
utan årtal: without date of
  publication
utan band: without binding
utan ort och år: without place and
  year
utarb. see utarbetad
utarbetad: compiled, edited
utdrag: extract
utförd: executed
utförl. see utförlig
utförlig: extensive, detailed
utg. see utgåva, utgivare, utgiven
utgåva: issue, publication
utgavs: was (were) published
utgivare: editor
utgiven: edited, published
utgör: constitutes
utk. see utkom
utkast: draft
utkom: appeared, was published
utkommen: appeared, published
utl. see utländsk
utländsk: foreign, non-Swedish
utm. see utmärkt
utmärkt: excellent
utök. see utökad
utökad: increased
utomordentligt: extraordinarily
uts. see utsåld
utsåld: out of stock, sold out
utskuren: cut out
utsökt: choice, exceptional
utstyrsel: make-up, design
uttolkning: interpretation,
  translation
utvidg. see utvidgad
utvidgad: enlarged
utvikbar: fold-out

vack. see vacker
vacker: nice, beautiful
välbev. see välbevarad
välbevarad: well-preserved
vald: selected
välskband: quarter-bound
vältryckt: well-printed
vanlig: common, ordinary
vanligaste: most common
vänster: left-hand
vänstra: left-hand
vapen: arms
vapensköld: coat of arms
vår: Spring
varav: of which
värdefull: valuable
värderad: valued
variant(er): variant(s)
varibland: including
varje: each
värs: verse, poetry
vattenfläck(ar): water stain(s)
vattenstämpel(stämplar): water-
  mark(s)
vävband: cloth binding
vävbd. see vävband
vbd. see vävband, välskband
verk(en): work(s)
verkställd: executed
versal(er): capital letter(s)
vikt: folded
vinj. see vinjett
vinjett(er): vignette(s), tail-
  piece(s)
vinter: Winter
vitterhet: literature, belles-
  lettres
vitterhetsarbete(n): work(s) of
  literature
vol. see volym
volym: volume
vyer: views
vyplansch(er): plate(s) of views

xylografi: wood engraving

ytterligare: further, additional
ytteromslag: dust wrapper(s)
ytterst: most, extremely

213